# REMEMBERING WHEN

# REMEMBERING WHEN

## Memories of the
## Great Northern
## Cascade Division
## and Beyond

TED & NANCY CLEVELAND

Skykomish Historical Society
P O Box 247
Skykomish, Washington 98288

www.skyhistory.org

Front cover image: Walter Ainsworth Collection PNRArchive.org

Printed by Gorham Printing, Centralia, Washington
Book design by Kathryn E. Campbell

# Dedication

This book is being dedicated with gratitude to Bob Kelly. Bob is the Curator of the Skykomish Museum. It is Bob's faithful commitment to come to Sky on Tuesday of just about every week and giving his time freely that makes this museum so great. Bob has the ability to talk to people and to draw them out. He makes them feel a part of the history.

Bob knows more about railroading and railroading history than some of the actual men and women who work in the industry. Without Bob and his knowledge it would have been a difficult job finding the railroaders who have been interviewed for this book.

We appreciate Bob's ready smile, sense of humor and his positive attitude, as you come through the doorway with yet another question. Thank goodness Bob discovered Wellington. It was a bonus for our town.

*Ted and Nancy Cleveland*

Bob became interested in railroad history when he took our son Jeff and headed north for a workshop given in 1992 by Grant Sharp and Willie Jones. It was about the Railroad History of Stevens Pass. I believe that was his first encounter with the word "Wellington" and he was smitten!

His early interest was anything and everything concerning The Great Northern and Wellington. Since then his interest has expanded to Great Northern History in the Northwest and helping at the Skykomish Historical Society and the Railroad Archive in Burien WA.

*Pam Kelly*

# Contents

# Introduction

Most of the time most railroad men and women don't know how to tell stories about their careers because they don't think that people would be interested in the years that we have worked as railroad employees. The same things that went on trip after trip, day after day and year after year.

To get the stories out of these engineers, brakemen, conductors, switchmen, telegraph operators, dispatchers and section foremen and their crews, the section gangs you would have to be willing to spend the time listening to their lives as railroad employees.

My wife Nancy asked me to be a partner in writing this history of the railroad. I personally knew most of these men and women, so it was very easy for me to get them started with the words, "do you remember when?"

I honestly know that whoever reads these stories will truly understand why we all loved our jobs.

*Ted Cleveland*
*Skykomish 2016*

The single thing that inspired me to do an oral history book on the Great Northern Cascade Division is the very fact that all of the old "rails" are becoming a dying breed. This book is a collection of oral stories told by these workers. They all have their own way of speaking and thinking. They each have their own memories of what they believe happened.

We lost our old friend Bob Miller and all of his fantastic memories. I look at my own husband Ted who worked for forty two years on the Great Northern and the Burlington Northern as an engineer. I hear stories that will be lost to all time.

This idea has been sitting in my head for quite a long time and it was time to make it a reality. Who best to conspire with me? A railroad man who knows the language and can talk to the storytellers and say, "Do you remember when?"

These men and women all have a strong sense of history and the role that they played in creating it. They have been willing to share their memories of a time that is now gone. We married young and I grew up with these "rails" and grew to love and respect them and the jobs that they did. As my very small grandson Patrick said at a time when I was feeling especially sad, "Gramma, no one ever dies as long as someone remembers them."

It has been an honor and a privilege to preserve these memories. Please enjoy these stories and by doing so, help to keep the "rails" alive in memory.

*Nancy Cleveland*
*Skykomish 2016*

# Editor's Note

Why, you might ask, is a person with no railroad history editing a book of railroad stories? That question certainly crossed my mind as I started into this project.

My first reason is simple: I have read and enjoyed Nancy Cleveland's first two books of oral history. I said yes because I admire Nancy for preserving the stories told by these men and women, which would surely be lost without her tireless efforts to interview and transcribe their recollections.

The second reason for agreeing to do this, dawned on me only as I started to immerse myself in these stories. I realized how universally awe-inspiring these great machines on tracks really are. Whether the masterful engineer at the helm, the simple passenger further back, or an onlooker at a railroad crossing, who among us has not felt the thrill of experiencing a great train in motion? Or even stationary. I was struck by the words of Karl Warren, track inspector, who worked for forty-two years on the railroad: *"Sometimes I'd get to Sky and there would be some of the big old Mallets sitting there by the building and you'd walk by those things and you'd look at them. You were kind of insignificant alongside of one of those things. It just amazed me."*

The common thread amongst the hardworking people represented in this book is how much they appreciated their jobs. They found time for fun in their daily work, and they found awe in their environment, from the roundhouse and switching yards to the colors of the sunrise in the mountains that they travelled through.

These memories of places, people and events are unique to each storyteller. As such, great care has been taken to preserve their individual voices, in their own words and manner of speaking. Not always grammatically perfect, sometimes rambling, but we have chosen to print these words as they were spoken. The sequence of stories is arranged in order of hire date, from oldest to most recent.

It has been a privilege to learn about the railroad through these stories, and a task not near as daunting after Nancy's hard work of gathering and organizing them with respectful care. And Bob Kelly's guidance and consistent encouragement.

*Beanne Hull*
*Seattle, October 2016*

# Preface

Bob Miller and Ted Cleveland were "Comrades of the Rails." One from Granite Falls and one from Skykomish. Both worked for the GNRR and the BNSF. Lifelong friends

They were known to each other as Comrade C. and simply Comrade. "Where are you Comrade C.?" "Oh, headin' south, Comrade and its foggier than hell."

The loss of our friend Bob Miller became the inspiration for this book. Bob was a storyteller. He loved Sky because he said that it was full of stories. You always think that someone will be here forever, but with each loss all of their wonderful memories are gone forever. For this reason we are doing this book.

*Ted and Nancy Cleveland*

*Join us now for a Journey,*
*When there was a Railroad*
*to Run and Tales to be Told.*

# A Special Thank You

To all of the "railroaders" who are gone, but live on in memory. A memory of Pat Burns a Great Northern engineer who lived in Sky comes to mind.

One dark and stormy night our teenage kids called from Sky. They couldn't get home after skiing Stevens Pass. What are we to do was the question. We called Pat and sure enough he said to send them his way. He took all of those wet, tired kids and kept them the night. Regaling them with tales of who knows what and strong, hot Irish tea. They will always remember.

To George and Bill Leu, two more Great Northern engineers from Sky. Thank you because you and your comrades inspired the making of this book.

To all of the participants who donated their time and their memories so that this book could become a reality. It wouldn't have happened without your stories. The life that you led deserves a place in history.

To our family who supported us throughout this project. They all know how important it is to save our memories.

To Glenn Eburn and JoAnne Boggs you set a fire under us with a desire for yet another book.

To Joan Keaunui you were a lifesaver for me, taking the time to do the interview with Ted. I couldn't have done it.

To Dave Sprau and his wonderful memory of events and people. The spelling of names, places and event has helped us with our goal is to give honor to these stories.

To Father Dale Peterka for taking the time to write the history of the area. Nothing is complete without its history, thank you for this thorough, interesting addition to the book.

To Mike Bartenstein for his skills in producing such a detailed map of the places written about in this book.

To Beanne Hull our editor who was gracious enough to take our project into her busy life. A joy to work with, she was always willing to go the extra mile. The quotes at the beginning of each story were Beanne's idea. They help to draw the reader into each memory. We are glad that she came into our lives.

To the Skykomish Historical Society for supporting and funding this book, preserving the railroad history that founded the Town of Skykomish. A special thanks to 4Culture for again assisting our oral history project with a grant.

And lastly to Bob Kelly who was always able to find the answer to the problem of the moment with grace and aplomb. We could not have done this project without you.

*Ted and Nancy*

# HISTORY OF THE GREAT NORTHERN RAILROAD

## Fr. Dale Peterka

The year was 1893. The Territorial legislature had incorporated the town of Seattle just twenty-four years earlier. The only rail connection from Seattle to the east coast was the Northern Pacific Railroad, which ran east by way of Tacoma. Seattle was at the north end of a Northern Pacific branch line!

In fact, in 1893, most of Washington State was branch line territory! A few brave pioneers were settled in places like Wenatchee and Waterville, but most of the state was isolated from the rest of the country.

It is that picture of empty forests, impassable mountain ridges, and dangerous river crossings that helps us to appreciate what happened in 1893. On January 6 of that year, the last spike was driven on a new railroad that ran from St. Paul across the Pacific Northwest, over the Cascades, through Stevens Pass and down to Seattle. It was the Great Northern Railway.

Stevens Pass was given its name by railroad explorer Charles F. B. Haskell, who reached the top in 1890, naming the pass for his boss, John F. Stevens, the Great Northern's chief locating engineer. Stevens had directed Haskell to explore the headwaters of Nason Creek above Lake Wenatchee. According to the famous story, Haskell reached the top and chopped the name "Stevens Pass" into a nearby tree. The pass retains that name to this day; the tree has not survived.

## The Birth of the GN

The Great Northern Railway, under the ambitious name, Minnesota & Pacific Railroad, began in St. Paul, Minnesota, in 1857. Two mainlines were planned, one heading west across Minnesota into Dakota Territory, the other swerving northwest to the Canadian border. The builders of the new line soon ran out of money, and the five-year-old railroad went into bankruptcy.

In 1857, the halcyon days of railroad building in the U.S. were already fading. The history books contain the names of dozens of 19th century railroads that had begun with great optimism and had quickly gone broke. The famous Union Pacific, for example, built with generous government grants of cash and land, went broke soon after it was completed. And again in 1893.

The new owners of the little railroad in Minnesota renamed their railroad the Saint Paul & Pacific. Since local investors had become very leery of putting money into railroad building, the owners went overseas and borrowed money from banks in Holland and England.

The new company was moderately successful but greatly in debt. When a great depression hit the country in 1873, the railroad failed again, and the Dutch bankers who held the bonds asked for bankruptcy protection.

In 1876, a new group of eager investors persuaded the Dutch and other bond-holders to sell the railroad to them. The new owners renamed the railroad the St. Paul Minneapolis and Manitoba. Among the names of the new owners, one stood out: James J. Hill.

In a short time, the line to the Canadian border was complete. But Hill's plans for the Manitoba Road were just getting started. By 1879, GN tracks had crossed into North Dakota. In 1883, the tracks reached Devils Lake. In 1886, they were in Minot, two thirds of the way across the state.

## To Montana

On a summer's day in 1884, the people of Helena, Montana, saw an unusual sight. The daily Northern Pacific passenger train from the East had arrived in town with an extra car on the rear. A business car. The exclusive car of the president of the *St. Paul Minneapolis & Manitoba Railroad*, Mr. James J. Hill. When the reporters surrounded him and inquired about the purpose of his visit, Hill insisted that he had come to Helena to visit two old friends, Charles Broadwater and Paris Gibson. Hill was an enthusiastic fisherman; the three would do some fishing in local lakes and streams.

Hill's reply was half true. Broadwater and Gibson quickly took the visitor in tow, but their purpose was more business than pleasure. Hill was a railroad man. Broadwater and Gibson were local businessmen in need of a railroad. In the space of a week, the pair gave Hill a tour of the Missouri River Valley from Fort Benton to Butte City, showing him a dozen promising areas of development and insisting that a new railroad in Montana would be a success, even with the already-established Northern Pacific as a competitor.

In 1886—two years later!—the people of Helena gave James J. Hill an official welcome at Ming's Opera House. The rails of the Manitoba—under auspices of the locally-owned Montana Central Railroad—had reached Helena. The railroad had built five hundred and forty-five miles of new mainline from Minot, North Dakota, to Great Falls, Montana, in one season! The following year, the rails would continue south to Butte and soon would be carrying copper ingots from Butte to the refinery in Great Falls and coal, machinery, and a hundred other products from the East to Great Falls, Helena, Butte and central Montana.

## To The Pacific

Hill was not yet satisfied. In December of 1889, John F. Stevens, chief locating engineer of the newly named Great Northern Railway, was sent to seek out a rumored low-level crossing of the Rocky Mountains. At the same time, Stevens's lieutenant, Charles Haskell, was sent from Kalispell to explore the western approaches to the same rumored pass.

Stevens set out from Fort Assiniboine, near Havre, and made his way west to the Blackfeet Indian Agency at the foot of the mountains. With an Indian guide named Coonsah and with instructions from locals at the agency, Stevens made his way to a promising opening in the front wall of the Rockies.

The men stopped for the night at the foot of the pass and built a fire, but Stevens was certain that success was only a few miles off and he continued his trek alone. At last, he found the summit which was later named for the nearby Marias River.

But Stevens had used up all his daylight in the effort. As night came on, he found himself trapped in the darkness without shelter and unable to build a fire or retrace his path back to camp. To lie down and sleep was to risk freezing. To walk in the dark invited a fall and serious injury. The only thing to do was to stay where he was and try to keep himself awake. Stevens found a level stretch of ground and began tramping back and forth in the darkness and the cold.

The light of dawn was a welcome sight to John Frank Stevens! At first light, he made his way back to the camp and revived the nearly-frozen Coonsah. Together they returned to the Indian agency and to safety.

A month later, Charles Haskell followed the Flathead River and Bear Creek up into the pass from the west. The discovery of Marias Pass was complete. Marias Pass was the lowest crossing of the Rockies this side of New Mexico. Rails over the top could be laid down with only a modest grade. And no tunnel at the summit would be needed.

## Stevens Pass

Out in Washington, the conquest of the Cascades would not be that easy! The entire range between the Columbia and the Canadian border had been explored. There simply was no easy crossing.

Stevens Pass was the final choice, but putting a railroad over it would not be easy. A two-mile tunnel would be necessary, but, in the meantime, Hill chose to put down a "temporary" line that required twelve miles of zigzag track. Trains would have to saw back and forth to gain the required elevation. Photographs of the switchback route show trains of only a few cars with engines on front and back making their way up the steep approaches. In addition, on the west side, a nine-mile detour was necessary to allow the railroad to wind its way back and forth down the hill. In one stretch, a westbound train was actually traveling east!

The two-mile tunnel that would relieve the bottleneck on Stevens Pass was completed in 1900. It allowed the line to bypass the switchbacks completely. But the tunnel brought problems of its own. The coal-burning steam engines filled the tunnel with smoke and steam, choking the passengers and the engine crews, and coating the rails with a slippery mixture of soot and condensation.

There was a narrow escape in 1903 when an eastbound passenger train arrived at the entrance to the tunnel. An extra helper engine was coupled onto the front of the train, and the train entered the tunnel. Some distance inside, the coupler between the two engines broke, and the train was unable to continue. The engine crewmen were overcome by smoke and collapsed. Soon the passengers were choking as well. Finally, one of the passengers, a railroad employee, guessed what had happened, went forward and released the brakes, allowing the train to roll back out of the tunnel safely.

## Electric Locomotives

In 1909, the problem of smoke and moisture in the tunnel was solved with the installation of overhead trolley wire and the purchase of four electric locomotives. Freight and passenger traffic could now move silently and cleanly through Cascade Tunnel. The new system served faithfully until 1929, when a more modern system was adopted and the overhead wire was extended all the way to Skykomish and to Wenatchee. The new electric locomotives served until 1956.

## The Eight-mile Tunnel

With the Cascade Tunnel, the switchbacks were abandoned, but the rugged stretch from Wellington down the hill to Scenic was still a major hurdle. Heavy winter snow often caused the line to be closed. A snow slide in 1916 covered both the upper and the lower level of track and took out bridge 402. Fighting back, the Great Northern built massive wooden sheds or galleries that kept snow off the track. Steam-powered rotary snowplows were purchased to clear the line. Large numbers of men were hired to shovel snow off the tracks where there were no snow sheds.

"Some of you will live to see this line eliminated!" was James J. Hill's comment about the steep, winding mainline from Wellington to Scenic. In 1925, the decision was made to dig a tunnel from Berne on the east side of the pass to Scenic on the west side, bypassing the old two-mile tunnel, the town of Wellington, and some seventeen miles of troublesome trackage.

The new 7.8-mile tunnel was completed in January 1929. Young Lee Pickett from Index made a photographic record of the entire project. His fourteen-thousand photos in the University of Washington library show the massive investment in money, time and equipment that was necessary to dig a tunnel nearly eight miles long.

## The GN Today

The long-abandoned roadbed down the mountain from Wellington has been transformed by the Volunteers for Outdoor Washington into a first-class hiking pathway, the Iron Goat Trail. The Volunteers hoped to continue the trail through the old Cascade Tunnel, but the tunnel partly collapsed in 2007-08. Entering today is extremely dangerous.

The Great Northern name disappeared in 1970 with the formation of the Burlington Northern Railroad. The BN, in turn, became part of the Burlington Northern Santa Fe in 1996. In 2005, the name was shorted to simply "BNSF". The name of the premier passenger train, the Empire Builder, survives as the popular stainless steel Amtrak Empire Builder.

The Great Northern Railway Historical Society was formed in 1973 to preserve the Great Northern story. The GNRHS has published over four hundred reference articles on every GN subject from dining car china to cabooses.

Over a dozen books have been written about the GN, including works on such related subjects as locomotives, equipment, depots, the memoirs of former employees, and Glacier National Park. The Pacific Northwest Rail Archive in Burien, Washington, contains over one-hundred-thousand photos and other Great Northern-related items for researchers.

# WHAT IS A RAILROAD MAN?

A different breed of man. It is my understanding that at one time rail workers were classed as unskilled labor, yet they handled millions of dollars in freight and equipment and were responsible for thousands of lives each day.

Not a nine-to-five job with weekends and holidays off. Working an extra board, never knowing when you would be called next or where your next job would take you. Whether it was the hard physical labor of laying the rails before big equipment came into the picture, building the eight mile tunnel through the mountain from Scenic to Bern. Or snow slides, derailments, broken rail and mud slides, forest fires or hauling tons of freight, thousands of passengers and your mail. The danger and the speed to get the train from one point to the other on time, the job has the same requirements. Long, long hours and being ready on short notice. This is what draws these "rails" together. Simply by virtue of the job and the hours that they work, tends to isolate them from others and draws them together as a family and a closeted industry.

With the thousands of miles of rails to maintain, freight and passengers to get to the right destinations it took hundreds of employees working in different positions to accomplish this monumental task each and every day. They worked together as a family and knew each other as family. The steel gangs, tie gangs, B&B

gangs (bridge and building), gandy dancers, switchmen, engineers, brakemen, firemen, conductors and the dispatchers are a few who held the whole thing together.

The romance of the rails persists as a myth for most who do not work in the industry. The lonesome whistle blows, the shining rails stretch endlessly. The people working on the rails what are they doing? The figures up in the cab of these powerful locomotives as they travel by the crossings, who are they and where are they going. Surely somewhere that you will never get to see if you are not up on the locomotive with them. It all adds to the romantic allure and the mystery.

These men and women are proud to be a part of the railroad industry.

*Nancy Cleveland*

# JOE F.N. GAYNOR &
# JOE M. GAYNOR

*On our list of names of people to interview was the name Joe M. Gaynor, The
son of Joe F.N. Gaynor Superintendent of Electrical Operations for the GNRR.
The very reason that we are doing this book is to collect the living memories
of the people who worked the Cascade Division. I was diagnosed and treated
for a major medical problem so our plans went awry for a few months. Finally
calling Joe M. Gaynor we were dismayed to find that he had just recently died.
To keep the memory alive the following stories are from people who remember.*

*Nancy Cleveland*

I knew Joe F. N. Gaynor when I went to work on the Great Northern. Joe would
talk to anybody. He was an electrical engineer and was the Superintendent of
Electrical Operations for the Great Northern Railway, between Sky and Appleyard. Even though he was very intelligent he was able to make friends with anybody. He was friendly, yet if you had a problem he could solve it.

Joe always dressed for his work. He wanted to be prepared to work if he had
too, he wasn't afraid to get his clothes dirty. Joe always wore a whip cord Filson
jacket, a semi dress shirt and pants and tall work boots.

He was proud of the fact that if he had to, he could make the trip from Sky to
Appleyard in an hour in his car.

L-R: Joe F. N. Gaynor with Dell Williams, Henry Surles and J. C. Wright at Cascade Tunnel
Station in May of 1927. Lee Pickett photo, Skykomish Historical Society collection

The reason that the Gaynor Tunnel was built was because the 5018 and the 5019 couldn't make it around the curves. The reason being that the trucks on these engines held three traction wheels instead of two. Some places in the valley are really wide but at this particular place in the valley it is really narrow.

The track followed the route of Nason Creek. On this section of track, the mountain narrowed and they had to make an abrupt turn. To eliminate these sharp turns, Superintendent Gaynor convinced the company to make a new straight route. That would involve building a new straight track and a tunnel that would allow the 5018 and the 5019 to go through. The curvature was such that they had problems all of the time with speed, derailments and the fact that cars were getting longer and they had to go around this curve with longer cars.

Joe had to make the decision of whether to electrify into Seattle or put in a new bridge and tunnel to solve the problems. There was only so much money and he felt that it was more important to make that portion more efficient, which would allow higher speed and safety by doing away with all of the problems of the old line. So he chose to put the new bridge and tunnel which eliminated the curvatures and allowed a more efficient trip. The Bridge was number 385, a two-hundred foot steel trestle across Nason Creek. The tunnel was named the Gaynor Tunnel.

It is too bad they couldn't have electrified into Seattle also because electric engines are so much better than diesels.

*Ted Cleveland*

I met with Joe M. Gaynor (Joe F. N. Gaynor's son) at his home in Seattle in March of 2014. Joe and his twin brother were born in 1938 at Wenatchee after the family moved from Skykomish. He worked as a machinist for the railroad for more than forty years (1960 to 2003) until he retired.

Joe was quite a story teller and seemed content to embellish a few his tales. He had lots of stories about his father including taking him and his brother to many locations along the line at all hours of the night if there was a wreck or some problem with the electrical system. While telling stories he would mention a "who's who" list of people associated with the Great Northern Railway in the Cascades.

While a kid in Wenatchee, Joe said he and his brother were able to get on any locomotive and travel with the crew for the day, east or west out of town. The crews would switch the kids to other trains heading back toward the end of the day. Often he noticed how his father would meet the kids when they got back to town. Later he said he found out that the crew and depot operators were keeping track of their location and sending telegrams to his father during the day.

When asked about the name of Gaynor station he recounted that it was named for his father's uncle, "the Mayor of New York City" who was a friend of Jim Hill. He said, "Mayor Gaynor was shot while in office." (Checking the facts William J. Gaynor was Mayor of New York City who was in fact shot while in office he served 1910—1913, Ed).

Joe M. Gaynor died in 2015.

*Bob Kelly*

# KARL WARREN

Birthplace: Cashmere, WA 1927
Date of Service: December 17, 1947
Position Held: Track Inspector

*Sometimes I'd get to Sky and there would be some of the big old Mallets sitting over there by the building and you'd walk by those things and you'd look at them and you didn't amount to very much. You were kind of insignificant alongside of one of those things. It just amazed me. They used them out of Interbay up to Skykomish.*

I grew up in Cashmere. Me and my dad hiked a lot, mostly over in the Icicle River area. Started out when I was about six or seven. He took care of the dams on those lakes up there for the Icicle Ditch Company. He'd go up in the spring and clean out the outlet and close the gate. The Icicle Ditch Company provided irrigation to take care of the apples in Leavenworth, Peshastin and Dryden down as far as Monitor. We'd take off early in the morning and hike in, do dad's work and hike back out. We'd go into Eight Mile Lake, Square Lake, Aqua Lake. They all had dams to hold the water back till they needed it for irrigation. So I'd get to go into those lakes, probably a couple times a year. There were a lot of guys on the railroad who liked to go fishing too and we'd hike into the Enchantments and we'd go fishing.

What led me to get into the railroad business was this: I'd just come back from the army, I was just nineteen years old. I came home to Cashmere with my wife. First day I got into town I took my wife down to see the warehouse, where I used to work and I ran into a fellow I worked for before, in the warehouse. He said, "Hey I'm glad you're back, you got a job yet?" I said, "No I just got in last night." He said, "Well, be here in the morning!" Just like that I had a job. I knew he'd done it 'cause he didn't like labeling apple boxes in the cold storage room. And he was about the only one who could label fast enough to do it, other than myself. So he put me to work on the labeling machine. There are five-hundred and ninety-eight boxes on a car and I'd do five and six cars a day. I did that for maybe a month and then my brother Homer came home. He said to come over when he got home from work. "Do you want to go to work on the railroad?" I said, "well I don't know." He said, "You can go to work tonight with me, on patrol." So I said, "Okay." Went that night with him on patrol, he worked with me a couple of weeks and then he turned me loose out there by myself, on the road with the motor car. Luckily I didn't get killed. Everything progressed from there. Working on patrol means running the track ahead of the train to make sure the track was clear. We just had a big wreck down by Wenatchee so they were running patrol there to get the trains through and make sure it was clear.

The warehouses didn't pay that much and the railroad paid ninety-six cents an hour when I started. I got $1.80 an hour when I ran the motor car. A motor-car was a speeder. In 1948 we had a big flood over there. We lost about one quarter mile of track, down by Monitor. And we almost lost the track this side of Cashmere. We were working eight hours a day, six days a week. That was our regular work week. I drew a paycheck for $318.00 for the last half of June. If you figure that out, after you take out retirement, which wasn't much then and six dollars or so in income tax, my take home was $318.00. Ninety-six hours at $1.08 an hour. The rest of it was overtime. So you could figure out just about how many hours I worked. I was out there for three days straight before they sent me home to take a shower and a little nap. I couldn't go to sleep, couldn't unwind. Then went back out for another couple of days. I was young in those days and I could do it.

I think probably we were the only family who had seven of us working here on the Cascade Division at the same time. Homer, Kenny, Norman, Glen, Wayne, Dean and myself. Homer, Wayne and I were all Track Department. Kenny was Signal Department, Norman, Glen and Dean were Train Service.

I started out on the Great Northern railway, it was a great railroad to work for. More like a family than a company. They always took care of their own. Up until the merger it stayed that way. I worked all kinds of jobs from slide patrolman to track inspector, section foreman, extra gang foreman. I always had a lot of good men working for me. Spent many, many nights down along the Puget Sound digging mud with the ditchers. There was a slide down by Mukilteo, at Naketa Beach road. We spent several days out there digging out the houses. We received some very good letters, sent to the superintendent from the occupants of the houses, thanking us for what we did.

I never worked on the trains at all, only the work train. Worked snow dozers there with Bill Coughlin, conductor on the dozer. Worked with all the old section crewmen on the line, John Micone, section foreman in Skykomish. John's son, Ted Micone was a conductor. Harry Nambu, section, Harry Hamada, section foreman at Scenic. They sent him over to Harrington during WWII to avoid "Executive Order." Steve George, section foreman in Merritt. Steve had two sons, Jim George who later became section foreman in Merritt and Paul George who became the roadmaster in Skykomish. Harold LaBounty, section foreman in Cashmere. I went to work for Alex Hasson in Cashmere when I first started out. Then there was Bill Hogarth in Edmonds, John Solga, section foreman at Mukilteo. These were all section foremen that I knew.

I knew all the old guys, even some of them who were on the Wellington slide:

Ben Nowak, conductor, I.E. Clary, superintendent of the Cascade Division and Ed Carter, was the trainmaster of the Cascade Division. His wife Ella was the agent in Sky.

Then there were the gang foremen. Mike Quaranta, extra gang foreman worked the gangs all of the time. Sarapo Evangelico Wicco, everyone called him Wicco, the only reason I knew his full name was because I made out the time books behind him, was an extra gang foreman and then a section foreman. Fe-lipe Labuguen was down at

Gang foreman Mike Quaranta worked the Cascades with complete railroad camps that traveled with his men. The large crews had bunk cars, cook cars and dining cars as well as all their tools and equipment. Skykomish Historical Society collection

Interbay. A lot of them at that time were Filipino or Japanese. Adamore Heppell was in Ballard. Adamore was more commonly known as Ernie Heppell. Bill Hogarth was in Edmonds.

Extra gangs were known as outfit car gangs. Outfit cars were just boxcars fixed up for sleeping quarters. Then they had a diner where they fed the all the men, self-contained. They sent the groceries to us from an outfit in Seattle called Addison Miller. Wasn't always the best but it was something. Had a cook and a guy that cleaned up the cars.

"Gandy dancers" were the extra gangs. They were the guys that built the railroad, right from the beginning to the end. They were the guys that did it. They worked hard with very little equipment. I heard that Jim Hill once said, they can ride his railroad anytime they wanted to because they built it. Sometimes they'd ship the gandy dancers out of Seattle. They weren't in very good shape. Mostly all winos. For the most part it was a way of life for them but they were all good guys. After they got three or four days out on the track working, they sobered up. That was 'til they earned a time check and went back to Seattle. As time went on of course they kind of faded away and we got more local people. If we were away from home we also lived in the outfit cars. I had an outfit car gang for about four years.

We had no big equipment not even when I started. Matter of fact everything was by hand. You cut the rail with a sledge hammer and a chisel. If you had to make a rail shorter that's what you did. Then a little later on they managed to make a saw that cut the rail. Then they came up with an electric tamping machine. Before that it was all done by shovel and the foot. There was nothing mechanical during WWII. It just stayed the way, it was during the Depression. Nobody made any machinery for them at all. They were too busy making tanks for the war. That's the way it was. Out there in all kinds of weather, it didn't matter. Whatever needed doing you were there. I spent a lot of nights along that bay, standing on the seawall watching for trains, while the guys were digging mud. They did have some steam ditchers but they were kind of fading away. The last one that I knew we had was in 1957 down in Interbay and we were using it for singling the track in Ballard. That was the last job they did, then it went to the scrap yard, the steam derrick ditcher. A lot of stuff went the same way. Everything was a lot of hard work. Everything you did was hard work, there were no easy days, especially working with some of those old foremen. They were really dedicated. When you found one that didn't care, he'd go along pretty easy, but very few of them didn't care.

You know really I didn't find many that didn't care until after the merger. I went down on the south end and put in ties from Tacoma to Centralia. We put in about 80,000 ties. Went down one track and back the other. I never saw one section crew who would lend you a hand in any way. They had all disappeared. You might see them sitting on the hill up there in a truck. All they did was sit around and wait for something to happen. My crew was doing the work. I had eighteen men and about a million and a half dollars worth of machinery. I had a good crew, always had a good crew, all good men. In fact they didn't come to me if they didn't want to work.

The only thing I remember about the steam trains, they were big and heavy

Nine members of the track gang throw their weight into pry bars as their foreman gives direction to align the track. Skykomish Historical Society collection

Locomotive #1453 in passenger service east bound at Monroe in 1947. Karl Warren remembered riding #1453 many nights in the snow, shoveling the switches for the crew as they crossed the Cascades. Walter Ainsworth Collection, PNRArchive.org

and made a lot of noise. That's about it. I rode a few of them, the #1453 that used to be over at Appleyard, the Leavenworth Local, rode it many nights in the snow, shoveling the switches for them. Sometimes I'd get to Sky and there would be some of the big old Mallets sitting over there by the building and you'd walk by those things and you'd look at them and you didn't amount to very much. You were kind of insignificant alongside of one of those things. It just amazed me. They used them out of Interbay up to Skykomish. I guess they used them back east too but not on this side.

There were a lot of good people back on the railroad then, when it was the Great Northern. Everybody took care of everybody. Everybody worked, everybody was happy. They were good people, really good people you worked with then. I absolutely enjoyed my work. Wouldn't have done it for forty two years if

I hadn't. I was away from home when I was on the gangs relieving the foreman, I'd be away for weeks. But I always managed to get home on a Wednesday night. I think there were only two or three Wednesday nights I didn't make it, because the machinery would break down or something.

There has always been trouble down on that line by Mukilteo. At one time they had three steam locomotives (ditchers and clamshells) out there working all the time. They worked twenty-four hours a day, during WWII and before. It always slid and its always going to slide. They can do whatever they want. They ain't going to keep it up there. If Mother Nature wants it down, Mother Nature's going to bring it down. I've seen them all talk about it. Everything they do is just a lost cause.

Our first introduction to a diesel electric ditcher was diesel electric #1841. Homer and I were sent down to Cashmere to put ballast into the counterweight on the #1841. Homer and I spent two or three weeks putting track railroad steel around the back of the counter balance weight so the machine wouldn't tip over. The company then started getting rid of the old steam derricks. The first decent diesel electric ditcher we got was #1843. They put it in the electric shop in

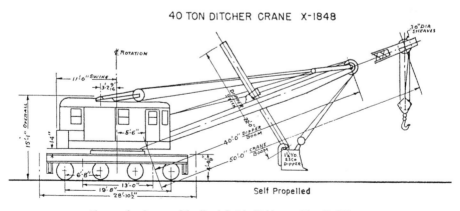

Diagram showing one of the diesel electric ditching machines Karl Warren
mentions as taking over from the steam operated equipment.

Appleyard. Arnie Bogen came over from Montana. He bid the job as the operator of the new electric ditcher #1843.

Adamore Heppell Sr. was the foreman at Mosher back around 1900, when they were putting in the sea wall. Mosher was a cross-over on the double track near Mukilteo. There were houses on the west side of the track, the only place between Everett Junction and Ballard where there were houses right off the west side of the track. Adamore had a crew out there building that seawall. They say he had a hundred Chinese men working with him. The Oriental Trading Company brought them over here to work. There was a Filipino man working there who came over with that company. He kept sending money to the Trading Company. The other Filipinos said don't send them that money, and he said, "Oh I have to or they'll send me home." Even after they cut off the Mukilteo Section Crew and he went down to Interbay to work he was still sending money back to the Trading Company. I don't know whether he did it up to the time he retired or not. He was by himself. He lived in a little old shack off someplace and had enough money to buy rice. That's the way he lived.

On a gang there would be anywhere from seventy-five men to the smallest gang of five or six men. After I got done with the tie gang, they allowed me twenty-five men for that job. Then I would go back to maybe seven or eight, depending on what they wanted me to do. When they built the hump yard at Interbay, I was the first gang in there. They sent me down there to start receiving all the material. The engineering department designed the list, I had a timekeeper to do all the book work and stuff. Then I'd just take care of the unloading. They started putting in lap switches and I'd never seen any of them before. When those things started coming in I didn't know what they were. They had two frogs, instead of one or two sets of points. Then on each one of them they had a color marked on every piece of it, every tie plate all color-coded. I didn't know what it was all about. Must mean something, so I kept all the colors separate. I started stacking up everything according to the color codes. Damn good thing I did. We had to unload over one-hundred thousand ties down there in 1968.

On a gang you had a basic number of men that stayed with you all the time. Then you had others working with them. Those old gandys, they knew what they were doing, you didn't have to tell them. They were a tough old bunch they didn't put up with any crap. When I first went down to that hump yard, I thought I was going to be in there all by myself with eight or ten men. Finally they brought in an extra gang that Carl Peglow had. Then they brought in the steel gangs, the West Steel Gang. They laid most of the rail.

Homer, my brother, was the general foreman on that job. Homer was all over the railroad, relieving the foremen, working the gangs and stuff like that, until they promoted him to steel gang foreman and then to roadmaster back in Great Falls.

Went to work on the section in Cashmere to make a living. I started out as a slide patrolman and held positions with everything up to extra gang. I finally retired on December 31 1989. Forty two years of service. I've still got all my check stubs from the first time I started working on the GNRR.

# REMEMBERING
# THE GANDY DANCERS

### Sis Javier & Sharen George

*Gandy Dancer is a slang term used for early railroad workers who laid and maintained railroad tracks in the years before the work was done by machines. In the U.S. early section crews were often made up of recent immigrants and ethnic minorities who vied for steady work despite poor wages and working conditions and hard physical labor. There are various theories about how the name came about but most refer to the dancing movements of the workers using a specially manufactured five foot long lining bar, which came to be called a "gandy" as a lever to keep the tracks in alignment.*

Taken from Wikipedia the free encyclopedia.

The Gandy Dancers, here in Skykomish, lived in the outfit cars across the tracks. They worked between Skykomish and Merritt. They had little cabins at Merritt and some of them would go over there and stay. They didn't go very far, they didn't go to Monroe or anywhere like that. They rode the bus back and forth between Skykomish and Merritt The work that they did mostly was putting in the railroad ties.

In the winter they shoveled the snow off the crossings. There were six to eight feet of snow in those days. They worked very hard, they even worked on the weekends shoveling crossings. I can still see the snow on the tracks, it was so

Gandy Dancers with their bus at Merritt, Washington in 1950. Not all individuals have not been identified. Gang Foreman A. W. "Buster" Norris is the second from the right in the back row. Others possibly identified are Paul Javier, Rusty Soloman, Andy Strom, and Ben Javier. Javier Family photo

high and they had to clear it all by shovel. They were hard workers.

They made a lot of good food, they ate a lot of rice. When they went to Merritt they took their own lunches with them.

Ben Javier was my father-in-law. He lived right by the track here in Skykomish. His son Paul Javier worked here with his dad in the wintertime. I had a friend in high school named Andy Strom Jr. and he did the same thing, working with the gandy dancers here in town. It was a summer job for them.

We had other Filipinos who worked here. They came from the Philippines. Teddy Arrabelle and Martin Busk were friends who lived together. They lived in a little white house by the Masonic Hall in Skykomish. Teddy went back home because he had left his wife there. He passed away back there. Martin went back with Teddy and he died there too.

Boxie lived here in town. Boxie and Paulie Allejo live on the same street. Boxie lived in Bob Pierce's house and Paulie lived two houses down.

*Sis Javier*

I remember Wico, a Filipino man who was a foreman for many years at Winton. There was the family of Benny Javier who also lived in Skykomish. Benny and some of his children and a little guy named Teddy worked with Jim back in the fifties and the sixties.

Jim was always late for dinner because they would invite him to eat with them. He loved their spicy foods, except for a dish that they called blood pudding.

*Sharen George*

# ELMER WALCKER

**Birthplace: Turtle Lake, North Dakota 1929**
**Dates of Service: Fireman: August 19, 1950, Engineer: June 10, 1964**
**Positions Held: Fireman, Engineer**

## Conversations with Uncle Elmer, written by Mike Walcker

So many times I complained about growing up in a town of only three hundred inhabitants. Now, after considerable time away, I look back on growing up in that town as a blessing. Especially since it sat squarely on the Great Northern mainline at the foot of the mighty Cascade Mountain Range, and every eastbound train that thundered through was about to battle the grades and topography of the last great obstacle that Jim Hill faced in completing his transcontinental railroad from Chicago to Seattle. By the time I was old enough to love trains (about eight years old) the transition from steam to diesel was

Elmer Walcker, the man who tied up locomotive #229, called a cab and went dancing with Stella, thus ending his career with the Great Northern Railway.

well under way. I vaguely remember smaller steam engines pulling freight loads up to the town of Gold Bar, where there was a small yard. This was known as the "Gold Bar Turn" and it terminated two miles east of my town of Startup, Washington. But the prize for us kids was the twice-daily appearance of that beautiful orange and green Empire Builder, taking lucky passengers to places that a kid could only dream about, being muscled along by those spectacular and sleek E7 and F units, followed by matching streamlined hotels on rails.

Fast forward about fifty years to the other side of the Cascade Range. Still being a GN fan and still living in a town that hosts the same mainline rail, all GN Historical Society members had been asked to reach out to any relative or friend that may have worked for the mighty GN and talk to them about the history and lore of their experiences. Enter Uncle Elmer. Elmer Walcker to be exact, and he was not really my uncle. His father, John Walcker, and my grandfather, Fred Walcker, were brothers. He was actually my father's cousin, but they looked and acted like brothers. We all lived in Startup where about seventy-five of the town's three hundred occupants were relatives on either my dad's side or mom's side. It made getting into trouble without being caught nearly impossible, and, as the rest of these stories will prove out, made for some great family gossip at all our holiday gatherings.

I love talking to Uncle Elmer. He has a very strong resemblance to my dad, who passed away in 1977, and spending time with him is like being with dad. Elmer was an engineer with the GN and worked out of Interbay. He would blow the horn every time he came through town and us kids would always try to be around the tracks to waive at him, proud as peacocks that our "Uncle" was at the throttle. This habit of his would eventually lead to my first question, in which I would try to prove or disprove one of our family's most recounted stories of my dad, and the day Uncle Elmer denied being related to ANY of us! To lay the groundwork for this story, you must know that my grandpa and grandma's house was located on State Route 2 in Startup, situated between the highway and the railroad tracks on about three acres. Grandma was a nurse and the downstairs of the house was used as a makeshift doctor's office for locals who needed medical care, but in 1960, they were in a car accident and grandma was seriously injured. The noise of the trains and the traffic bothered her as she tried to recover (the injuries would eventually take her life), so we "switched houses" with them. Mom, dad, my two brothers and I lived about six blocks north and far enough away from the highway and tracks to give grandma some much needed quiet time. The grandparent's house was a three-story farmhouse with a large porch running across the entire front of the house. If you stood on the right side of the porch, you were close to the tracks, and on the left side, you were closer to the highway. The door going into the house from the porch went directly into the kitchen, where mom spent a quite a bit of time. All of these bits of information will soon become relevant, as events of that day played out.

The Gold Bar Turn would go eastbound late in the morning, work the yard, and sometimes switch out small industries up to Baring and for a year or more, Uncle Elmer would draw this duty as engineer. When on time, the train would head back westbound around 4:00 p.m. If dad was home, he would wait for them to come into town and Uncle Elmer would blow the horn as he rounded the curve just off the Wallace River Bridge, giving dad ample time to come out on the porch and wave. On this fateful day, they were late, and dad was already home and had taken the paper and took refuge in the bathroom, giving him some rest from three boys and assorted friends who were usually at the house. Mom was cooking dinner and had grown tired of the wooden screen door slamming shut every time one of us chased in or out, so she hooked the door closed and ordered us to stay out. The stage was set for what was about to become one of my dad's *least* shining moments.

Elmer was on the throttle and he had a new fireman on board. He warned the newbie that as they rounded the curve into town, he would be on the horn, not for a crossing, but to signal his cousin, who liked to greet him as the train passed by. The ritual went forth as planned, but dad was in...uh... no position to greet the fast approaching geep (nickname for the EMD GP7 locomotive) that was at the head end of the westbound consist. In a panic, dad jumped up, hustled his trousers up and ran for the door only to find the screen door securely locked. I must mention at this point that dad was a little over six feet tall, about two hundred and fifty pounds and had been a successful football player and boxer in his younger days. The momentum of this mass moving at light speed towards the porch could not be stopped by a flimsy wooden-framed screen door, and it simply wrapped itself around him as he passed through it. The shock of having a screen door attached to his still moving body as he continued to the corner of the porch caused him to loose grasp on his trousers, which quickly fell to his feet. At that moment, Uncle Elmer looked out the window of the cab with his fireman and saw a large, disheveled man fighting to rid himself of a screen door in his underwear. "That your cousin?" quipped the fireman. And without missing a beat, Elmer shot back, "nope, don't know who that crazy bastard is, he must work for the U.P.!"

After wiping away a tear of laughter, Elmer confirmed the validity of the story and the answered first of my several questions.

In 1977, many of us were singing along with Johnny Paycheck to the country classic "Take This Job and Shove It". What I didn't know was that someone in my own family took up that mantra a decade before Mr. Paycheck ever sang one note of that song.

Flashback to Lake Chelan, Washington. I was spending the day with my "uncle" Elmer Walcker at his home on the lake along with his wife, Stella. We were talking about Elmer's career with the Great Northern Railroad, mostly working out of Interbay and Everett. At some point, Stella asked Elmer if he still had "that stack of your old railroad stuff" put away somewhere. Elmer responded that he thought it was in the closet, and Stella offered to find it. A few minutes later, she rejoined us with a handful of papers and schedules, at which point I lost focus on the conversation as I could see paper gold (to a rail fan) and priceless documents being handed over for my inspection.

In this stack were some time-tables from the sixties, some GN advertising, various schedules and work documents and other work-related papers. I then came across a seniority list of engineers. I nearly fell out of my chair reading the names of the men who were on that list and seeing the most senior man was Joel H. Arnold who showed a fireman date of September 23, 1903!! Here was a complete list (for Spokane west) of the men who powered those monster steam giants over the Cascade Range, over the switchbacks, through the hazardous old tunnel, surviving the Wellington disaster and so many other amazing acts and events. The list was inclusive of engineer and fireman up to January 1, 1959. I'm sure Elmer said something while I was pouring over this gem, but darn if I heard him!

After several minutes, I felt that I needed to move on to other documents and carefully asked if I could keep all the paperwork to copy and share with other GN folks, and if that was possible, I would have plenty of time, say, around bedtime, to carefully and completely digest the list, despite my wife's woeful looks of angst. So I plugged on through the stack of papers. The next was a book entitled: "Form 1404, Time return and delay report of engine and train employees—for enginemen", or in street language, a time card. It was a full book for 1966, time on duty, what locomotive, where, when, employee number, etcetera. Each page was carefully filled out and each page was worthy of careful examination. Switcher was #229, train was #9 in Delta yard. Conductor was Adkins, engineer was E.E. Walcker, date was December 31, 1966, time on duty was 2:45 p.m., train departed at 3 p.m., time off duty was…let's see, where is the time off duty? After a careful search, including looking for a following page dated January 1, 1967 and finding none, I had to ask Elmer why the log was incomplete? Did they use a different coding system in 1967? Did something happen that delayed him over or changed his duty status? I never expected his response. I had always believed that Elmer left the GN when the merger took over. It was never really an issue in family circles of why or when he left the railroad, we just knew he did leave and started a construction company with his boys and went on to own and operate a resort hotel at Lake Chelan, Washington.

There were two other things we all knew. Elmer was married to Aunt Stella, and every boy in the family had a secret crush on Aunt Stella. She was, and still is, a stunning woman in both her personality and stature. Elmer certainly married up! The second thing I knew about Elmer was that most Walcker men are independent and are prone move in directions that some would consider unwise. Or at least, act impetuously when the situation called for a calm head. Turns out Elmer wanted to meet Stella at the Everett Eagles at 11pm to dance in the New Year. He had requested the time, he had seniority, he had the time coming, but he also had, what he called "a total jerk" for a boss and he was denied the time off. So, at 10:30 p.m., he called a taxi cab, tied up old #229 in the yard, and went off to dance with Stella, thus telling the GN and his boss to "take this job and shove it!"

As a post script, at the Monroe swap meet in February, Bob Kelly introduced me to an old GN head who knew Elmer. We talked about this incident and he laughed out loud, remembering the same event, and agreed that Elmer's boss was a real nasty man, and that Elmer quitting nearly cost the man his job and upset many railroad men who knew and liked Elmer. Finally: "Way to go, Uncle Elmer!" I would have done the same thing.

So far, my visit with Uncle Elmer was spent talking about family and friends. The subject I really wanted to talk about was his role as an employee of the Great Northern Railway. I had been taking notes, so now I opened a new page and changed the subject. "Tell me about your career with the GN", I asked. "Well, let's see…" Elmer paused and thought. And the stories began to flow. Without quoting, I will try to highlight his recollections.

Elmer hired on with the GN in 1949. He recalled that the war had ended and many men who were drafted into military service were returning home and going back to their jobs, and many of them were engineers, so that job was hard to come by. Elmer started out on a section crew, then a tie gang and would often run ahead of the Empire Builder in track car looking for rocks or slides. All of this was out of Interbay, and the biggest problem area for slides was around Index, just as the railway started to challenge the Cascade Mountain Range. He said there were a few times they had to delay the Builder to clear a rock or two off the mainline, something the dispatcher never enjoyed doing!

Movement was quick during those years, if you worked hard and were a company man they moved you along when openings came up. Elmer was promoted to fireman in 1950 out of Interbay and ran routes to Vancouver, Washington, Portland, Oregon and Wenatchee. He said at that time, there were seven crews in Skykomish assigned to the big electric engines and he was assigned to the extra board and also plowed snow in the winter months on the Stevens pass section. Seniority at that time was very important and over a few years, he worked on Train 28 (the mail train), worked the Gold Bar turn, worked a switcher and helpers to Vancouver, BC, and was on the extra board in Vancouver, Portland, and Wenatchee. He said that at that time, most engines were oil fired steamers and recalled the 1147 (now in Railroad Park in Wenatchee). He liked that loco and said it used to be an old passenger locomotive that had been put into switcher service and was a "darn good" piece of equipment. He really enjoyed the steam engines, but said the mallets were tough locos to run and they really swung wide, which made them tricky when pulling into yard tracks or going around tight curves.

The transition to diesels was not a problem for Elmer, they were more comfortable and easier to service. They solved a lot of problems for the railroad, especially on the "hill". He recalled that some of the early F units had electric brakes and could easily run up to one hundred miles per hour, and said that on a trip to Vancouver, somewhere around English, they hit just over that speed on a trip north. There were no speed recorders then, they came later, and engineers were very proud of keeping their train on time and in one piece! He said that when they took the Builder out of King Street station for the eastbound run, they would depart around 4:10 p.m. and would pull into Skykomish close to 7 p.m.. He said overall, working for the railroad was good, but they kept a tight handle on expenses. There was no meal pay, no expenses, and they allowed $1.20 a night for hotel expenses. It was not unusual for an engineer to work until 3 p.m., get eight hours of sleep and then be called back to work and stay on duty for the maximum time, which was fifteen hours and fifty-five minutes. Any more and they would have to allow you ten hours of rest.

I asked him what the most frightening experience he had as an engineer and he instantly said it was coming down the hill into Wenatchee on Train 28 when it was foggy. They ran seventy-nine miles per hour and you couldn't see the blocks because of the thick fog in winter that would come off the snow. He said that was very unnerving, but they had to be on time, so they did the best they could. He did recall one other thing, when he was a fireman he would ride to work with an old engineer friend. One day they were talking and the engineer mentioned that he never had gotten a Washington driver's license. Elmer said he yelled "Why the hell don't you have a license?", and of course, the old hogger calmly explained that you don't need a damn license to drive a train!

I think, all in all, even considering the fact that he walked away in disgust when he finally had his fill of the railroad management, Elmer truly enjoyed working for the GN. Especially the friendships and long relationships that came with the job. He never had a bad word for the working class men and women of the railroad, except for one particular supervisor, and still recalled the names and faces of many of his co-workers with great fondness. I try to visualize what it must have been like to be in the cab during the steam to diesel transition, running up Stevens Pass, or up and down the coastline to Vancouver, Washington and Vancouver, BC and must admit, it had to be a great ride.

Many of the stories that Uncle Elmer had talked about involved our family. At first I thought it might not be an important part of the dialogue on the impact that the railroad had, but then realized, that without the GN, or Jim Hill's vision of having a transcontinental railway, all of our lives might be different. To emphasize that point, I often wondered how a family of German-Russian-Austrian immigrants ended up in Startup, Washington, when most of them had settled in North and South Dakota. The Great Northern railway was the answer.

Grandpa Fred Walcker was one of fourteen children, and was the third oldest. The youngest was Jake Walcker and when their father died of what they then called the plague, their mother remarried and the three oldest boys moved out and went north for work. Six months later, their mother also died and the remaining kids were scattered. Jake was adopted by a family in Wenatchee, Washington named Schoe, or Schoo (we never really tracked that down) but they didn't change his last name. Fred last saw Jake when he was about six months old and never knew his fate after his mom died. My dad was an only child (I guess grandpa learned something after being part of a family with fourteen kids!) and when my dad graduated high school, grandpa and grandma moved to Everett to work in the shipyards. At times, he would come out for extra work at the Startup cedar mill (the town was named for George Startup, owner of the mill, not because it's where you "start up" the mountains). Jake Walcker worked on a track gang for the GN and they were doing work out of Gold Bar. One day, after work, Fred stopped in at the Cedar Stump tavern to play pool with the guys from the mill. The GN track gang had finished up their work and they too felt the urge to refresh at the only watering hole in Startup. At some point, someone yelled "Hey, Walcker, you going to join us in a game?" and at that point, two men seated at the bar both turned to respond. They both laughed and Fred said something to the effect about both of them having the same last name. That's when Jake said the words that our entire family has repeated since the dawn of time ..."Yea, but my last name is spelled differently, it's W-A-L-C-K-E-R".

I don't know exactly what happened after that, but I get choked up thinking what my grandfather must have been thinking when he realized he had located his brother that he had not seen in so many years. And it was mostly due to the Railroad (and a tip of the hat to beer and taverns!) Not long after that, grandpa and grandma bought property and a house in Startup. Jake met and married Maggie Fadden and they too, located in Startup. Dad gave up his teaching job at Mayfield college and moved with mom, to ... you got it ... Startup, and within a decade, both maternal and paternal grandparents, six sets of aunts and uncles, and GOD knows how many cousins ended up in that cursed little town, that fifty years later, still holds a place in our hearts, and still has that ribbon of rail that was pounded down at the turn of the century for the GN railroad.

I must end with this last story, because it could only happen on Stevens pass. And pretty much only to my two older brothers, who were so bad growing up that I was considered a good kid because I could never get into as much trouble as they did. Elmer corrected himself as I was getting ready to leave that the worst thing that he remembered from his engineer days might not have been the fog going into Wenatchee in the winter, but it might have been one particular trip from King Street Station to Skykomish on the Builder. He was deadheading that day, he could not really recall why, most likely heading up to stay in Sky for some extra board work or to bring a train back to Interbay, but what he did recall was that as the train rounded the curve east of Sultan and onto the long tangent into Startup, the engineer said "I hope those damn kids don't show up on the Wallace River bridge again." "Kids?" Elmer responded. "Yea, last couple trips there have been three kids who climb the bridge and have been…uh…relieving themselves on the vista dome as we pass underneath." As quickly as the conversation progressed, the train approached the bridge, and sure enough, the shapes of three people could be seen on the east end of the bridge. There was, I'm sure, a long string of curse words thrown about the cab of the loco, and as they passed under the girders. Elmer said he looked up and there they were. My two brothers and the neighbor kid, all in position, zippers down, to anoint the Builder as it passed underneath, to include many startled and shocked patrons in the unfortunately named "vista dome". "When you see your two brothers, you might remind them of that day the three special agents came to your house. They still don't know how they got caught, but you can now tell them that their favorite Uncle Elmer made the call to the agents the second he got into Sky". Laughing as hard as he had all day, he said he wished he could have been there when dad found out. As I went out the door and said my goodbye's I could still hear him laughing and saying "them damn kids!"

As a post-script, one of "them damn kids" became a Washington State elected representative and respected insurance agent, another became a captain in the Washington State Patrol, and the third, an Everett Police officer and later a business owner specializing in antiques and collectibles.

Life in a small town happened because of and in spite of the railroad, and if it would not have been for one man's dream, and the labor, blood, sweat and tears of many men…none of it would have happened. Thank you, Jim Hill!

*Much appreciation to Mike Walcker who was prompted to collect these stories from Elmer Walcker after reading a request in the GNRHS magazine, asking members to collect information that may soon be gone. Born in Monroe, raised in Startup, and graduated Sultan high school and Everett Community College, Mike's career in criminal justice eventually led him to become a senior special agent for BNSF in Spokane and he worked a number of details in six different states. In addition to his earlier career in the WSP, he and a partner owned Side-Tracked Hobbies in Monroe for about fifteen years.*

# BOB MILLER

**Birthplace: Arlington, Washington, 1925**
**Date of Service: Fireman, September 19, 1950, Engineer, June 10, 1964**
**Position Held: Fireman, Engineer**

## "The Whistle Blows" by Fred Cruger

*Fred was Bob's friend and is the Curator of the Granite*
*Falls Museum, he wrote this testament to Bob's memory.*

*Bob loved old cars and old trains...heck he loved all old equipment, and respected*
*the men who knew how to operate and maintain it. That love of "how things work"*
*drove Bob to life-long learning in virtually all things mechanical and electrical.*

About twenty years ago, I moved to Granite Falls from the suburb of Machias and made friends with Bob Miller while talking about antique cars. On Monday January 9, 2012, Bob died after a multi-year battle with cancer.

Bob had spent his formative years in Granite. His grandparents Austin and Laura Miller had come to Granite in about 1902 with Austin's sister and her husband Hugh Sharp. Austin named his own son Hugh, honoring his brother-in-law. Hugh Miller married Belle and in 1925 their son Bob was born.

Bob was born into a family of self-sufficient men and women. His great-uncle Hugh owned and operated one of the successful taverns in Granite. Hugh's wife was an early milliner in Granite. They lived in the house that is today the Historical Museum.

Bob's granddad Austin had worked in the mining industry, then operated heavy steam equipment (steam donkeys and locomotives) in the logging industry, as an engineer on heavy Climax and Shay logging locomotives. Bob would spend a career as a railroad engineer, after an early stint in the navy. And as the saying goes, "You can take the boy out of the train, but you can't take the train out of the boy!" For years he presented lectures and slide shows on northwest railroad history. Bob set up the display in the Granite Falls Museum a few years ago, and provided countless stories and artifacts for visitor enjoyment. Bob loved old cars and old trains...heck he loved all old equipment, and respected the men who knew how to operate and maintain it.

That love of "how things work" drove Bob to life-long learning in virtually all things mechanical and electrical. He had a compulsion to "experiment". And he had a personal bias that said, " If you can't fix it you probably shouldn't own it." So we spent hours talking about antique engines, cars, crank telephones, magneto ignitions, telegraph keys and early radios.

But what fascinated me about Bob was his love of animals and his sense of humor. In the 1930's Bob's dog had his own "handout" route in town. Bob was never without a dog and even a few years ago, when Bob's old dog died and Bob found out he himself had an early cancer, his biggest concern was that he couldn't get another dog because he wouldn't be around long enough to raise it. Fortunately his doctor said, "Miller, something else will kill you long before this does, so get a dog and make it (and you) happy!" Tonight, I'm sure four legged Lucy misses her best friend Bob, but she has known for months that he hasn't been well and together they enriched all lives that they touched for the last six years.

I can see Bob's eyes twinkle with his lips set straight, as he spins a yarn for an unsuspecting listener. His amazing understanding of "how stuff works" seemed to compel him him to create fanciful variations of the truth for the gullible—the more gullible the listener, the more fanciful the explanation. Bob could spin some pretty wild yarns before finally letting his catch off the hook. It was a cross between a sport and pure entertainment—let the listener beware!

Bob loved animals, he loved "heavy rusty guy stuff", he loved teasing an unsuspecting innocent listener, but most of all he loved his family and an angel he called Rosie, his wife. He could tease her too, then in the next breath say something like, "You know, without Rosie, I likely would have never survived my mistakes, and if I had, I'd probably be behind bars anyway. She's kept me straight all these years and still puts up

Bob Miller with his first locomotive.

with my nonsense. We know at least one person in this family is going to heaven."

Bob has gone and the sense of loss cannot be expressed. But his memory makes me smile, as he did when helping to install the cast iron belt-driven fans in the museum. Bob was tightening bolts while I was supporting one fan, when one of the wives walked in and started to say something about being careful. Bob at eighty-two, on a ladder and a lift about twenty feet off the floor muttered something akin to. "At this point, advice is not likely to increase the margin of safety." Gee I miss him.

# ROSIE MILLER,
# WIFE OF BOB MILLER

**Birthplace: Wisconsin 1932**

*Life on the home front. Because of the very nature of the job on
the railroad, marriages had a tough time surviving the test of
time. This is a story of one that did for sixty-two years.*

To begin with I think that Bob's love of the railroad started when he was just a
little boy. His folks and Bob lived in the Webb logging camp over on the Olympic
Peninsula. They had a bunkhouse, which
they would move from camp to camp.
To move it they would put it on a flatcar
and moved it that way. For most of Bob's
railroad days he was on the fireman's extra board and then the engineer's extra
board. Bob was always catching ten days
in Vancouver BC, ten days in Wenatchee
or Portland. It was really great if he
caught ten days in Everett.

Rosie and Bob Miller and their dog Lucy

We spent almost a year in Canada in 1952 and 1953. It was slow on the railroad and with Bob's seniority he would have been laid off. So he took a job in Vancouver BC, hostling, where he would take care of the engines, fuel them and get them ready for the crews to take out. The hostling jobs were bid on for six months at a time.

The kids (Tom and Elaine) and I ended up coming back to Everett in the late summer of 1953 so Marilyn could be born in Everett.

Now for a few stories of what happened when the kids and I were by ourselves. The car wouldn't run, it needed a coil, so Bob ordered it. For some reason the parts store didn't have it and he had to order it. When it came, Bob was in Vancouver BC, so I installed it. My brother-in-law thought that was amazing that I could do that. He wasn't a mechanic either.

I think I ran a taxi getting the kids to Little League, dancing lessons, skating lessons, swimming lessons and ball games. On one of these taxi trips the Mukilteo police stopped me for speeding. I told him I was sorry, that I was picking up kids from one of their activities. He just talked to me and let me go. Think all the kids in the car helped, no seat belts then.

At one of Tom's Little League games not enough men came so they were short a referee. They wanted me to fill in. Thank goodness a man came at the last minute. Bob missed most of the kids' activities. When you worked the extra board you were on call 24/7. If you laid off a day you may have missed several days before your turn came up again. No cell phones then so you couldn't go anywhere. Without a cell phone, you had to be at home. If you missed your call you went to the bottom of the list again.

The kids earned money during the summer. My folks had a berry farm at Granite Falls, the kids and I helped them each summer for many years. We would pick berries all day then I would haul them to Snohomish to the cannery. The kids made pretty good money. Tom would also pick blackberries where the Everett Boeing plant is now. We would take them to Mukilteo to the Sea Horse restaurant. We had to go to the back door, they would buy all the berries Tom could pick, for their pies. Now that blackberry picker is a doctor.

We did have some good vacations. A couple of times to Disneyland, the ocean, Crater Lake. The all-time favorite was Yellowstone Park with my sister and her family. A bear got into their car and did some damage. Kept us inside the motel so we couldn't get out. The bears were on the porch of the motel. Another vacation was our first razor clam digging with a bunch of our friends and their families. We filled the whole motel. I think it was Pacific Beach, Washington. We cleaned clams in the room and we weren't supposed to. Lots of kids, adults and razor clams.

Another funny story happened when we were at a viewpoint. All of a sudden, Marilyn, age five, started shouting, "Lookee, lookee, my mother is a movie star." Embarrassing moment, no one knew where that came from. She sends me flowers now from time to time and says, "I still think you're a movie star."

Bob was always a jokester. He had a hearing problem, the railroad asked him if he used earplugs when he used the lawnmower. Bob said no and they asked, "Well why not?" Bob said, "Because my wife mows the lawn!" That was the truth because I did always mow the lawn. I had a Snapper lawnmower, we bought it brand new and it was still going after about twenty-five years. I would say, "The reason it lasted so long was because it had a woman driver." I always painted our houses, inside and out, thank goodness they were always one story.

The kids and I were always by ourselves. We were going somewhere when we were on Broadway in Everett. Three kids were in the backseat in this old '37 Ford and we were stopped at a red light. I looked in the rearview mirror and two big wheels off of a semi truck were coming right at the back of us. Thank goodness there wasn't anybody in front of me. I quick made a right turn around the corner, it missed us but it went clear across the intersection and smashed a sign all to pieces on the other side of the street. That was before free right turns.

It was hard being alone, but it is only as hard as you make it. We didn't think we had it so bad. We had a job and plenty of food. We could do all sorts of things to entertain ourselves. Holidays were like any other day, normally Bob would either be called in the middle of dinner if he was home or he wouldn't be home in the first place. He'd be someplace else. We usually had Bob's folks and my folks for dinner. We weren't alone during the holidays. Bob did end up getting to the kids high school graduations. I can't remember how it happened.

There was one thing. Bob and I had completely different friends. I took up bowling and ceramics and things of that sort. Where Bob was mostly involved with railroad people. Really the kids and I didn't have many railroad friends other than Nancy and Ted and their family. At one time Bill Sundvor used to come by the house. Bill was a railroad man. I really didn't think it was unusual, it was just the way our life was.

Bob did a good job, he worked all that he could, he loved his job. It wasn't boring, he did something different almost every day, for most people their jobs aren't that way. If you were a good employee the company covered you. I think that railroading must have been in Bob's blood when he was born. He had always been in a logging camp or working for the GNRR. Bob's memory was so good, even when he got old he could remember about the things when he was young. Actually I found a letter from the company congratulating Bob because he got one hundred percent on one of the tests that they would give you. That was really unusual that someone would get all the answers right on a rules test.

When little kids used to come to our house, Bob would tell stories. The Cleveland kids used to love to come and hear Bob's stories, and none of them were true. He could entertain kids for hours. We had a piece of aluminum slag and he told the little kids that was a "selenium diaglot". It was just a piece of slag from the aluminum plant. Then he told some other kids about the "Island of Platformate". Can't remember what all he told them about that one. They'd come to visit again and they wanted to be sure and hear about the selenium diaglot and the Island of Platformate. He had the operator up at Sky so terrified of the "Sleeth" ripping the car up that she wouldn't go out of the depot.

I guess we must have done something right, we ended up with three honest hardworking adults, Tom, Elaine and Marilyn. And a good life.

I think that railroad men are poets. In Bob's desk I found a poem by Garry Johnson a switchman at Delta. I remember the story, it's really a true story. The poem is on the next page.

# Wiley Coyote

by Gary Johnson

There once was a hoghead named Ted
Who had a coyote he fed
He missed many a sign
As he watched the thing dine
Thank god now old Wiley is dead
But then there was a conductor named Berget
Who said of the coyote, "Don't fret
I adored him so highly
That I kidnapped old Wiley
And have him locked in my caboose as a pet.
To which an engineer named Miller replied
I don't think we should be denied
We'll storm the caboose
To turn Wiley loose
And hope that old Bergie hasn't lied
But wait said a janitor named Fred
Have you guys considered whats been said
At the price of those scraps don't you think that perhaps
You would be much better off with him dead?

**Ted Cleveland's "Wiley Coyote" at Delta Yard**

# TED CLEVELAND

**Birthplace: Everett, WA 1930**
**Date of Service: Fireman May15, 1952, Engineer: October 6, 1964**
**Positions Held: Hostler Helper, Hostler, Engine Watchman, Fireman, Engineer**

*I worked for the Great Northern, Burlington Northern for forty-two years before retiring in 1992. I worked every job on the Cascade Division. My favorite job was the hill job between Interbay and Wenatchee. Going down the Chumstick was the highlight of my trip. The area was beautiful and the pioneer people who lived there would come out and wave to us. After darkness fell some would come out and wave using their lanterns.*

## Memories

I have so many memories of my career on the railroad that it is almost impossible to put them all down. As a kid I grew up in Skykomish. I knew the town and the men who worked here. I begin my career on the Great Northern with these memories.

Wayne Williams, my cousin was working the helpers and I was on an east bound freight. He was just coming down the back lead when I threw a glass of water and I got him right square in the face. Wayne was the engineer and Elmer Dahl was the fireman. Later

Ted Cleveland, master storyteller, who worked on steam, electric and diesel locomotives.

48

on we were going up the hill and I was running the engine through that rock cut just below Deception Creek. Wayne and Elmer had driven up with a bucket of water. They were up in that rock cut and as we came by, the whole bucket of water came right in the window!

I remember John Micone, the section foreman who had a hell of a garden down by Maloney Creek. He had the local freight crew from Delta bring in some livestock cars and park them down by his garden. Then he had the section crew shovel the manure out of those cars into his garden. He had the best garden around.

I was working as hostler helper when I went down there to John's garden. He had a whole bunch of garlic, so I had an idea for a practical joke. One night I jerked a bunch of it out and wrapped it up. Out in the office in the roundhouse there was a hole in the ceiling that they used to put all the records up in there to save them. I took this garlic and I threw it up there. They had radiators for heat in the office. The smell got terrible. They thought it was on the radiators but they couldn't figure it out. When it had finally died down and it was all dried out, it was the best dam garlic you ever saw.

I was twelve years old when my uncle, Delbert (Red) Williams took me up to the Tonga Bridge. He was an engineer on the GNRR. Number Twenty-seven had wrecked. What happened I think was this: Verle Kilde, was head brakeman on this mail train, and they came around the bend there at Tonga on the straight stretch. The fireman went back to check the charts. On the electrics you had to do that before you got into Sky. He was back in the motors and Verle was on the head end and apparently didn't realize that the engineer, Blue Barrel, was not paying attention or was momentarily distracted.

At the top end of Tonga the engine kicked out of regeneration, that's what you control the speed of the train with, and down the hill they came. When they got to that curve coming onto the bridge, the engine was a 5011, the old GE. The engine went off, the cars started peeling off. Luckily at that time they had several people who worked in the mail cars sorting mail before they got to Sky. They had all got done with their work and gone back to the last car, a passenger car where they had coffee back there.

As all these cars were coming into that curve they were peeling off. Luckily the second to the last car peeled off and it had slowed down enough that the head car went clear across the bridge and stopped over there by the Blue Mud Cut. Verle lost his arm, but the fireman who was marking the charts, it crushed him, killed him. The engineer got banged up. You couldn't see where it had left the rail. The rail was just as good as ever.

After the mail train wreck, Verle Kilde became a telegraph operator and was promoted to dispatcher.

When I got out of high school I started working in construction. I worked in Eastern Washington driving heavy equipment. Then I got married and came back over to Sky, driving a logging truck. My dad was a logger and he told me I should go to work on the railroad. "Talk to your uncle about getting a job on the railroad. Logging is too seasonal and too dangerous." At one time, to get hired on the railroad you had to have an "in" and my uncle Delbert, engineer for the GNRR, was working out of Interbay. My uncle put in a word for me. My uncle Delbert hired out on the railroad in 1910, he ran the steam locomotives. Uncle Delbert also took me fishing a lot. He was a great uncle.

My first job here in Skykomish was working as a laborer in the roundhouse. I was an assistant to everybody in other words a gofer. On a typical day you would do what the mechanic wanted you to or superintendent wanted you to do. There wasn't a heck of a lot to do around Skykomish. We only had about six freight trains a day, in fact there were more passenger trains than freight trains. Hard to believe isn't it?

There was the Empire Builder, #1 and #2 both ways, east and west. The Western Star, #3 and #4 both ways. The local between Spokane and Seattle, #5 and #6. The mail train, #27 and #28 both ways. That was the extent of the passenger trains. We had to uncouple the trains here from electrics to steam, then when steam ended, it became to diesels. They all had to be cut off by the depot and transferred to the other mode of power.

Then I started hostler helping. You moved all of the engines as an assistant to the hostler. Basically all that he did was run the engines. He moved all of the engines while the hostler helper did all of the throwing of switches and so forth.

As an example, when #4, the Western Star, came into Sky at eleven o'clock they had a steam engine on it. You would climb up on the steam engine and the hostler would take it up to where the electric engine was. The train engineer and fireman would get on the electric and the hostler and hostler helper would go up to the upper part of the yard, go through the crossover and around the wye so the engine would be heading the right way going west and check the water and oil. On the west bound you would do just the opposite, take the electric and bring it around (the electric had a cab at both ends), and dump the heater car off.

The electrics didn't have steam on them like a steam engine. So they had to have a heater car. The heater car furnished heat for the train. Then you'd take sand on the electrics on both sides. Going uphill with the train if you started to spin the wheels, you'd put sand on the rail, you did that on the steam engines too. It was up to the hostler helper to do this. They had a sand tower and you had a hose you used to fill the tanks full of sand.

When I was the hostler at Sky I had a hostler helper who didn't show up for work. I was hostling nights. We went to work at 11p.m. I knew where he lived of course so I went over and knocked at the door and no answer. So I walked in and yelled his name several times. Finally I went into the bedroom and he was laying there with some woman. Course I shook him up and told him you're supposed to get over here and go to work. This woman's face was down in the pillow. I noticed on her arm she was wearing a bracelet. Anyway I went over to wait for my helper and he finally showed up and we did our job. I wondered who that woman was.

I've never said anything to anyone up to this day, this is just a funny story. For days and nights I looked at all of the women for this bracelet. Finally three weeks later I found out who was wearing the bracelet. And I knew who it was!

When I worked here at Sky I was also an engine watchman. What an engine watchman did was to work on a whole bunch of steam engines that would be idle (shut down). In order to have them ready all the time, you had to go around and start the fire in each engine, and fill the boiler with water.

This is how I met William M. Cogdill, a fireman on the steam locomotives. You meet a lot of people on the railroad. Some of them you really form an attachment for a lifetime because you really like and respect them.

How I got to know Bill was because I was having trouble lighting the fires on the steam engines and Bill saw me having this problem. He said, "I'll teach you how to start a fire on a steam engine." This required taking a piece of waste (a bunch of threads from clothing wadded up). The first thing that you would do is soak that with kerosene, light the wad of waste, open the steam door and throw that down on the bottom of the firebox. Then you had to make sure your oil was hot from the tank, then you'd turn on your atomizer, steam and your oil and that would kind of splash out there. You had to be careful to get that fire going without dripping that oil down on the ground. If it would fire off and go down on the ground it would burn the engine up.

You had a water gauge right there in the middle of the cab. Usually it would be down so you would have to pump the water up till it was full and get your steam pressure up to two hundred pounds pressure then you could shut it down. You had to keep circling all these engines and make sure the water was up, the oil was hot in the tank. How you made sure the oil was hot was you would shoot hot steam into the oil tank. After I learned that, they would start right up. That was my job as engine watchman.

Bill was kind of a proud guy, kind of aloof you might say, but he took a liking to me and I took a liking to him. He knew so much about railroading. He started out someplace in the south and then came out here. At first Bill worked for a logging company. Then he transferred over to the GNRR as a fireman, that's when I got to know him. He was working a local between Everett and Skykomish. They stayed at Sky when they got here and then the next day they went back to Everett.

The engineer that Bill worked with was a big guy by the name of Louis Oien. I remember that Louis always had oatmeal for breakfast and that didn't seem like much for such a big guy.

Then later on after I came out of Skykomish and was working at Delta, I ran into Bill again, he was working on a switch engine. Believe it or not I was one of a few guys that liked him and he liked me. He'd talk about his old times in the south and working the steam trains up here. We had some good conversations.

Anyway later on I became an engineer and I was working a switch engine at Delta in Everett and this young kid, Mitch Cogdill was working summers as a switchman in the yard and going to college to become an attorney. He turned out to be Bill's son. He's been my good friend and lawyer ever since.

The lesson learned here was that I was lucky to have had a good teacher. I never saw an engine burn up and didn't want to, but I saw a rotary burn up. Fact of the matter was, the superintendent's son was firing the same time I was. He came up and his prime job was to fire an old rotary over here and to make sure that the oil was hot all of the time. He didn't have the oil hot enough and he finally got a fire going in the boiler and it dripped down on the oil below and it burned the whole damn rotary up.

From hostling to engine watchman I had a chance to go firing. Firing was learning to be an engineer. I wasn't old enough yet to go firing, you had to be twenty-one. I wasn't twenty-one until 1951. Then in 1952 I was promoted to fireman. I had to move down below because there were no jobs up here. I was low man on the totem pole.

This meant that my family was left in Skykomish because the job was too unstable to move them. I might be on a job out of Interbay and then called for a job at Sky or elsewhere. One time for instance, I came back to Sky as a hostler. You could bid on the job for six months at a time. I was working hostling and driving logging truck too. I was trying to make a lot of money because I knew damn well that when the electrics were done, we were done here in Sky!

When I wasn't working a job at Sky I stayed at a room in Seattle provided by Reynold (Reggie) Moline, an engineer who lived on Dravis Street in Seattle. Lonely times for both Nancy and me. The railroad life was hard on wives and marriages. It was hard because you were always away from home. Your wife had to take care of everything. Luckily I have a good wife. Believe it or not the railroad was noted for engineers and brakemen and so on, who had been married several times, because the wives couldn't put up with what the railroad really amounted to.

The older men didn't seem to have this problem. The husbands and wives seemed to stay together more. The generation after the second world war was just a different class of people. Marriages on the railroad didn't seem to last long. Still it was a hard job for women to more or less run the show because more than fifty percent of time you were away from home.

We have been married for sixty-six years and raised five good kids. My wife more or less raised them and the good thing, I always thought, was that my wife never said: "Just you wait till your dad gets home." She just took care of the problem, unless it was really serious. Nancy is my partner and my best friend.

The railroad leaving Sky was hard on the town. They shut down the substation and lost probably five jobs. There was the high car that took care of all of the lines from here to Wenatchee. Maybe ten people on that lost their jobs. There were probably about twenty guys who worked in the roundhouse here. They didn't have to haul oil anymore, there were a lot of jobs lost. Of course there were jobs made. They put in the fan house to blow the diesel smoke out of the tunnel. That probably required five men.

I think that basically the average person doesn't know what it means to run an engine. You sit up there and don't even have a steering wheel because you are on a track. When you first start out on the railroad you started out as a fireman. In the olden days the engineer was the king and you wouldn't even think of touching anything or getting in the driver's seat at all!

In my time, what happened was that during WW2 a lot of the firemen had to go into the service. After the war when they came back their many years of seniority had accumulated to the point where they were almost engineers. Of course they had already kind of learned the basics of how to be an engineer.

These guys were young engineers, like when they got to Portland, as an example, they wanted to go out and have a good time and consequently they didn't get much sleep so it was to their advantage that they would teach the firemen how to run an engine so they could sit over there and kind of half-ass sleep. So that is how I learned to be an engineer.

When you are promoted to engineer you are then responsible for the safety of the train. When you are completely responsible you are more conscious of everything. You don't know the tonnage and what it is going to take so you are very careful. You get so you have a feeling for the train, the tonnage and everything. What its going to be, what its going to take. How much air to take, whether you can use your dynamic to control your speed. Coming into a thirty-five mile an hour curve, how to set the speed, how to kick it off just right to keep the whole train going at thirty-five until you get through that whole area. It all comes from experience, you are slow at first, you are cautious. As time goes by and you get more familiar with the territory you know how to go around a curve better and at what speed.

I trained younger people to be engineers and they were required to be trained by several engineers. I was rough on them, I think that they were half afraid of me. I always told them when they left, I'd say, "When you leave me, don't say, well, Cleveland does it this way. You do it his way and the next guy his way and the next guy his way. When you get done with all five guys, then you run it the way you think best after learning from those five people. If you do this you will turn out to be the best engineer of them all."

The best engineer that I trained was Nancy McLaughlin. She listened to everything I told her. There was not a soul that would ever say anything about her. She was a very upstanding person that everybody respected.

Passenger trains, it takes a lot of seniority to hold a passenger train and I never had the seniority to hold one regularly. But you could mark up on them if the regular guy went on vacation. I marked up on the International going into Vancouver BC. Coming out of Vancouver on New Year's Eve, it was snowing to beat hell. The switches were all screwed up, me and the fireman had to dig them out, nobody else would help. Every time we came to a switch we'd have to stop the train and shovel the switch out. I got in real late with the passenger train. I was cold, wet, tired and crabby and when I got home I told my wife Nancy to cancel the New Year's Eve party. Well that went over like a lead balloon!

I had the best years out of the railroad. Why you might ask? The railroad always protected us, we were a family. Now they don't. Its no longer if you are a good employee and look out for the railroad, they will look out for you. This is the reason that when I was working if our train had any kind of a problem I would work to keep the main line open and running. I did this because the railroad provided a good living for my family and me.

As an example, as I left Sky one day with this freight train, this tank car had projected itself up on top of this boxcar, wheels and all and we were going along and the air went at Baring. We went back to check on what was the matter and the air line had gone. I don't know how we made it as far as we did across bridges and all, but the two cars were stuck tight together and finally the air hoses stretched as far as they could and busted and that's when the air went on the train.

There was a trainmaster involved in this one. He said, "We'll see if we can lower it down." The superintendent had told him, get rid of the car, shove it into the brush, we want the main line open. He didn't follow orders and they put him into Interbay for the rest of his life. What we should have done was not to have called anybody and just taken the cars and separated them and taken them down to Baring and put them on the side track and left it there and call them up and tell them what we had done and taken the rest of the train and gone. But with the trainmaster involved we couldn't do that.

I'll tell you about Frank Marabelli another engineer. We were on two westbounds. I had to set out at the Everett Junction. There are two sets of tracks there, there's the oil track down by Howarth Park on the eastbound track. I was setting out and Marabelli came down the other mainline and was setting out at the oil track by Howarth Park. Well, he got out ahead of me. If he gets out ahead of me he goes back to Wenatchee ahead of me. So I called the dispatcher and told him put me down the east bound main at Mukilteo. The dispatcher put Marabelli down the westbound track along the bay. The dispatcher put me down the eastbound main. Marabelli thought he was out ahead of me and I kept gaining on him and gaining on him. Before we got to Edmonds I went by him and he looked over at me and I gave him a wave and I got ahead of him all the way to Interbay.

This was kind of neat. I can't remember the conductor's name, but I really liked him. He was working a work train. He was in the clear for a train that was supposed to be coming. This trainmaster got on the radio and called him and said, "Where are you at?" Well I'm in the clear. The trainmaster says, "Well I want you out of there!" The conductor says, "Well I can't go because of my orders. Can't hear you, you're breaking up." All this time he's getting his tape recorder out. He came back and said, "Can you hear me now, can you hear me now?" The trainmaster says "Yes! I want you out of there, because I said so, I don't give a darn whether you want to or not, you're going out of there."

It came to an investigation because the conductor came out without the train orders to do so. At the investigation the trainmaster denied saying anything. The superintendent was there listening in on it. He asked the conductor to step out into the hall with him for a moment. They went back in and the superintendent said, "This investigation is all over." He said, "YOU" pointing at the trainmaster, "In my office."

Stu Aldcroft was the freight agent and station agent at Everett. He was right under the trainmaster as far as authority. He didn't bring himself above the men. As an example I came up Hewitt Avenue by the bank. Stu was standing outside the bank with someone telling him something. And as I approached Stu said. " Well hi there Ted, how's it going?" What I liked about Stu he never held himself above the men, he was very fair and he ran a tight ship.

I was offered the job of traveling hoghead. A traveling hoghead (engineer) is assigned to a territory. It is his job to keep track of the engineers there and make sure that they are doing their job correctly. Because I knew what the job amounted to I did not take the job that was offered. It meant moving all of the time. I wanted my family to be stationed in one place.

Mark Cleveland, 8 years old, testing his skills in one of his father's freight locomotives.

But another good friend of mine, Al Hedrick did take the traveling hoghead job. Al and his family went to Whitefish, Montana and to Klamath Falls, Oregon.

I'll tell you about our friendship. We were both working the east end pool. We had a room that we rented by the month at the Columbia Hotel in Wenatchee. My wife Nancy and I had driven my pick-up over to get some peaches. Nancy and Al's wife Evelyn were both canners. And of course we brought them home for all of our friends too. We always did free peaches for everybody.

We absolutely loaded that pick-up full of peaches. We had gotten them for free because they were through picking the orchard and we were able to go through the orchard and pick what was left on the trees. When we got loaded we were full of peach fuzz. I had parked outside of the hotel and gone up to wash. When I came back down the fruit inspector was there. He was going to give me a ticket because you had to be a cash buyer to have that many peaches. He said, "You're going to have to come up to the office at the courthouse." They were having a meeting of the growers. I walked in and started raising cain and making all kinds of noise. They finally said, "Well let's forget about this, all we want you to do is, cover most of it and take the rest down and load it on an engine and take it back on the engine." "The Peach Express."

Al and I were good friends, we always had a good relationship with Al and his wife Evelyn.

I worked the extra board at Interbay and you'd catch jobs where the regular men would lay off. If you would miss a call, not home when they called, you had to wait until that guy got back before you could go back on the board. So you had to be very careful about being around when that call came in. That went on until you could hold a steady job as a fireman, on a freight, local or switch engine in the yard.

If you caught a job in Vancouver BC for ten days, for instance, you would pay your own lodging and meals you would pay it all on your own. If you got stuck with ten days it was like making nothing.

Thanksgiving day, a day when everyone wants to be home with their families. The phone rang and I was called to take the caboose hop from Interbay to Skykomish, to pick up the snow dozer and plow snow. Can you believe it had snowed enough on Thanksgiving day to use the dozer? In any case I was the fireman and Don Pulver was the engineer. We had one engine and a caboose, heading for Skykomish.

We were going up the coastline. We were a little bit worried about slides on the coastline but we had a clear block coming into Edmonds. We came around the curve and all of a sudden there was a slide about eight feet deep and a hundred, or two hundred feet long covering both main lines. We hit that thing and we left the wheels and trucks right at the first part of the mudslide and we rode the engine over the top of that thing. It was like riding a bucking bronco. It never tipped over and we finally ended up on the other side of the slide.

The caboose though, didn't fare as well. It rolled over but fortunately the crew on the caboose didn't get hurt. They said that the tools that were there for repairing cars were floating around like flies. Would you believe though that everything went right and we were home for Thanksgiving. The thing of it was we had planned a Thanksgiving dinner with everyone there. Nancy and the kids were preparing it when I was called and I had to go. By the time I got back from the wreck dinner was all ready.

I got promoted to engineer in 1964. But that doesn't mean that you work as an engineer right then. You stay on as a fireman until they need engineers. Once they call you up as an engineer, then you are working that board again. The same deal as when you were a fireman. Work your way up. You try to work road jobs because you make more money. I always worked the extra board until I could hold a steady job as an engineer. The best job really was this hill job. It was a piece of cake as far as I was concerned.

I was working between Interbay and Wenatchee. I was on an eastbound freight and Ian Mcdonald was on another eastbound freight ahead of me. At Sky he went out ahead of me and up the hill with his train. We were using diesels through the hole (the tunnel). I called Ian and asked him when he got to the tunnel, to let me know exactly when he hit the hole. Course I was following him up the hill. When he called me I knew how long it would take him to get through the hole. I knew how long that it took to blow the tunnel out.

So anyway, when I got to the west end of Scenic I had a clear block. I pulled up to the depot at Scenic, there was a clear block and the fan lights were going. I stopped at the clear block. The dispatcher came on the radio and he said, "Are you having trouble between the switches at Scenic?" I said no. He said, "Are you moving?" I said no. He said, "Well what are you doing? Haven't you got a clear block?" I said, "Yea I got a clear block." He said, "Why aren't you moving?" "Well" I said, "you haven't blown the damn tunnel out yet."

The block went red, fans started blowing, smoke came boiling out, finally the tunnel was blown out, I got the block and I proceeded ahead. If the tunnel wasn't blown out properly you would breathe that smoke until you would finally run out of it. From that day on, I never had to worry about the tunnel being blown out.

Here's another good story and one that I learned something from. I'd pulled up on the siding at Berne going west. I had a long train and it was heavy. I stopped at the block which was red and was waiting for a train . After your stops and the train is pulled in tight you can release the air on your train and hold the whole train with your drivers. I sat there for quite a while and then the dispatcher called and said, "You're going to be there for a while." So I thought I'll get off and go down to the old dump and see if I can find some old bottles.

There was a depot right there at Berne and for years the operators lived right there and they'd throw their discarded bottles and garbage over the hill. I was down there churning around and all of a sudden I heard the train start to move. Boy, did I come up that bank fast, run up there, got on the train and stopped it of course.

I was telling Bob Smith what had happened and he said, "You know I found a remedy for that. As soon as you get stopped and everything seems to be holding, get down there and run a dime underneath the wheel. Believe it or not that will hold the train." The weight of the engine has to be lifted in order to start moving. And believe it or not that absolutely works.

Another time I was coming out of Wenatchee. I had a tank train (oil tanks). This happened just a little bit east of where the Espresso Chalet (the coffee shop) is, there on Highway Two by Index. It had been raining to beat hell for weeks.

I was in dynamic braking because it was downhill and at that time the speed limit was probably thirty-five down through there. I was going along and all of a sudden, BOOM! The pilot (the front of the engine) hit the ground. I dumped it (put it into emergency) just as soon as that happened. Of course we have all of this weight. I called the caboose and said, "I hit something up here." He said, "I just felt it." We stopped, took probably half a mile to stop. I said, "We had better back up and find out what's wrong." So we started backing up. We were still on the rail. He said, "STOP!" So I stopped. He said, "There is about seventy-five feet of rail hanging in the air." There was a culvert under the track there plugged up. This whole seventy-five feet, which was just like jello, had gone down the hill when we went over it.

Of course my whole train was bunched tight, so it was acting like a solid piece of steel going over. I don't think that it completely washed out until we were over it. But by the time we got backed up with all the shaking that there was, that whole damn area went.

I called the dispatcher and said, "You'd better get a work train up here with a bunch of rock." We got over it, but somebody else would have had a hell of a wreck.

Most of the men were good employees. One engineer, Keith had a lot of trouble with speed as all of us did. But defective rails by the manufactures caused him to have a wreck here at Miller River on the curve. The rail exploded. The rail wasn't manufactured right and it just crystallized.

The same thing happened at Peshastin, that curve there is a thirty-five miles an hour curve. We'd always hit that at forty-five. Well he hit it at forty-five and the rail exploded. He got fired over it and six months later they brought him back. They should have brought him back right away because it was the rail not the speed that did it.

Here's another one. Leaving Sky here going east at about Scenic the air went. I sent the brakeman back to see what was wrong. Fifteen cars back, we got a car off the rail. What happened was that you have a coupler and where that coupler goes into the car is into a socket. Where it goes into the socket there is a hole you can shove a piece of steel through. Where this goes through there is another hole there that you can shove this piece of steel in. There is a pin on the other side that holds that pin in. Well the pin had busted. The coupler pulled out and dropped on the rail, hit the axle and popped the car off.

We went into emergency, there was only one set of wheels off, it was snowing hard. I called the dispatcher on the radio and said, "Get hold of Bob Pierce." He was the section foreman in Sky. "Have him bring me up several pieces of hardwood wedges. I think that we can put this car back on. In the meantime I'll take this head fifteen cars up to Scenic and put them in the siding there. By that time Bob should be there with the shims. Bob and I put that car back on."

There was no drawbar so we had to put a chain around the hole that holds the drawbar, hook it to the engine, take that one car up to Scenic and put that on the house track. Then come back and get the train and take it up. The main thing was to get the mainline clear so they can run trains. By that time they had sent the hook out of Seattle We told them to send it back. That was it, no investigation, no nothing.

The next real bad one was, I was going through the crossover at the Toutle River. The funny thing is that the speed limit used to be fifty through the crossovers. When I first started going south everything going north was on the land side and going south was on the bay side. All the switches were hand thrown at that time. Then they went to automatic switches run by the dispatchers.

They were crossing me over at Toutle River. The speed limit was dropped to thirty-five because the conductors were complaining about tipping over the caboose. This particular day, I went through there and the air went. The first thing I did was look at the speed recorder and I was right on thirty-five. I sent the brakeman back. Well we got three cars against the girders. Off the track against the girders. There are two tracks across the bridge. I asked, "is the other track clear?" Well yes it was.

I called the dispatcher and said, "we got three cars against the girders, coming through the crossover there we must have split a switch." I told him we just passed that local, and to have him come back and pull our train back over on the other main line. I'll take these cars up to the next station and leave them. We'll spike the switch (forcing it over to make it tight). He said, "Well go ahead." We did it and never an investigation.

Again I was working the south end into Portland. When I was working down there it was foggy, it was always so bad. You are right on the river most of the time, you had to be alive and watching that block. You couldn't see the track but you could see the block go by so you had to have your eyes open all of the time.

Bud Worthington, an engineer on the GN told me this story. We were working sixteen hours a day at that time. In those days you worked sixteen hours, now you can't work over twelve hours. You'd leave Seattle and you would get what you called a buckshot train. Everything going south was thrown into that train. So you would have to stop and switch them out and get them all together so that when you did make the set out you could just shove them in and leave. That's one of the reasons that it took sixteen hours.

Anyway Bud said he left Longview. It was foggier than hell. The fireman and the head brakeman kept dozing off. Bud would wake them up and tell them we have to watch these blocks. The blocks are about a mile or a mile-and-a-half apart. Pretty soon they'd be dozing off again. It was easy to go to sleep working the hours that you did.

It's so foggy down there that you have to have your eyes open all of the time because its immediately that you see that block for only an instant. There are two things that you have to watch for. That's the whistle board sign that means a crossing is coming up and you have to start your whistle. And the block signals every mile or so.

So Bud went by a clear block. He was going along about fifty miles an hour. He immediately made a bunch of noise and pretended to be asleep. They woke up and saw him sleeping, came over and shook him. They said, "What was that last block?" Bud said. "Oh, it was probably clear. I guess." Bud said after that their eyeballs were just about out of their head looking for the next block. They stayed awake after that.

A few incidents happened to me on my life on the railroad that made lifelong friends for me. Engineer Bob Miller and I lived close together in the south end of Everett. Our families knew each other, our kids went to the same schools. We became lifelong friends. Bob and I used to play jokes on each other. How we communicated on the radio so no one would know who it was, we decided to call each other "comrade". I'd call him and he'd call me, we'd always end by Comrade C. and Comrade M. This way nobody knew who was actually talking.

I can recall one time my wife and Rosie were making soap. It got so lye (for making the soap) was hard to find. And it was fifteen cents a can. I can always remember that being as how we were traveling all over the state we started picking up lye where ever we could.

One day Bob went into a store he found a whole case of lye. He put the case in his basket and on his way up to the counter he passed the wine counter and he picked up a bottle of wine. He got up to the counter and the clerk said, "My god, what do you do with all of the lye?" "Oh", Bob says, "You take that and mix it with that lye and it makes a hell of a drink!" Bob could say things that you would actually believe what he was saying. The clerk looked at him like he was a strange person.

There was another time with Bob, I was coming home from a job and I found a hamburger stand that said, HAMBURGERS TEN CENTS A PIECE. I flew in there and would you believe the hamburgers were about the size of a silver dollar. So just as soon as I got home I called Bob on the phone and I said, "you'll never believe this but I ran into a place that have hamburgers for ten cents!" I told him where it was at and him and Rosie jumped in the car and went down. Rosie told me this later. Bob came out with those hamburgers and said, "That Cleveland sucked me into a bunch of bullshit like this." Bob loved hamburgers, but not those!

I remember every year around Christmas time Harry Root, the foreman, and his crew on the high car decided that there was the perfect fir tree between Berne and Merritt to decorate as a Christmas tree This was the perfect tree and area to share the spirit of Christmas for all crews and passengers who passed by. Icy Point the place was called, where the tall fir stood. The canyon at this point squeezed real tight and it was very, very cold, snowy, iced and sparkly.

The high car crew maintained the catenary system that ran over the tracks and supplied electricity to run the electric locomotives. They devised a way using a transformer to reduce the power of the catenary system from 11,000 volts to 110 volts to supply the power to light the tree. There was no power in this area other than the catenary system. The crew spent their own time making this scene happen. Stringing the lights, supplying the electricity and all of the labor to make things work. After the electrics were gone the scene was gone also.

Picture this scene in the winter time. Down in the canyon where it is pitch dark with only maybe the light of the moon. The Empire Builder and the Western Star came to this area of darkness and suddenly a spectacular scene appears out of the blackness...a lighted Christmas tree standing maybe thirty or forty feet tall. The engineer would always slow the train down to a crawl as they went through this area. The conductor would go through the train alerting the passengers to look for the sight that was about to appear. I can still see this spectacular Christmas scene. It was beautiful.

I was the local chairman of the engineers union and I went to a lot of investigations and represented many engineers. I felt that employees should respect the fact that the railroad has given them a job to support their families.

I worked for the Great Northern, Burlington Northern for forty-two years before retiring in 1992. I worked every job on the Cascade Division. My favorite job was the hill job between Interbay and Wenatchee. Going down the Chumstick was the highlight of my trip. The area was beautiful and the pioneer people who lived there would come out and wave to us. After darkness fell some would come out and wave using their lanterns.

The railroad was a lot of fun when I worked and there were a lot of good men who were always willing to work with you.

# THE LAST ORDER
# TO THE ELECTRICS

## July 31, 1956

Andy Strom and I worked together as Engineer and Fireman. We were first out in the helper pool. We knew this was going to come up, the end of the electrics from Skykomish to Appleyard was going to end. It's funny the company didn't disband the helper pool until that particular day.

We were called, Andy Strom, engineer, Ted Cleveland, fireman and Al Holevas, conductor as the helper crew to take engine number 5018 and several Westinghouse helper engines over to Wenatchee Appleyard.

We left Skykomish with several double cab engines. We took pictures on the mainline in front of the depot when we were departing Sky. We stopped at Scenic and took several photos departing Scenic. When we

Printed in U.S.A.

**GREAT NORTHERN RAILWAY CO.**

**CLEARANCE FORM A**

Date *July 31, 1956*

To C&E *Eng 5018 east*

At *Dryden*

No._____ To_____
    *Rule D-97*

I have *1* Orders for your train.

No. *245* No.____ No.____ No.____ No.____

No.____ No.____ No.____ No.____ No.____

No.____ No.____ No.____ No.____ No.____

There are no further orders for your train.

Do not leave before_____

O.K. *402P* M. *R H S* Supt.

*Hudson* Operator

4-1-46  RP     Over

**The last Clearance Form A was issued to
GN 5018 at Dryden on July 31, 1956.**

went through the Cascade Tunnel we stopped at Berne, the east end of the Cascade Tunnel and we took several photos of the engine coming out of the tunnel. We left Berne to pick up a train order at Dryden to meet the high car number X838 at Cashmere. After meeting the high car we proceeded to Appleyard to the

L-R Ted Cleveland, Andy Strom and Al Holevas pose with #5018 on the way to Wenatchee, the day the electric locomotives left Skykomish for the last time. July 31 1956.

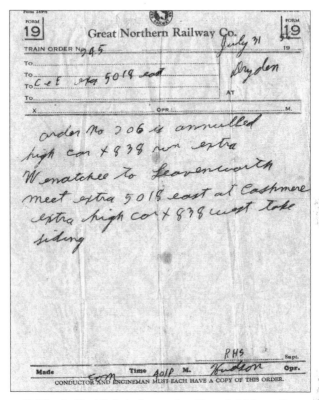

**Ted Cleveland kept the last orders ever issued to an electric locomotive in the Cascade Division. The orders arrange to meet at Cashmere with High Car X838 as the #5018 proceeds to Wenatchee.**

electric shop where the electric juice was shut off. There was no longer electric power between Skykomish and Wenatchee.

We deadheaded back to Sky. The helpers were disbanded and we all had to move to different jobs on the Cascade Division.

The end of an era.

*Ted Cleveland*

# JIM GEORGE

**Birthplace: Leavenworth, WA 1939**
**Date of Service: June16, 1955**
**Position Held: Foreman and Track Inspector**

*Every winter we'd have to go up and down the track knocking all the
ice out of the tunnels, clean the slide fences and all the switches. Knocked
the ice out of the Winton Tunnel and the Swede Tunnel, I hated that Swede
Tunnel, you could never hear a train coming. You better hope nothing was
coming. I always figured I'd lie down on the side and hope and pray.*

I started work as a laborer then I began running maintenance machines. I ran
every kind of machine there was except for cranes. I could have run them if I had
to, but I just didn't feel good on them. Never went to school for nothing. In those
days you just climbed on the machine and started. Of course there was always
somebody that knew how to run them and you'd get on and they'd explain to
you what this did and what that did. It was altogether different back then than
it is today.

We had respect, and that's something these guys today don't have. Basically
they knew if you were trying to do your job, learning how to be safe, they'd go
one hundred percent for you. I went to work for the railroad in 1955. During the
summer I'd work for dad on the railroad and then I'd go back to school. We'd get

out of school in May. I'd work from May to September. I worked for dad on the gangs. Actually I went to work when I was about fifteen for dad. He knew all the road masters, superintendents, so they didn't give dad any guff about it

My dad would tell the crew "Okay, time to go eat." We'd get our lunch and go eat and soon as we got done eating we'd start throwing rocks,

Jim George and his son Steve. Jim started working for his father's GNRY gang when he was 15 years old and worked his way up to Section Foreman. Steve works for the BNSF and has fond memories of his dad's ability to organize men.

cans, whatever. Dad would wake up, "HUH" he'd say. "That's railroad rock! You go bring them back." That was the end of throwing the rock. Not only that, he'd say, okay its time to rest and he'd sit there under the tree and put his hat over his eyes and we learned real quick that if we didn't sit still and be quiet he'd wake up and say, "Okay, time to go back to work."

The railroad was a good place. Basically I did everything and anything. I worked from Wenatchee to Spokane, that was off our division. Then I came back and worked from Wenatchee to Tacoma. Worked all of the yards in Everett, Seattle, Interbay, Edmonds all those. Up north to the Canadian Border. In fact I went into Vancouver B. C. the first year of the World's Fair. We had to go in there and pull all the rail from the old rail yard at the Expo site so people didn't trip over them. We'd go across the border. Sid Pierce was the conductor on the work train. He said, "Well we got permission to go in there, but you guys got to get on the floor so they can't see you, cause we don't have any visas, Okay!" We were

Buster Norris, with back to camera, gives hand signals to his gang aligning the track. The alignment was completed "by sight" as can be seen with the foreman eying the rails and giving instructions to his men.

there two or three days pulling rail. We'd come back and stay at Blaine.

Went to Tacoma, worked the Tacoma yard. Then I finally came back to Merritt where I got a gang to run. I ran a gang for many years. I had from eight to forty people on a gang working for me. Depending if it was a tie gang we'd have more people and I'd have an assistant foreman with me. I had a cook car, everything was right there. In the wintertime you either tied up the gang at Skykomish for the snow conditions, or you'd tie up in Monroe and work the yards. I knew Pete Nisco, quite a guy. I knew Mike Quaranta, he and my dad were great friends. I never worked for Mike, he was actually before my time. He'd come around and see my dad, Steve George.

I remember the time I had the gang out here in Merritt and a fight began. They were playing cards and one guy didn't like another guy and he pulled a knife. I called the sheriff. The sheriff had a big German Shepherd. He came in with that dog named Ripper. George Carveth was the sheriff's name. He said, "Okay boys, you better shape up or ship out, one of the two, or this dog will have you by the nape of the neck." The guys said, "Okay Boss." My wife Sharen and the kids were hiding out in the bushes watching. Most of the guys were good. If you didn't like it, it was "Hit the road Jack"! I gave them all the breaks I could. They'd go out there and work their fannies off, putting in ties, rails. Didn't have the machines they have nowadays. Everything was by hand, pick and shovel. The guys of today don't realize what the guys back then went through. They all worked together. These guys today wouldn't even know how to do it. They did better work then than they do now with these dang machines. Those were the good old days! When they got paid they'd come over here and knock on the door and they'd say, "We're going to town Boss, will you keep my money so I don't spend it all?" So they'd have me keep most of their money till after the weekend.

Worked in the tunnels, you had to be careful in there especially in the winter time. With the water, you'd have ice. One time I was knocking the ice out of the Gaynor Tunnel. I had a big pike pole, I hit the ice and it broke off and it came down the pike pole and hit me right in the chest and knocked me flat on my butt. That taught me right then, be aware of what you're doing. Other than running tie gangs, I ran surface gangs. A surface gang is where you have the machines that are raising the rails, surfacing the track, putting elevation in the curves, stuff like that. I ran rail gangs too.

You know, when we first started knocking ice out of the tunnels, we didn't have the Gaynor Tunnel. When the Gaynor Tunnel was built, that's when we ran into problems. I remember the passenger train hitting ice in that tunnel, it took the cattle guard right of the engine. Knocked the windows out of the cars, especially the dome cars. After that we had to go check the tunnel before the passenger trains could go through them to be sure nothing could take the dome off. Of course back then we had snow. We'd have to snowshoe into them with a pike pole. 'Course no one else would do it except ME. The ice in the tunnel was caused by cracks in the roof. Water got in the cracks and expanded the crack and made bigger icicles. There was a hell of a wind through there, they all had wind, even the Eight Mile Tunnel. Even with the fans they got now, they still get wind.

Every winter we'd have to go up and down the track knocking all the ice out of the tunnels, clean the slide fences and all the switches. Knocked the ice out of the Winton Tunnel and the Swede Tunnel, I hated that Swede Tunnel, you could never hear a train coming. You better hope nothing was coming. I always figured I'd lie down on the side and hope and pray.

Here's a memory from our son Steve: "They had a derailment in the big tunnel the Eight Mile Cascade Tunnel. Not a lot of room to work. All gangs were called to the tunnel everyone was running around like chickens with their heads cut off. Nobody knew what to do. Somebody said call Jim George. Pretty soon, here comes my dad. Course in those days I was young and didn't think my dad knew anything. But here comes my dad and I was never so proud because he walked in there and said, "Okay you do this, you get that, bring this and everything just kind of fell into place. They were in there two days. I was so proud of my dad I didn't know he was so good at that. After they worked in there they all came out black."

They wanted me to go to Montana as an official. I had no hankering to go, this was good enough for me. One big boss told me: "If you take that job you can't talk with the men, or pal around with them. You can't go out with them, you can't associate with them in the evenings or even go to lunch when you're the boss." I don't believe in that. If I can't have the men I don't want the job. The men are what make you. If they believe in you, they'll work. I came to Merritt as a foreman.

I was track inspector including all the yards. Worked in Tacoma for about a year. I stayed in a cabin down there. I had a burner, a sleeping bag and a shower. Instead of running all over trying to find a place to stay I just stayed there. I didn't care for that yard.

The water tower over here in Merritt, that's where we got our water. In the wintertime dad said, "Okay son, go fix the water. Get the ice out of the intake so we'll get water". When I was a kid I'd have to go down to the east switch and go about a mile and a half up the hill. I'd snowshoe down there and snowshoe back, that was fun. My dad was from the old country, he was very strict and very strong. In 1986 they took the water tower down.

That water tower reminds me of the worst time I ever had when dad was alive. I was eight or nine years old, somewhere in there. There used to be a walkway all the way around and on one side was a water spout for the steam engines. I went up there one winter and was playing around. There was eight to ten feet of snow on the ground. I thought oh that would be fun to jump off of. I landed in the snow and luckily I put my hands up, because that's all that was sticking out. The old man came out there on a pair of snowshoes and reached down and pulled me out. "Don't you do that no more!" I'll never forget that as long as I live.

༄

When I was a kid, the one-room schoolhouse here in Merritt went to the eighth grade. Once you got out of the eighth grade you had to go to Leavenworth to go to high school. So we would end up going down to Leavenworth to find and stay with a family for the school week. I'd get out here and they'd flag the train down so I'd get on it and tell the conductor where I was going: I wanted to get off at the Leavenworth Depot. Then I'd have to walk into town of course. No big deal. I'd go stay there and then Friday night I'd go back home the same way.

In 1949 a slide came down and took the school out. I was the only kid in school then, me and the teacher. I think that year we got about six or eight feet of snow. Dad wouldn't let me go to school that day. A guy came running up to find dad and said, "A slide just took the school out!" I said, "Hey dad, I'm going to put the snow shoes on and make sure the teacher got out". So I snow shoed out to the highway and here comes the teacher, walking up over the hill. I looked behind me and there went the school." Piano, bricks, the whole thing across the highway into the river.

I remember Jess Nostrand the operator here in Merritt, holding up the orders for the train. He'd hold them up there and the engineer put his hand out and the caboose would put his hand out to get the orders from that Y stick. Jess was a funny old guy, smoked a pipe, he'd sit back there and he'd think he was king of the island.

Dad always watched the mountain goats up there. Me and these friends went up there to see if we could scare them goats. That's the worst mistake I ever made. They were dad's goats, he thought he owned them. Yes sir'ee, you leave them alone. Then I made the mistake of shooting one when I was hunting. Dad got upset about that. He told me you shoot them you eat them. I said, "Okay dad whatever you say".

We had from fifteen to twenty feet of snow in Merritt. Nobody plowed the road, you had to snow shoe in and out. Come spring dad would put the guys to it, five guys. They would shovel snow from here to the highway. They'd do it in just a little over a week.

Basically, the railroad was fun. It was work, but it was fun. There were a lot of nice guys and a lot of dingbats. I enjoyed my job. I worked for the company for

**Sharen and Jim George were married on May 10, 1958.**

over forty-six years and my brother Paul worked close to forty years. Paul went to Montana to become a roadmaster, then came back as roadmaster at Skykomish and lived in Monroe. I met a lot of good people here.

# SHAREN GEORGE,
# WIFE OF JIM GEORGE

**Birthplace: Wenatchee, WA 1932**

*Life as a railroad wife, keeping the main line running.*

This is the story of just one of the many railroad wives who were left in charge of running the home, kids and just about everything!!!

You know in those days Jim would be gone on a gang and I'd be here alone with three little kids. First one, then two and eventually three. He had our only vehicle. For entertainment I'd either go over to the depot and talk to Jess the operator or take the kids and walk up to the Merritt Café which was right up here on the corner and drink a pepsi, that was my entertainment. No television and one car. Those were the days.

I was fifteen and a half years old when we got married. Jim was eighteen. He had just graduated from high school, we met in high school. He had signed up for that draft, when you get out of school you go in. Well by then we'd been seeing each other for about six months. He decided he wanted to get married because he said, "If we get married now you can finish school and I can go in the service and you will draw my allotment and when I get out we'll have that money saved up to buy a house. And I'll have the service behind me." So it was a wonderful plan!

We went to our parents who weren't thrilled but they gave us permission anyway. We had gotten married on a Saturday, May 10, 1958. We spent Saturday night in Monroe. Came back and I had to do a thirteen page book report for school the next day. Jim's mother had moved over to the little house, and here we were rattling around in this big old house. I can remember Jim made me a ham sandwich while I'm trying to do this book report. I got a B+.

Then Jim had to report to the National Guard, May 12, 1958. July 1, 1958 he had to go to Fort Lewis for two weeks of training. When he came back I got pregnant. Ten and one half months later I had our first daughter. Jim didn't pass his physical to go into the service. He had cracked his wrist on a machine and they turned him down. But the following January when I was seven months pregnant living up here in the snow bank and him out running around on the crews, they drafted him.

So he went in and told them I've got my mother and a pregnant wife who doesn't drive yet. So they let him out on a hardship case. Then we had Tamera at the end of March in 1959 and we had our son the following year in August, 1960. We had two kids like right off the get go. And here I am up here in the snow bank, still a kid myself and Jim is off on a crew.

Jim's mother lived next door which was my salvation. Because I could take the kids over to her house and I could go up to the Merritt Café and have a Pepsi and talk, that was my social life. Finally Jim got a pickup and I had a car. Jim's mother was here at Merritt and she moved immediately over to the little house and said, "You kids can have the big house." I was not real pleased about it because I thought, oh no, I'm going to be stuck up here in a snow bank. There I was! In fact one time when Jim was gone, Jim's mother called me and she said, "Sharen, Sharen my water tank, the pipe froze and broke. There is water going all over the house." The shut off valve was outside the house under about six feet of snow, and it was me and her. So about that time one of the railroad guys drove a cat operator. I went over and got him and he brought the cat over. He pushed the snow off where the valve was so we could get to it and get it shut off. Got the water shut off finally. Seemed like in those days everything was twice as hard.

The funny thing I remember about just living here in this little railroad berg, they had a snow train that would go to Leavenworth. It would come through here and stop and let everybody off to play in the snow. In those days the snow outside would go clear up over our windows. Jim would have to shovel the windows out. There would be about a foot of the window open at the top One day I hear this noise and I look and here is all of these people up on the snow bank looking in the window at us. So I walked out there and they said, "You live here, all winter? Do you have water?" I guess we were really something different. They were quite amazed that people lived here and survived.

Women of today wouldn't last as railroad wives. Back in the sixties when Jim was gone, it was up to me to do the shoveling. Jim had gotten a cow and some chickens and they were way out there past his mothers house in the barn. Snow banks were like seven feet tall. I'd have to try to get up that snow bank with five gallon buckets of water and carry water out to the cow (we were raising it for beef) and the chickens. I think I'd have drawn the line on milking a cow! You shoveled and it was like you were in a tunnel. Jim decided to let that cow loose. I could never figure that one out. I'd go out there and I'd meet that cow in the walkway which was very tunnel-like, not a lot of room. And she'd lower her head and start dancing like she was going to butt me. So finally told Jim one of us is going to go, either me or the cow. The cow tasted good. Those were the good old days back then.

Jim and I have been married for fifty seven years. We raised three children, Tamera, Steve, and Traci all at Merritt. They all went to the Winton one-room school. We took care of our parents and buried them all in the same year. Raising our children here has made us a very close family. Now our great grandchildren come to visit and play at Merritt. After fifty seven years of marriage and three generations of railroaders, at our ages of seventy-three and seventy-six, we still live at this great little place called Merritt.

# DEAN WARREN

Birthplace: Cashmere, WA 1939
Date of Service: April 27th, 1960
Positions Held: Track Department, Switchman and Trainman

*I enjoyed my career, I was there for forty years. I was the youngest of our family and I believe between all my brothers, my brother-in-law and a couple of my nephews who worked there for a while, we had right around 350 years combined service for the family all under the GNRR.*

I was born in Cashmere to Homer and Mary Warren. I was the youngest of eight boys and one girl. All eight of us boys worked on the Great Northern. Starting out with Homer: Track Department, Kenny: Signal Department, Norman: Track Department and Trainman, Karl: Track Department, Glen: Track Department and Trainman, Wayne: Track Department, and me, Dean: Track Department, Switchman and Trainman. Don Stone, my brother-in-law: Track Department and Trainman. My oldest brother Bower worked on the Great Northern before WWII. He chose not to return to the GN after the war.

When I was nineteen years old I was building houses in Cashmere. I got married on March 25, 1960. A month later I was laid off and I knew I needed a job. On the Friday I went over and saw my brother, Homer. On the Monday morning I went to work on the crossing section in Monitor for Homer. I worked for Homer for about three months, then I went up and worked on the Chelan section.

On October 10, 1960, I went down to Wenatchee and started switching. Worked as a switchman in Wenatchee for two years. There wasn't enough work there as it was seasonal.

Then I got called to go over to Everett to talk to a train master, Al Foote. He asked me if I would like to come work for him as a switchman. So I went to Everett and worked for him. Worked the various crews there, worked down in Interbay for a while. Really enjoyed the job switching and being home and then I found out they needed brakemen on the weekends, so I volunteered. If they needed me they would call quite often on week ends. It was like I didn't have a home. Out working the "extra north" with a lot of nice people, working on the Great Northern. There were some interesting folks working that north end. There were a lot of things going on in Vancouver when you were off duty. Never did get involved in those good times in Vancouver. Those guys were pretty heavy hitters up there. I worked with Tom Kenny, conductor. Nice guy to work with, also Victor "Porky" Rengstorf and Al Holevas,

I remember one day in Interbay. I'm sitting there watching this train come in from Canada. Looked at this one tank car and I couldn't believe it, there was a whole double set of trucks missing from under the front end of that car. I came into the yard, went down and looked it over. The conductor was Howard Welch. I told him about it and he couldn't believe it either. We walked down with the car man, looking at it. They didn't know where the wheels were at that time. Fortunately, the knuckle on both cars had a lip underneath it so they wouldn't slide past. That's the only thing that kept it from derailing. So they backtracked everything and they found that set of trucks at an industry track in Everett called Nord Door. That thing had switched itself right out, travelled down there and was sitting right where they spot cars for lumber. That was one of the most amazing things I'd ever seen.

We were just talking about a hobo at Delta Yard, down the old caboose track. Went down there, walked by an empty boxcar and I happened to glance in. It was about two in the morning. I shined a light in there and there's a guy lying on the floor, so I reached over and poked his foot with my lantern and told the guy, "Hey we're going to be moving this car, you're going to have to get out." Didn't get any movement so reached up and touched him and I knew right then something was wrong. Got the yardmaster down there, he took a look and called the coroner. He'd been hit in the head or something, cause he was dead.

I had a number of experiences with guys who were riding the train. I was walking down through Interbay yard one night, just a quiet, beautiful night, I'm just enjoying all the silence, All of a sudden this voice says, "Hey buddy". Damn, I almost jumped over top of that boxcar. I didn't expect anybody to be there. He says,"what time is it?" Wanted to know where the train was going. You know back in those days we had a lot of guys riding trains they just wanted to get from point A to point B. Never really bothered them and they didn't bother us.

There was one old gentleman, every Wednesday he'd come down to the south end of Interbay yard, he was probably in his seventies. He'd want to know where the train was that was going to Portland. I just happened to be working that train. I was knocking the brakes off. Well this train is going to Portland. He said: "Well, where's the car I can ride in?" I said, "We got some empty ones back there, kind of hard to get in. You're going down to Portland? I think I've seen you here before." He said, "Yea I go down about every other week if I can. My wife is in a nursing home in Vancouver and I have no other way to get there, so I ride the freight train." I said, "Well, you're not going to ride in the boxcar this time." So I took him up on the engine. The engineer was Carl Molander. I said, "This gentleman's going down to Vancouver to see his wife in a nursing home, I told him he could ride up here with us, what do you think, Carl?" "Set him down", Carl said.

After that he pretty much rode the cabooses or he rode the engines when he'd go down to see his wife. After about a year we never saw him anymore. Apparently either he passed away or she did. But I just couldn't see that old gentleman riding back there in that boxcar. It was back in the days of the GN when you could do things like that. I loved working for the GN. After the mergers and all the changes, things like that, it just wasn't the same. I'm glad I'm outa there now, with all the things that go on.

The Warren family L-R: Glen, Norman, Bower, Homer Jr., Daphne, Dean, Kenney, Karl, Wayne. Seated: Homer Sr., and Mary, September 19, 1965.

My brother Glen, he kind of had a black cloud following him. Every time I would mark up on his crew working with him, my wife would have a fit. She said, "you're going to get fired." I said, "No honey I'm not going to get fired, I'm going to keep Glen, from getting fired." Glen was a conductor working the turn up at Ferndale. The guys were up at the top end of the Ferndale yard switching out their train and going to put the engine in the grain spur and then go over to the hotel. So Glen drops off at the depot and lines up the switch to the grain spur, so when the guys come back they can go right in. They are switching up there at the top end of the yard and it's quite a hill coming down towards the depot. Some mistake was made up there. The cars on the main line got away from them, about a dozen cars and the caboose came down, went into the grain spur, hit the end of the track and took out the Ferndale Phone Company. People up there were without phones for at least a month. Glen got fired, whole crew got fired on that one. Glen was off thirteen months, got back to work, marked up on the East End Pool as a conductor. I was working that crew and my nephew, Jerry Warren, was working as a brakeman. So there were us three Warrens all on that crew. We worked a trip over and back no problem.

The next trip, I got called to work a passenger train to Vancouver BC. So I took that and they had an extra man go make the trip east. Coming back they had a grain train with helpers. At the west end of Berne a car derailed, about six cars in front of the helpers. They went into the tunnel and they tore up about six miles of ties and rails in that tunnel. Shut that down for a while! Usually I was on the caboose, working the east end. I was always out on that back platform when we went over that west switch at Berne, watching for any problems.

I remember one trip, I was called off a switch engine to go out on a work train. They had a derailment on that big curve at Index. I'm out there, working with the wrecker using hand signs. The superintendent, Jerry Wicks, was there and he comes up and starts giving signs to the guy operating the crane. I'm giving the guy stop signs. Mr. Wicks says to me, "I want him to move." I said "Mr. Wicks, I'm supposed to be giving him the signs, he's supposed to take no signs but from me." He says, "Well I'm the superintendent." "Well sir, I know who you are but you're backing him right into those high power lines right above him." He looked at that and turned around and walked off. Later I got a letter from him thanking me for being so vigilant. Jerry Wicks was a real gentleman for handling it that way.

Another trip I remember, we came into Wenatchee. I had Jimmy Smith (Bobby Smith's boy), as the engineer. He had a fireman, Jeff Aldcroft. Lloyd Oxentenko was the head brakeman, a good man. I worked the caboose with Gilbert Bjorling. Gil and I dropped off at the caboose at the yard office. They went down to head into seven track to put most of their cars over to six track. It was a pretty long train and they ran through a switch! This young trainmaster decided the whole crew was going to go up to the hospital for a urinalysis test. So they take us up there, give us the test, bring us back and the young trainmaster calls and says, "Well they tell us these guys can't work now until the results come back?" Which was normal, we knew that, but he didn't when he had us take the UA. So they had to put us on a passenger train and send us home The results of the UA got lost and we were off nine days! Everybody came back clear, we knew we were all good, and we knew we were going to get paid. Nine days off with pay! Next trip I got back to work we came over to Wenatchee. First person I saw was that young trainmaster. I walked up and I shook his hand and said, "Thank you for the paid vacation sir." He just looked at me and he didn't know what to say.

How the railroad affected my home life. One time I was getting ready for my days off and it was in the middle of the week, it was the summer time and we were going to go out camping when Barbara, the crew clerk, called. My youngest son Dean, about eight years old then, answered the phone. Barbara says to him, "This is the crew desk is your dad there?" Dean kind of hesitated. I was outside putting stuff in the trailer. Dean said, "No he isn't." Barbara asked, "Well where is he?" Dean said, "I think he went skiing." Now this is in the summertime, so Barbara said "are you sure?" "I think so," said Dean, then he hangs up. Three or four days later when I got back to work Barbara needed to talk to me. I walked over and she tells me this and says, "I asked your boy where you went skiing." He said "I guess you'll have to figure that out for yourself." "Barbara, I was outside putting stuff in the trailer and I didn't even know you'd called. She says, "You got him trained pretty good." We had to do things like that sometimes.

I remember one trip, I came in off the hill, I was working again with Lloyd Oxentanko. Lloyd went over and he wanted to lay off one trip. Barbara says, "We don't have any men." I was just wandering around the office and Lloyd leaves and I said Barbara I need to be off one round trip?" I was always polite with them, if they can't let me off, I just say, "Maybe next trip?" You know I never had any problems laying off anytime I wanted because she knew if she called me for an extra shift, I'd work. Barbara was quite a character. George Pete was another and Charlie Northrup, he was another. He called me a lot for those "Extra North's".

There was one trip I made on a passenger train up there. A bunch of GNRR officials wives had the use of a private car. They had this one young trainmaster riding with them, these were wives that were from the GNRR, but it was the BNRR at that time. I was working the train as the rear brakeman. I decided, Ellen my wife was going to Vancouver with me on the train. Spend a night up there with her and then come back the next morning. We did that quite often. We got on the train and I'm standing outside talking and some of these women from the private car walked by and asked, "How long is it going to be before we leave?" I said, "Probably about fifteen minutes." Ellen steps in the door there and looks at me. I said this is my wife, I brought her with me. They said, "Oh, well she can come back and ride in the private car with us". I said, "Thank you very much." Ellen goes back with them, we get up to Blaine at the border, we get everything cleared to go across. We have to stop over at White Rock for customs. Well the Canadian Customs go in and check out the private car. The booze isn't locked up like its supposed to be so they make us back that train up and unload all that booze at the Blaine depot before that private car can go into Canada. (Booze had to be locked up, or special paperwork done). This young trainmaster hadn't done any of that. We get back to Blaine and they're unloading it. I'm standing there, one of the officials wives comes back, she says to this young trainmaster, "You were supposed to have had this all taken care of!" "Yea, well I just didn't get it done." The official's wife said, "Well when you get to Vancouver, you get on an airplane and you go to St. Paul and you exercise your seniority in any department you worked in prior to becoming an official." She fired him right on the spot. She'd been on the phone with her husband. Wives have power!

It was a lot of fun out there but a lot of sad things happened too. We were coming back from Wenatchee once, I don't remember who the engineer was. I'm looking down the track and there's a guy standing along side the track, he's maybe half mile from us, I can see him up there on the curve. We get about fifty yards from him and he drops down on his knees and lays his neck right across the track and never moves. Come to find out he had a fight with his girlfriend, so he showed her! We kind of get a thick skin to that stuff, but not completely.

A tonnage train probably takes a mile, mile and a half at least, in full emergency braking to stop. People don't understand, trains don't stop like a car. Been in several situations where we hit people. It is just not something you get over. The guy I really felt sorry for was an engineer, Jim Buss. Out there in Everett he hit a little boy. Oh Boy! That was at Picnic Point. I don't think Jim ever really got over that one. Somebody would get hit out there and then for weeks after we'd have people throwing rocks at us. I remember one time we were going to Wenatchee. and they threw rocks and hit the windshield right in front of me. I'd just taken my glasses off and was wiping my face. That windshield exploded right in my face. Bobby Smith was the engineer. I told Bob we're going to have to stop at the depot, I got a face full of glass and I'm not going to even open my eyes. I was an emergency medical technician at that time for the fire department. They took me up to the hospital to wash my eyes out. The doctor said "Glass like this is more like sand you get in your eyes, it doesn't have the sharp edges on it." I said, "There is no way I'm going to open my eyes until you ask me to. He said, "That's a good idea".

I remember another trip with Bobby Smith. We were leaving Leavenworth going up the Chumstick on a beautiful sunny day. All of a sudden we lost the air. Bobby said, "I wonder what caused that?" I said, "I'll go take a look, Bob." So I walked back, about ten cars. A shiny box car that looked like it was brand new was pulled right in half. It was an old box car and they'd given it a brand new paint job! I said, "Bob you've got to come back here and see this!" Just pulled it apart and set it down. Bob came back and said, "Hmm they gave that a "Sherwin Williams overhaul", in my career it's the first time I've ever seen that one".

I was working with Chuck White. We came out of the tunnel into Berne. I was on the caboose and we lost our air. My nephew Jerry was on the head end, so we started walking the train We got seven knuckles and the caboose stopped just in the clear, so a train could get by us. One spot we got both knuckles between the car. Chuck had to make out reports on that one, he couldn't figure out why it had happened. They were really ripping on him about it. Chuck told me, I had to write letters and make explanations for six months on that." They wanted to fire me, but they couldn't find a reason.

Christmas—everybody was trying to find out some way to be home for Christmas. It didn't always work, but I got to spend most of my Christmases at home. The job interfered a lot with our social life. We'd have something planned but you could never really plan things.

Christmas and holidays, you just hoped that you could make it home. There were times we had our celebrations the day after. Ellen and I always had a joke between us, the way paydays were the first and the fifteenth. As kids we were living pretty much paycheck to paycheck for a long time. Ellen always got her Valentine's Day card and box of candy the day after Valentine's Day That was kind of an understanding and a joke all those years. Even after things were a lot better that's the way it was. That was a tradition. We grew up together that way in our marriage. We've been married fifty-five years.

Finally I got enough seniority where I could have all my vacations at Christmas. I fell down a flight of stairs at Interbay and tore my shoulder. I was off for six months. They offered me a good retirement and I left. Stu Gordon helped me with that. Stu started out as a switchman, his dad was a bridge tender on bridge #12 in Marysville for years. Stu went to work very young as a switchman in Everett. Worked his way up through yardmaster, trainmaster and became terminal superintendent. He knew the guys. He was never transferred out of the area like they did with most of the guys. Stu knew what went on out there. If you were having problems you could talk to Stu.

I enjoyed my career, I was there for forty years. I was the youngest of our family and I believe between all my brothers, my brother-in-law and a couple of my nephews who worked there for a while, we had right around three-hundred-and-fifty years combined service for the family all under the GNRR. Almost all those were on the Cascade Division. Homer was made a roadmaster over in Montana for a while but almost all of our careers were on the Cascade Division.

# DAVE HALL

**Birthplace: Everett, WA 1942**
**Date of Service: May 26, 1960**
**Position Held: Section Gang, Gang Foreman, Switchman and Brakeman**

*You know, I admire the company, they worked for*
*everybody and helped. I can say it was a real pleasure*
*working for the Great Northern.*

I was a junior in high school when I started working for the railroad. I worked pretty near forty years for them I resigned at age fifty-six because of hardship in the family.

I started working for the railroad when I was a junior in high school, but I became involved with the railroad long before then. We lived in Milltown in Skykomish. We lived only about three-hundred feet from the railroad. The steam engines on the head of a train would always come by our house. As kids we would throw rocks at the hobos. It didn't work out so well when they would crawl out and start chasing us. We went back to the house and didn't do that again.

We'd walk from my house to Sky and fish along the river. One day I was coming back from town, I believe it was around 1951. I was down toward the sawmill when this happened. I was just a youngster. A "covered wagon" diesel engine train came by and a guy stuck his head out the window and said "Would you like a ride?" I looked up at him and looked at the ladder and said, "I don't know if I should." He said, "Come on up here, we'll give you a ride." So I climbed up there, I had to stand on my tiptoes to see over the cab. Red (Gilbert) Lyon was the engineer. I grew up with his kids, Barbara and Darrell. Red said, "I'll give you this ride, but don't you tell my kids." He started moving and I thought we were going to fall off the tracks or something. That was my first deal with the railroad, riding in that cab.

Right in front of my house when I was a kid in Milltown, they had an underground cable that went under the tracks to this power pole by the road. The ditcher had dug up the track and it broke the cable. The line was abandoned you see, and it was coated with lead. Us kids didn't have any mold to make fishing sinkers or anything, so we took a double bitted ax, put the line on the chopping block and pounded on it till we got little chunks of it off. Someone said why don't you put them on the railroad tracks to flatten them? I wonder what the guys in the engine thought was going on down there because we had about ten or fifteen of them laid out and they looked like silver dollars

Dave Hall and his daughter Tonia, who is a conductor, visit the William Crooks in Duluth, MN

three inches across. Then we took tin snips and cut them to put on our fishing lines to go fishing.

I went to school at Sky up to Junior High. My dad worked for Northwest Portland Cement. They had a mining pit in Lake Wenatchee. My dad helped to get it started. When I was in the eighth grade he decided to move to Lake Wenatchee and I moved with my dad.

In my junior year I decided to go to work for the railroad because a friend of my dad's, Homer Warren. He and dad were real close, they played cards (pinochle) a lot. Homer asked me, "Do you want to go to work for the railroad? You got to be eighteen to work, but never mind, I'll just put you on." That was fine, I went to work. A few years later they wanted to know my birthdate, I had an awful time getting that straightened out.

My first day at work we were under the first bridge that goes over the track at Cashmere. Homer Warren was the foreman. We had this coarse gravel. You had a square shovel trying to get this coarse gravel tamped in and raised up. I worked hard that day. It was like doing it twice cause you'd pull it in, it rattled out, pull it in, it rattled out. That was a hard day's work.

I worked for the railroad on the section of the Cascade Division. It was Wenatchee to Seattle, repairing tracks, putting in ties, surfacing, any emergencies, fire fighting, all of that. I worked there for a couple of years and they decided to put me over on the west side on the slide patrol. I wasn't too sure about coming to Edmonds on slide patrol because I didn't know how to get there. I'd just got my license for driving when I was eighteen, but I decided to go ahead and do it. I came to find out it wasn't as bad as I thought it was going to be. There were several times I had problems with the track because there was snow and slush on it. Had an awful time moving the motor car through that stuff because it would spin out. I went from Golden Gardens down to Edmonds, and Edmonds to Everett, working different shifts.

One day I was at the depot at Edmonds, John Skucy was the operator. The Empire Builder was coming by. The engineer was George Miller. George left Edmonds going west. He got out by Richmond Beach when he called in and said, "We just hit a boy out here, you're going to have someone come out and get him." He was trying to free his dog off the tracks. John asked me if I could get the motor car and go out there. The coroner came out there to pick up the boy and dog and I brought them in where they could be reached.

I had another one about a year later near Mukilteo. I looked out and there was a body floating in the water. I called the dispatcher and told him to have the coroner or somebody come out here to get this body. The Everett coroner came out and between the two of us we got her on the motor car. I took her into Mukilteo and got the ambulance to pick her up. She'd been missing for thirty-one days out in the Sound.

There was another incident on the slide patrol. Someone broke into a store in Richmond Beach and dumped a safe out into the bay, I reported that. There were lots of incidents I ran into. There was a work train that would work the Chevron storage tanks. I told the dispatcher we've got problems outside of Golden Gardens. They had rail pilings and timbers piled there to shore up the bank. And above that the leaves were rolled up, like someone had just rolled them up. Something was moving and sure enough it wasn't too long after that about a hundred foot slide came down by Golden Gardens and covered one track. I worked there on the section for six years.

I was working at Mukilteo when they started the new line up to Boeing Field. The new line raised five feet for every one hundred feet of track. The track from Sky to Merritt raises a little over two feet for every one hundred that you go forward They started that grade up to the field, I thought, oh man, that's an awful steep grade.

Homer Warren helped me get my foreman's promotion. I had surfacing gangs at Everett. One day we were running ties (putting in ties) in near Mukilteo. Stacked them all on the east bound track while we were putting the ties in on the west bound lane. There were orders there for the trains to slow down. I watched these guys on the train come around the curve and we moved the ties. I kind of wondered, those guys are hardly working up there, we're out here with these black bananas (creosoted wood ties) we called them, working hard. So I went to Adolph Holmes, the roadmaster, I asked him could I take a leave of absence and go into train service. He said, "Well it's up to you." Henry Ferryman was Division Roadmaster then. Dick Tangy was Assistant Superintendent in Wenatchee. I talked to him one day and he said come on over, we'll get you to work right now.

I only had two days of training and they put me to work nights. I started my switching that day in 1966, went into train service. I worked for several years before the NP and GN railroads merged. They tried to get the merger started in 1968 but it didn't materialize. The government postponed it. Then in 1970 they got the merge and ended up calling it the Burlington Northern. At that time they threw our seniority into one big pot where you got switchman, brakeman both. So we were eligible to go on the road, work trains or wherever they might send us. Worked an extra board most of my life.

I had a lot of problems with the people getting off and on cars. They would want to go up to Oroville to pick apples or whatever. They'd get on these flatcars, we had the Wenatchee Oroville Local working one day and they pulled up by the roundhouse. Arne Wheatcroth and I were coming off work and I saw this guy trying to get on. He couldn't get his foot in the lower stirrup. He let go and fell between the rails. I told Arne, "You better get the coroner down here, he lost his life there." We dealt with this many a time. People get hurt on the railroad. We don't like to see that happen no matter what they do.

I worked there for quite a few years and then I got a job regular on the Alcoa Local, which put me to work at five in the afternoon til five in the morning, twelve hours. When I first went switching they had the sixteen hour law. Sixteen hours on, eight hours off, sixteen hours on. It got old after a while. "Hours of service". Now they've dropped it down to twelve hours.

It was bad over at Wenatchee working in the snow, digging switches out, a lot of problems. I'm not sure of the year but they had an explosion in Wenatchee as I happened to be going to work at 2:30 p.m. My late wife and I were down at the south end of Wenatchee by a laundromat doing the clothes. All of a sudden the power went off. Then the concussion hit and all those dryer doors just flew open like somebody had took them off. I went outside and saw people running up and down the street. I looked down toward Appleyard and I could see this funnel cloud coming up in the air and I said, "Oh my, there goes a tank car." That's what it was. Everybody thought it was Schroeder's oil tanks. He had a service station but it was further than that. It was amazing what was lost. Switchman Dave Jones was killed, he was my partner at work. There were some other people injured. The damage was terrific, six million dollars of damage in Wenatchee. It took years to get over that. I have pictures of the hole in the ground. It didn't blow up, it pushed everything into the ground including the ties. They tried to find the cause. It was a Dupont car containing some kind of chemical. They found more of this on a train in North Dakota and the railroad automatically set it out of the train because they had no idea what was in it. They tried to simulate the same process trying to figure out why that thing exploded. Still didn't know how it happened, but I'll tell you one thing, it shook the ground where we were at.

Those days are kind of gone now everything is computerized wherever you go. Infra-red track detectors for the rails pick up the hot boxes in various places, especially on a hill where you're using brakes. I worked several years and it happened my last few years on the railroad when I worked mostly the Alcoa local. Because I'm on call one day I come to work and the yardmaster says, "The whole crew goes upstairs, we got a drug inspector here, go take care of your sample here". I said, okay. A few days later I went on a different job and again, "You all got to go upstairs". I said, "What?" I walked in and they asked what was I doing there? Well I'm doing what I'm told. That was twice in one week so I should be safe for awhile. I enjoyed working for a company that every day was a mystery. Tough times, a lot of people didn't want to work out in the cold, but I was always there. I never had a any problems getting time off (personal leaves) because I worked all the time. They'd even call me sometimes, "Would you work an extra job for us?" One time I was supposed to go on vacation and they said, "We don't have the manpower." So I said, "Postpone my vacation."

One day I was switching in the yard, I don't smoke or chew but we had a brakeman on the job, Russ Allenbugh was his name. We were working together and we happened to pull up in the front of the yard and the yardmaster was hollering for me to tell him something. I happened to look up, Russ must not have heard me. He opened the window up, spit out the window and down on me when I was hollering at him. He looked at me and said, "I'm dead." There was spots all over my face. I went up there and he said, "Man, I'll clean you up." He got some paper towels and wiped it off my forehead and cheek. It was kind of comical. Things like that happened. I found out you got to have a good sense of humor and real keen judgment, working with this railroad cause if you don't, you can have a lot of problems.

Getting back to my section days, there was an earthquake when I was a foreman on this tie gang at Everett Junction. Roy Keenan was running the tie saw. Delbert Snelson was running the tamper and Wayne Warren was running the digger. I looked at Roy when he was cutting the ties, three pieces, the center and two ends. Roy looked at me and I looked at him "What's wrong?" Roy said, "You're making an awful lot of movement on this track." I happened to look on the hillside and all the maple trees were shaking, then I looked down the track and you could see the waves in the track like a rope. It was an earthquake! I got the crew away from that hillside. It was kind of a weird situation, we all stopped and we all looked at each other.

I was working in the Cascade Tunnel one day. I was Relief Foreman filling in for foremen on vacation. On my days off somebody called me at home said they ran into a big piece of steel in the tunnel and said I'd better go check it. It was at such and such a bay area. Here was a big quarter-inch piece of steel all bent. Whether it had fallen off a car or what, I could feel an awful draft. I looked up about six or seven feet and it had come off the wall. It was from a little side shaft to the Pioneer Tunnel. The Pioneer Tunnel was how they serviced the crews to the main tunnel at the time of construction. I got up in there and looked. I found a keg of little dinky spikes. The two-by-sixes and two-by-tens were just powder from dry rot. I went a little further and the water was running down to where it comes out at Scenic on the west end of the Cascade Tunnel.

I bought a new '65 Mustang Fastback. I had it up here in Sky. We were working up by the Foss River on the tie gang. It was raining. I parked down by the outfit cars here in Sky. The big crew bus, was in and out all the time. The bus was all fogged up and the guy who operated it, he backs up and mine was the only new car there. I got back from work and I looked at my car. "What happened here?" "Well the crew bus backed up and he didn't see your car and caved in the rear driver's side." The car was kind of a metallic blue color. It was kind of hard to match those paints. I drove that car till it had forty-four-thousand miles on it before I got rid of it.

I was working in the Tacoma yard. There were two helpers and a foreman back in those days. There was a clean-out track they used to clean out all the grain cars, scrap lumber, the bands and stuff. I stayed in an old box car that was sitting on the ground. The floor was nearly eaten away. Had a bunk and a stove in it. It was a place to keep you warm. In those days the railroad didn't pay for your lodging.

We had kerosene lamps mounted on the switch stands for night switching, and of course everyone had to light their cigarettes. They would open the cap, get their cigarette lit and never turn the flame back down, so we would run out of fuel. The lanterns had green lenses on two opposite sides and two yellow lenses on the other two sides. The lanterns were permanently mounted on each switch, so when we threw the switch it turned the lantern. Green for the lead track and yellow for the storage track One day the roadmaster said they were shipping about fifteen of those reflector lights. They wanted me to pull those old kerosene lights and get rid of them. I thought, what am I going to do with all these lights? I kept four but should have kept them all. What do you do back then? To this day I wished I would have kept them all.

A friend of mine had an old GN bridge sign. Jerry said, "Do you want this? You can have it for five dollars." I took it, but you couldn't read it, you could barely make it out. You could barely see Rocky the goat. So I got some turpentine to clean it, but that didn't even touch it. I scrubbed and scrubbed and didn't remove anything on it. So I got some rubber gloves and a little bowl of gasoline and real fine steel wool. From there it was all elbow grease. I got it all off and now you can put a light on that a mile away and it will just sparkle.

When I hired out, Homer Warren had the tie gang. It was 105 degrees at Cashmere putting in these railroad ties. The river is right next to the track there and Homer says you guys want to take a dip in the river? Man, everybody went in the river.

There was an incident I remember, a friend of mine had his leg severed in the

Wenatchee yard. It happened in the main yard. It was at night, and he was working down in the main yard. The foreman let these cars go into the track. Bill was down here hooking up air hoses. He was in there when those cars hit each other. He lost his leg when that happened.

Let me tell you of the time I stole a train out of Wenatchee. Me being on the extra board, the guys working regular got their orders out of Wenatchee. All I do is look at the orders because we know what work has to be done. Cars to pick up and what not between here and there. Pat MaGee was the engineer. Gilbert "Alabam" Allen was the dispatcher Anyway we took our train and left Wenatchee and did our job. We had a new dispatcher on the midnight shift. He was looking at the train orders and he said, "These guys are out of yard limits what are they doing up at Omak, switching?" Just a minor mistake. Every time I think of that I think, "Well, I stole a train out of Wenatchee!" They pulled all of us out of service, this was the first part of May. August 15th our union rep said, they want you to come back to work. That was the only big scar I had on my record. Nobody got hurt.

The trouble was we did all the work, we got the mill all switched, everything else in the yard all organized. When it was real busy they had two jobs there. There was so much work up there. Pat Lyman our conductor called it an endurance test. There was no place to eat up there, you just grabbed a sandwich and rode the rails and ate it on the way up.

I caught the second to the last trip on the Mansfield Line which goes from the Columbia River up to Mansfield, hauling grain. I knew it was being abandoned soon. They made one more trip and that was it. They abandoned the line. A friend of mine Roy Busk, was the engineer coming out one time. The track just gave way, no tie support or nothing. He remembers each car was a wooden boxcar. One car just disintegrated. Real soft, just buried the wheels, another car came up and there was grain everywhere. It put the engine on its side, rails coming through the cab. Roy was hanging on to the water cooler that was next to the controls when it stopped. I enjoyed that line. It was kind of sad to take it out.

I have thirteen acres in Plain, been there twenty-nine years. I built my chicken house out of switch ties. My brother-in-law, Bruce Dickinson, he got to tear down the Berne depot. He and I were up there tearing it all down, I got the hardwood flooring out of there. I got all the two-by-sixes out of the icehouse in Wenatchee when they tore that down. They were just throwing them all away. I got a lot of stuff from the icehouse. Used it all, it adds character to the place you know.

Back in those days everybody worked together. When I was switching in the Wenatchee yard by the bridge, it is downhill there. You have your work lead plus thirteen tracks plus the mainline. We were switching there right under the bridge and Ron Bird was foreman. I had to make a cut to get this car out. I came out with it and had to ride the car down to tie it down to the joint (slow it to a coupling). Where the joint was, I cranked on that brake but there was nothing. It went all the way up and it stopped like it was locked. So I just said, "well you got twelve tracks, its got to go into one of them. So I jumped off. You know what! That thing was lined right into the side of the train at the bottom end, Vic Caillier was yardmaster, Ron was foreman. I called him up and said, "You know we got a car on the ground here?" Ron had just got his foreman rights and he said, "what are we going to do"? I said, "Don't worry about it, I worked the section for quite a while." I got it taken care of, put the car away and Vic came and said, "Where's the car, where's the car?" I said, "Well, we put it on track seven over there."

There was another time, Pat King had just hired out switching. They had the cross-over between seven switch and eight switch to thirteen. One of us was working on the upper end. Apparently the person on the upper lead was watching the seven track and he stepped back to see what I was doing on the ten track and I saw that car hit him and knock him down. He grabbed his foot. I was about ten cars away, man did I run like crazy to him. Frank Boyd was foreman on the other crew. He saw it happen. We ran up there and got his leg out. He had these real thick cornered shoes, real thick heels, It caught the heel and drug him along and it peeled his leg right down to the bone. Maybe that's what saved his leg? His thick heel. They had to come up and interview me to see what happened, you can't blame the kid cause he was watching me and I was watching him. I saw he wasn't paying attention. It makes you think, you don't get a second chance on the things you do. Going from car to car you got all those ladders up and down so I just ran across the tops of the box cars, just hopped across till I got to where I wanted to go. This was years ago you could get away with it. Now you don't get up there. Everything is done from below.

We put them all over the ground at the Texaco spur one night. We had Standard Oil and we were east of Chehalis Street. We got up there and somebody cocked the switch yet the target was still green. Eddie Boyd was the engineer and he says, "Hmmmm, sure feels funny" and he dumped it. Had eleven cars for WO, had some boxes and one full tank. The tank and the engine went on the ground. We hit the power pole. All the wires came down. It was at night. Eddie said, "man we're going to get fired for sure for this." Then he shut the engine off. I said, "Hey, don't do that we got to have a little air." I told Eddie to start the engine and we had six cars of air out of an eleven car transfer. Everything turned out okay!

Another story to tell you. The engineer on the east end, Wenatchee to Spokane, they go through the wheat fields. Anyway they had firemen on board in those days. They were going along and the fireman decided he needed a little snooze when a pheasant flew up and hit the fireman's window side. Blood was running down the window. The engineer hollered, " Did that boy on the bicycle make it over there?" The fireman just about had a heart attack, he woke up fast!

I was working in the switch yard in Wenatchee. An engineer named Gary was working our shift. He came into Wenatchee after I'd been there several years. He was a small guy, but he was a real caring guy. We worked hard together. One day he had four units working in the north end of Appleyard. I was supposed to kick a tank car out into the main yard. Jim Caputo was the foreman, he pulled this set of cars off the main towards the bridge, when he stopped. I was on the brake and it slammed me into the side of the tank car. It knocked me out. I fell, and I came too when I was falling off the tank car onto the ground. I was a little worried where my arms and legs were cause the cars were rolling back until the slack was taken up. It knocked me out, hitting the tank with my head. Anyway I came too and pulled myself up and I couldn't catch my breath. Jim says, "You okay"? I said, not really. It knocked me for a loop. I had a nerve problem on my right side all the way down to my feet. They had another guy come and replace me and I went to the hospital to have myself looked at. It knocked a vertebrae out in my back and that's what caused the deadness in my leg. Gary was the engineer and he felt bad about it. He came to visit me periodically and he saw my barn and liked it. He ended up leaving, went up north to work the Kettle Falls turn there at Colville and he built a barn just like mine. I'd go and visit him periodically he had horses and Scottish Highlanders, the cows with the shaggy hair and the long horns. He had several of those. Its kind of nice to watch those beautiful animals.

Gary was a real good engineer and smart in rules. He knew the rules. When he first came to Wenatchee I said, "man where did this guy come from"? He had a long beard, no hair on his head, wore a baseball cap and was small. I thought he wasn't all there, but that was a mistake. You learned working with him. It was real pleasant working with Gary. I wish that we had more engineers like him.

I caught a job on the Spud Local. The engineer was the regular but the conductor was from Spokane and had never worked the yard in Wenatchee. I worked there for several trips. I caught this one on Good Friday. The dispatchers centralized traffic control system went out, so we had to hand throw all the switches from Wenatchee all the way up to Quincy. I was in the caboose the conductor said, "well you better go up and tell them how to throw an electric switch." I just went up and stayed on the head end. I was by myself the whole day. We died on "hours of service" at Malaga.

There are good people up there at Quincy warehouse where they process potatoes. They asked, "Could you guys stay up here, we want to get this other car out of here." So we waited. Then they said, "Would you like some potatoes?" They brought fifty pound boxes out for all four of us. We had some good times in those days I don't know what its like now. Its quite an industry. We spotted a lot of cars up there. Lyle Courtney, he was a good engineer too. Wintertime he was always sticking his head out the window telling me what to do and what not to do. One day I grabbed a snowball and threw it. He wore glasses. I didn't pack it that hard but I hit him right in the nose. His glasses were all snow and around his face, I started laughing, couldn't help it.

Keyes Fiber caught fire. Something blew up down there on the north end of Wenatchee just before Holly Street. Gerald Huber and I were at Orondo street and we saw the explosion and stuff flying all over. So we went down there and sure enough, they had a fire in that boxcar. It had merchandise in it and it was burning steadily. We worked all night. Then we worked all day getting that box-car cleaned out. Nobody wanted to do that, but we finally got the fire out. Dick Tanguy, the assistant superintendent said, "You guys can take an extra six hours for that." Gerald and I, it was like our eyes were on fire from the smoke. I looked in the mirror and my eyes were all red. But we managed, Gerald and I, we worked hard together.

We had a lot of scrapes, nothing major, nobody got hurt. You know, I admire the company, they worked for everybody and helped. I can say it was a real plea-sure working for the Great Northern. My daughter is a conductor working from Everett to Vancouver BC. She's been working about thirteen or fourteen years now, I got to keep somebody in the family there, cause it was a good job for me and now she can take over.

Dave Hall with part of his Great Northern Railway memorabilia collection.

# Switch Lanterns

Lanterns are used for everything.

At the railroad they are used mostly at night.

They are used to pass signs from the field man

to the foreman in case the train is too long

and one of its switchmen gets out of sight.

The engineer reads these signs just like you'd read a book.

He knows when to go ahead or to back up.

Or how many cars there are to go.

He knows when to give them a nudge so they can pull the pin.

He knows what alley they are lined for to shove the string of cars in.

Lanterns are used to see in the dark

when yard checkers walk down track.

Like the bum that jumped me at two a.m.

and scared me when I was walking alone.

That's when I looked at my watch and wished it was just time for me to go home.

Lanterns are used by car men as they prepare a train to go.

Maybe a drag has just come in and it has traveled through a lot of snow.

The car man walks the length of the train checking it over and bleeding off the brakes. He works in all types of weather. This is information I just wanted you to know. Lanterns are used by operators at bridge 10 when they have to know that the tracks are aligned, if they aren't a train will go on the ground, putting the operating schedule behind.

Lanterns are used by conductors who read from the list of cars to know where a cut should be made, then signal to the engineer to lift a pin so the train can pull away. In the daytime they are stored in your grip with an extra battery or two. Because you never know when you'll be called out at night, or maybe you'll have to double through.

Yes, lanterns are essential for they are the railroad worker's right hand. They are even used to stop a creeping car as it starts to roll away. Of course, when he gets it back, his lantern has seen better days. 'Tis then he goes to the yard office to find one that is new, hoping to keep it in one piece till his day is through. Now you know what lanterns are for, they help each and everyone out as they work every day.

So when you drive down the highway maybe next to a railroad track or two, should you see a lantern light flash, it is just switchman or brakeman as they work the night through. For each man has a job to do. But his extra lantern he keeps hidden and completely out of sight. For a switchman is not like the hoot owl who sits up in a tree. An owl has a really good pair of eyes, but a switchman has to have his lantern just so he can see.

*Leo Younglowe*
*May 12th, 2014*

# DAVE SPRAU

Birthplace: Snohomish, WA 1944
Date of Service: NP Telegrapher May 28, 1960, Dispatcher July 1, 1964,
GN Fireman April 1, 1969, Telegrapher February 27, 1970, Dispatcher March 1, 1970
Positions Held: Fireman, Dispatcher, Telegrapher

## Sprau Family Story
### By Dave Sprau

*As the blade began whirling at top speed, it flung what little bit of snow was on the rails like a missile. Looking out the bay window of the depot, the juggernaut was approaching, snow flying in all directions, just in time for me to dive under the telegraph desk. As the machinery passed, the blast of icy snow broke out every window in the front of the depot, along with most of the wooden frames, and filled the entire office with snow. Shattered glass was everywhere, and both stoves hissing away with snow steaming on top.*

Were it not for the Skykomish Valley, and its joined-at-the-hip connection to the Great Northern Railway, my own life, that of my parents, and a good number of other relatives would be quite different. Although spending several years working for Great Northern and Burlington Northern as a train dispatcher between Wenatchee and Seattle, and a lesser amount of time over the Stevens Pass route as a locomotive fireman (engineer trainee in days before simulators and schools), and an even shorter period as telegrapher at the Skykomish depot, this is a drop

112

in the bucket compared to the connection other family members have with the railroad, and the Valley.

On my paternal side, my grandfather, Art Sprau, established what became an ice cream and soda pop wholesale factory at Monroe in 1908. By the nineteen-twenties he was shipping cases of soda pop, and gallon containers of ice cream in cork-lined canvas bags via Great Northern trains to outlets in Skykomish, Scenic, Tye (Wellington) and Leavenworth. At Leavenworth we had two prime outlets:

I suppose "Sprau's Ice Cream" was the product our family was best-known for, because advertising signs were plentiful. A frequently-seen Pickett view of the Skykomish main street and depot shows an ice cream sign next to "CAFE".

"Mrs. Shipp's Bakery," also known as "Emma Day's Confectionery."

Lee Pickett and grandpa Sprau were good friends. One day Pickett encountered grandpa coming out of J.G.Henry's store at Skykomish. "Can you meet me down at Money Creek Park?" he asked. "Sure," replied grandpa. Here is the result.

Sprau jumbo ice cream bars were a treat
for kids up and down the valley.

Grandpa was puzzled. He asked Pickett "How come you wanted ME in that photograph? Couldn't anybody else have done the same?" Pickett replied " I wanted somebody everyone knew."

After 1932 when my father (Merle Sprau) took over the family business due to my grandfather's sudden death, Stevens Pass Highway was in good enough shape to substitute a delivery truck and driver for the Great Northern trains of old.

Wellington and Scenic stores had folded by then, and Leavenworth business eventually was lost to Wenatchee outlets, but we continued serving stores as far east as the "Summit Inn," then under ownership of Jess Maddox. We distributed beer, by the keg, for Sicks Rainier Brewery as well as our own soda pop and ice cream. Normally the deliveryman was Paul Gatterman, born into a family of loggers at Alpine, but sometimes others, including my father, substituted for Paul. Lucky for me. I'll get to that later.

On my maternal side, my grandfather, George S. Hawley operated a shake mill at Milltown below Skykomish sometime around 1900. I wish I had listened a little better to Grandpa Hawley, because when I was too young to know better, he told a couple of stories which I remember only vaguely. One involved employment

**Grandpa asked Pickett "How come you wanted ME in that photograph?**
**Pickett replied, "I wanted somebody everyone knew."**

for a short time as a mail clerk for the postal service, assigned to railway post office cars. For many years, he had an old railroad lantern hanging on his front porch lettered "CMStP (Milwaukee) RR." When I asked him about it, this is what he said: "I was a mail clerk for the post office; the Great Northern was awarded a government mail contract which resulted in establishing the "Fast Mail" trains for which they later were well-known. I worked on that train's first trip. Great Northern didn't own enough railway post office cars to run their mail train, so they borrowed one from the Milwaukee—that first train had a Milwaukee mail car, and inside the car was this lantern. I stole it for a souvenir of the first trip."

Grandpa gave me that lantern, and I still have it. I suppose I should add for posterity that he wasn't completely correct about the reason for the Milwaukee car. As it turns out, the Milwaukee Road had the contract for this same "Fast Mail" from Chicago to St. Paul. The post office car, and bulk mail cars arrived at St. Paul on the Milwaukee, transferring there to the Great Northern for a quick trip to Seattle.

Grandpa's second story involved a Great Northern wreck around 1908. This was before automatic block signals, which would have prevented such a disaster. A mix-up in train orders caused two freight trains to collide near Fern Bluff, three miles east of Monroe. The collision wasn't too bad, and little damage was done, but grandpa said, "I was riding on top of a car of shingles the westbound train had picked up at Milltown. It was going to California, but my intention was to jump off at Snohomish where my first wife and daughter lived. When the train crashed, I got off at Monroe; but not the way I would have liked—I went head first off the side of the car into the brush, and had to walk to Snohomish."

Another family member also figured in the May 7, 1904 wreck of GN's "Overland Limited" passenger train at Monroe. Some bad kids ages eight and eleven, walking the tracks home from school, opened a switch just east of the Woods Creek bridge leading into a short spur track serving August Holmquist's Mill. Train #1 went into the spur and crashed at the end, injuring engineer George Ziegweid and killing head brakeman Marshall and fireman Thomas Downey.

John Harvard Berringer a local preacher, had married Grandpa's other sister, Ethelyn Sprau, known as "Ethie." Aunt Ethie, sickly as a child, was not expected to live very long; resultedly, she spent a goodly amount of time in church and was quite pious. There, she met the young lay preacher who by his own admission had been a whisky-drinking miner during the Alaska Gold Rush. Ostensibly reformed, the young man swept Aunt Ethie off her feet and they were married. Berringer, hearing of the wreck, immediately went to the site and found the doomed man

The May 7, 1904 wreck of GN's "Overland Limited" passenger train at Monroe.

trapped against the boilerhead, from which live steam was escaping. His own words are here quoted in the M.E. Church's weekly column in the *Monroe Monitor* of May 10, 1904:

> *"It was our humble privilege on Monday evening to speak some words of cheer to the poor fireman, pinned in the wreck, and to present a Savior able to save the uttermost who will come to Him; later to have the man express fully trusting he was forgiven, and ready to meet God; and later to send some message to the sorrowing wife, intended to comfort her."*

Eventual "outcomes" provide vignettes of life. The sorrowing wife sued the Great Northern for $50,000 and settled for an undisclosed sum. As for uncle John, I remember him as a wonderful, pleasant man, fully dedicated in service to the church and humanity; but human frailty always seems to surface. Despite his participation in "Temperance Rallies" and "Epworth League" activities urging abstinence, Uncle John often smelled strongly of whisky! Some habits, I guess, are just too hard to break. His wife, Aunt Ethie, apparently overcame her frailty, outlived him, and all eight of her siblings, passing away in 1977 at age ninety-seven.

#

Returning to the Skykomish Valley: At Baring, a store and saloon once called "Royer's Pool Hall" stood to the south of the Great Northern tracks and gravel

Cloverest C. "Clovie" Parker (second from left, above) purchased "Royer's Pool Hall" in and promptly renamed it the "Baring Grocery—C. C. Parker, Prop."

highway. In 1924, using money saved after retiring from Puget Sound Power & Light Company, where he once was one of a large crew constructing the Snoqualmie Falls Powerhouse, Cloverest C. "Clovie" Parker purchased the saloon building and promptly renamed it "Baring Grocery—C. C. Parker, Prop." and installed a full line of groceries, along with a soda fountain and U.S. Post Office. The latter provided a tidy stipend which sustained the store during sparse depression years. Clovie had married my maternal Grandma Liz Evans's sister, Ruth Evans, in 1910. Ruth and Liz lived in Snoqualmie at the time, and were popular local girls squired, respectively, by Clovie, and Grandpa Hawley, who somehow took time from Skykomish activities to open a Snoqualmie shake mill, on the riverbank behind the downtown Bowling alley and Pizzeria. Grandpa's first wife had died in Snohomish several years earlier; this second marriage produced my mother and two sisters, joining a third sister born to his Snohomish wife. That third sister's daughter, Betty, married Harry Corliss of the well-known Puyallup Valley concrete and gravel business.

Skykomish pioneer Joe Gibson recalled Clovie's Masonic activities: Through the Masons, Clovie met a lot of business people from Everett and Seattle. He used these contacts to wangle a bunch of dentists and doctors into coming to Sky during the depression and take care of poor folks who were sick, or whose teeth were bad. He got one of the barbers to close up for a few days so the dentists could use the barber chairs to work on teeth, while the doctors used chairs and couches to diagnose sick people, all for free. He also twisted arms of some of his grocery suppliers to bring food that was still okay but too far gone to sell, to Sky to hand out to people down on their luck. Later, he insisted we remodel the Masonic Hall to include a room in the back where people—not just Masons, anybody in town—could go to relax, drink coffee, and read books or play pool. After the room had been fixed up and in use for many years, when Clovie and

Ruth sold their store to Turners in 1947 and moved to San Diego, we renamed the room the "Clovey Parker Room" in his honor." (The writer forgives the Skykomish Masons for spelling Uncle Clovie's name differently, after all, it's just a nickname).

In 1930, along the shore of the Skykomish river behind the present schoolhouse, an oil sheen appeared on the water and it wouldn't go away. It formed pools of goo along the river and caused a noticeable, unsightly mess along the shore extending four miles downriver, past Money Creek camp. The State Game department got involved and sent their Deputy Warden, William Dunstan, to investigate.

William "Billy" Dunstan was resident Superintendent of the State Fish Hatchery at Tokul Creek, below Snoqualmie Falls for many years and, on my paternal side, had married my Grandma Levina (Mrs. Art) Sprau's sister, Edith Kincaid. Edith and Grandma had two brothers, Warren, owner of a department store in what's now the Dolloff-Key Building in Monroe, and Arthur, killed at Triers in World War 1, just as it drew to a close. The Legion Post in Monroe is, therefore, named in honor of Uncle Arthur.

Back to the oil slick: Uncle Billy went to Skykomish along with GN Master Carpenter J.J. Dowling and Claim Agent K.C. Dorsett, and found oil flowing into the river from two sources; a sewer pipe from the depot, and a cavity in the river bottom north of the railroad's oil storage facility near the school. Obviously, there was no other source than the railway to which the leakage could be attributed. In a letter to the railroad's attorney, Dorsett tried to soft-pedal the matter and mentioned that Billy Dunstan had been an employee of the Great Northern many years before, "was not unfriendly," and that perhaps the matter might be abated or mitigated if a few steps were taken to corral the company's oil a little better. Alas, this was not to be; although "friendly" Warden Dunstan and the State Game Department indeed pressed the matter further and temporary measures stopped the direct flow of oil, enough petroleum contamination had occurred that as years went by, the problem persisted intermittently and Skykomish finally emerged as a "Superfund Cleanup" site, requiring seventy-five years later that the entire town be literally "jacked up," and contaminated earth under nearly every building be removed and replaced with clean soil and gravel. The task was monumental, made headlines all over the United States, and cost both the taxpayers and the Burlington Northern, who had inherited Great Northern's foibles of many years earlier (initially investigated and prosecuted by Wm. Dunstan) a bundle of money. I'd be neither vain nor egotistical enough to suggest that Uncle Billy gets any credit for the eventual cleanup debacle, but he certainly was the first state authority to get the ball rolling, back in 1930.

Earlier, reference was made as to Alpine's Paul Gatterman driving my dad's soda pop truck, and how his re-assignment on that one day was lucky for me. In having Paul deliver products around Monroe on that day, my dad took the soda pop and ice cream truck "up the line" as a trip to Skykomish or the Summit was then referred as. When making a routine delivery at the Baring Store, he was introduced by Ruth Parker to a new, young lady clerk at the soda fountain: "Merle, this is my niece from Sumner, Susan Hawley." They looked at each other, and Susan said, "Ice cream? You own an ice cream factory?" I don't remember what his supposed reply was, but Susan, who was dating Sumner High School's football hunk Fred Gratzer, dropped poor Fred like a rock. She and my dad were married in 1934. And that is how I got here, and how come Ruth and Clovie Parker were my aunt and uncle.

As for myself, there isn't much to say. I was a telegrapher and train dispatcher on the Northern Pacific from 1960 until 1969 and then chucked it and went to work for the Great Northern in engine service. Between assignments to Portland, Wenatchee, and Canada, I managed to bid "Helper Engine" assignments working out of Skykomish with engineers Wayne Williams and Forrest Witter, plus a number of trips with extra board engineers Bill Stevenson, Elmer Dahl, Mike Karakash, Eugene Kratzke, and Don Kirkwood. Wayne Williams was a good, patient trainer and spent a lot of time standing over me—but never micro-managing—teaching me how to run an engine and handle a train. He was an amateur artist and, knowing I had been a train dispatcher on the Northern Pacific, once drew a cartoon of a dopey-looking man taking a bath in a giant toilet, using the toilet brush for scrubbing, with soap bubbles and water all over the floor. He titled the work "NP Dispatchers' Bath Tub." I wish I had that cartoon.

Now it can be told: Once in February, 1970, Williams took sick with a sudden, legitimate case of flu. The train we were supposed to help was about an hour

A view of the Skykomish depot operator's desk. After a snowplow knocked out all the depot windows in 1970, remember when showing off the nice, "restored" depot of present times, don't let anybody tell you the office windows are "original,"—because they aren't!

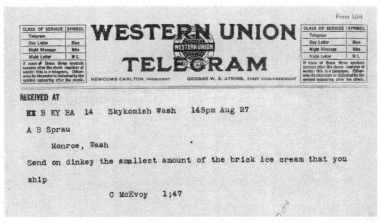

This telegram is an example of how Sprau's ice cream was ordered
for delivery by the "Dinky" a local daily train.

away and it was obvious Wayne wouldn't even be able to make it from his house
to the engine. So, pilot Conductor Roy Austin and I did what we had to do; saying nothing to anyone, we helped the train to Merritt, returned to Sky with the
helper engines, and tied up. On the way over, brakeman Walt Rose of the freight
crew being helped, was riding in the helper engine and kept asking, "Where is the
engineer?" My standard reply was, "He is in the rear unit." We arrived at Merritt,
still no engineer in sight, and Rose stated: "I don't think your engineer is aboard
this thing." My reply was, "Well, I am waiting for you to cut us out of the train,
so we both can get going." Rose went down the ladder, uncoupled our helper
engine, put the freight train back together, got back on the helper, and gave me
an "ahead" sign. I dropped him off at the caboose as we passed it, heading toward
Berne, and shouted, "See ya, Rosie,"

Right at merger time, I decided that being on call 24/7 for the rest of my
life was not a very attractive option. I had been offered a job as train dispatcher
by Great Northern management; as an experienced dispatcher, I could transfer

crafts and receive a seniority date immediately. Charlie McFarland was night chief dispatcher at Seattle during the week before the merger and, probably remembering that his brother Arnold had gotten a seniority date as a dispatcher on the Northern Pacific in 1968 because of my laying off, forcing the company to put trainee Arnie on my job, Charlie made a few phone calls including one to General Manager Wicks, and managed to get me on the payroll in time to have a merger "Job Guarantee."

Shortly after that, because I also needed to work as a telegrapher part of the time, I was sent to Skykomish. The only really memorable thing when working the telegraphers' job at Sky was one morning after we had a heavy snowfall and ice storm, Roadmaster Paul George wanted to take the rotary snowplow up the hill and clean off the main line, but beforehand, gave the machine a "dry run" in the Skykomish yard. Only problem was, Skykomish wasn't "dry." We had about six inches of snow, topped by a coating of icy stuff, above the rails; far less than the couple of feet at Scenic and Berne. Paul had work train engineer Jonas Patterson and Conductor Sid Pierce shove the rotary up the main line eastbound—fast—past the depot so he could try it out. As the blade began whirling at top speed, it flung what little bit of snow was on the rails like a missile. Looking out the bay window of the depot, the juggernaut was approaching, snow flying in all directions, just in time for me to dive under the telegraph desk. As the machinery passed, the blast of icy snow broke out every window in the front of the depot, along with most of the wooden frames, and filled the entire office with snow. Shattered glass was everywhere, and both stoves hissing away with snow steaming on top. The snow quickly started to melt in the warm depot, so I shut off the stoves which, thanks to all the broken windows, brought the inside temperature down to freezing. Just at that moment—shift change time—agent Russ Kvam walked in the door.

I remember Russ as a nice fellow, with even temperament. Not that day. "What in the &%$# is going on here?—What the *&^%# happened?.." he asked, face reddening. When I told him, he exploded again, got on the radio, and called the work train. Avoiding profanity this time, he told Jonas Patterson: "You tell Paul George to get back down here NOW. This place is wrecked. I want him to come here and take care of this mess." In the meanwhile, I was rounding up the section crew to shovel out the office and waiting rooms. Snow was melting all over the telegraph desk, ruining correspondence and papers on the agent's desk. I think it would have been funny, if Russ hadn't been so mad. Several hours later, I observed Bill Scrupps and the Bridge and Building crew from Everett hard at work, replacing broken glass and window sashes. By the next night, the place was good as new. But when showing off the nice, "restored" depot of present times, don't let anybody tell you the office windows are "original,"—because they aren't!

During my time both as fireman and telegrapher at Skykomish, the Cascadia was sort of a gathering spot and watering hole for locals. I remember one of the beanery queens, a girl named Minnie. Engineer Wayne Williams and I played practical jokes that would get us jailed, fired or both today. We tied a bunch of fusees together, strung some coiled wire to them, attached the wire to a ridiculous-looking old alarm clock, and put the whole thing in the front seat of Minnie's car. When she opened the door she almost had heart failure and got the Cascadia's owner, Rick Gillmere, to come out and see. Recognizing the ruse, Rick grabbed the device, "heroically" ran back into the cafe with it, and threw it in a sink full of dirty dishwater. Problem solved. Several months later, two helper engines collided in front of the Cascadia in the middle of the night. Mike Karakash and I were aboard the lead engine; we stopped because one of the rear units had gone dead. Another engine coming from the west, run by Forrest Witter from his west cab with a fireman named Sprague ostensibly watching from its east cab, collided with us and knocked me the length of the engine room. I blacked out for a second and awakened next to a main generator that had broken loose from its moorings and was flopping around. My scalp had a gash about two inches long, bleeding profusely. Operator John Sawetch came from the depot and took me to the hotel, where Rick and Mrs. Gillmere were awakened and stitched my head up with a sewing needle! Later a doctor re-did the job, commenting it almost was good enough to leave alone. I was supposed to return to the doctor to have the stitches removed, but engineer Wayne Williams and his girlfriend removed them about a week later. Wayne sent me a phony "bill" of $100 "for professional services."

Another time, I rigged some rubber tubing and a quart beer bottle "reservoir" behind the dashboard of the engine so when Wayne sat down and released the independent brake, a nozzle concealed behind the dash squirted him in the face with water. There he sat, water from head to chest, and dripping off his nose. He got even later, but I can't remember how, or with what.

I used to try to get to the Cascadia for dinner, or at least for coffee, when Minnie was working the afternoon shift because (a) I was trying to impress her, and (b) every night about six we would get a "floor show" when one of the Puget Power crewmen came in for dinner. I suppose this tale is unkind by today's' standards; but as most everyone knows, in those days, many things happened that we wouldn't think of doing today. One of the workers was an older gentleman, Glen Olson. He would have several drinks before and during his dinner, which usually was stew, or chipped beef and gravy on toast. "Regulars" at the cafe, including waitress Minnie and myself, had a "betting pool" as to when poor Glen would fall asleep, face down, in his plate of food. Glen never failed to disappoint, but always at different periods during the meal. The "betting pool" had many different winners, day-to-day.

Another memorable occasion in the Cascadia was when fellow Fireman Thomas "Nick" Hemmesch and myself were having a few drinks in the bar. An extra board engineer from Seattle was filling one of the three helper assignments (not ours—we had just tied up, and were not subject to duty), and this man soon would be called. Someone tipped off the management that, as was his habit much of the time, this fellow had been drinking, so Master Mechanic Tom Kotnour and Assistant Superintendent Hemmesch (Nick's dad) were dispatched to catch the miscreant "in the act," so to speak, and administer proper discipline. Apparently they believed their victim was in the bar at the "Cascadia," because suddenly Kotnour swooped in the front entrance while the senior Hemmesch came in the back. Unfortunately, the intended person was not present; the only drinkers available to be "caught" were the Assistant Superintendent's son, and myself. The embarrassment shone plainly on the officials' faces; Kotnour just stood there, while Hemmesch picked up his son's glass, held it to the light, and commented, "Just checking to see if you are drinking good whisky, son!" Both then departed, not to be seen again for months.

Another place I worked as telegrapher, but having a definite Skykomish link, was the afternoon shift at Interbay yard office, Seattle. The day telegraph operator was Ella. Depending on the time of life that you knew her, she was either Ella Oftedalhl, operator at Skykomish, or Ella Worthington, or Ella Carter, agent at Skykomish, or Ella Holevas, day operator at Interbay. Anyway, in September of 1969 when working as engine hostler at Interbay Roundhouse, I'd met Ella briefly while she was on duty in the telegraph office, but did not introduce myself. She knew me then only as "the hostler."

Ella was all business, well-known as very particular, even to excess, and didn't suffer fools or younger employees, which she likely considered "interchangeable." While at Skykomish, her reputation was similar. Night Chief Dispatcher Verl Kilde once told me, "When I was an operator at Sky, Ella was agent. She was awful persnickety and hard to work for. I'll never forget, one time I did something she didn't like and instead of just telling me about, it, she left me a nasty message with an E-number on it." Verl, a brakeman injured in the 1945 crash of the "Fast Mail" at Foss River bridge where he lost an arm and was forced to change to a desk job, was a very conscientious, dedicated employee; no funny stuff, no rules violations, and all business. But his disdain for Ella, by the tone of his voice while telling this story, was rather obvious. Messages with file numbers preceded by a letter (designating the author's name or title) ahead of their signature at bottom, were a prerogative of officers such as the superintendent, chief dispatcher, or company officials of like status. For a station agent at a place such as Skykomish to do something like that was indeed the height of ego, and disdainful. Verl was having none of it. Ella's reputation indeed preceded her, wherever she went.

So, here I was, reporting for the afternoon operator Job at Interbay, relieving someone whom I considered to be "Mrs. Iceberg." As I walked in the door, Ella said, "Are YOU my relief?" I thought maybe she recognized me from hostler days. Wrong! She was merely establishing pecking order; but foolishly I replied, "Yes, -- I remember you from when I was a fireman here."

Through narrowed eyebrows, she sneered: "I don't KNOW any FIREMEN." Gulp. A second try worked a little better. "Oh.... well, I am David Sprau. Nice to meet you... I met you once when I was a hostler."

Ella: "Sprau?" Are you from Monroe?

Me: "Yes."

Ella: "Are you Merle Sprau's son?"

Again, "Yes."

I never saw anyone change so fast. Ella broke into a smile: "Your father made the best ice cream! And supplied the beer to our town! And he used to come to our dances on weekends! Everybody was so glad to see him, because he always brought lots of goodies and donated things for our social affairs. And he was a good dancer, too! Now, let me show you some things you should know about working this job... " After that, Ella was always nice, and treated me well. Some of the trainmen, watching thru the window from their room next door, were puzzled as to how the cranky day operator they were used to, could suddenly become so pleasant to a guy walking in at shift change time. Blame it on "insider trading," because Ella was right, my dad always was a soft touch for charity or community events, often donating things like ice cream, soda pop, punch, and other amenities for which, as a businessman, he probably should have charged money.

But anyway, the story of how Ella "warmed up" pretty much sums up the response I've gotten whenever any of my predecessors were mentioned to the old-timers at Skykomish. The first time I met Mayor Joyce Timpe, she was a beanery queen at the Cascadia, as was her sister Katie. Like Ella, they both graciously bragged of having gone to school with Clovie's daughter, my cousin Nellie Parker. Billy Dunstan's name has evoked similar responses around Fall City and Snoqualmie, and one day when I was inspecting track around Lake Kapowsin on the Tacoma Eastern Railroad, where my very last job was serving for a short time as Superintendent, I encountered an old man picking blackberries. Grandpa Hawley had owned the grocery store at Kapowsin after leaving Skykomish; when asking the berry picker his name, and if he remembered grandpa, he replied: "Yes, I am James McDonald, and I remember George and Liz all right, but I remember your mother better. I used to date her in high school!

So, I guess my family ties and roots go pretty deep into the Skykomish and Snoqualmie Valleys, thanks to at least five predecessors on both sides of the family.

# MIKE PIERCE

Birthplace: Everett, WA 1945
Date of Service: December 29, 1962
Position Held: Brakeman and Conductor

*Always had money in my pocket and a roof over my head. I had a good career and I figured that I did alright for myself. Being a third generation railroader, I cannot think of anything else that I probably would have ever stuck with. I was riding trains when I was six or seven years old. For the life of me I can't think of anything else that I wanted to do. So I guess I can say I had a satisfying career on the railroad.*

My grandfather was born in 1885 back in the Midwest. He moved out here and hired out in 1911 on the GNRR. He retired in 1955. His name was Sydney John Pierce. My dad hired out working for the GNRR in 1936 in Seattle as a brakeman. His name was Sydney Richard Pierce and his brother Edward John Pierce hired out in about 1938.

I had a grandfather on my mother's side and when he first settled out here he worked in the roundhouse in Skykomish. He eventually gave that up and bought Richardson's Tavern here in Skykomish. My mother had a brother Glick Gordon aka Buster Richardson who hired out after the war as an engineer on the GNRR.

My cousin Robert who was Edward Pierce's son hired out in the mid-sixties as a fireman on the GNRR. Then they found out that he was color blind so they wouldn't bring him back in train service. So in about 1972 he came to Skykomish and started working on the Section. I think Bob worked until 2003, when he retired. I retired in 2005. I had bounced around a little bit. In the middle seventies I moved to Wenatchee for five years. Then I came back to Seattle, went to Spokane in 1984 and stayed there till 1999. Then came back over here and decided that Skykomish was where I wanted to retire. So I bought a house here. I worked my last six years out of Everett. before retiring. Always liked Skykomish, been around here off and on all of my life. It just seemed like a perfect fit.

Third generation railroad man, Mike Pierce; his grandfather Sydney John Pierce hired out in 1911, his father Sydney Richard Pierce hired out in 1936 and Mike hired out in 1962.

My mother Ethel was born and raised here in Skykomish. She is a graduate of Skykomish High School with the class of 1943. She and dad got married in 1944 and moved to Everett. She had three brothers. Glick Gordon went to work for the railroad. Older brother Nathan was an attorney. He was mayor of Port Angeles many yeas ago and he represented the Indian tribe in that area for a long time. She also had one younger brother William who was a school teacher. Glick and Nathan both served in WWII and my uncle Billie was in the Korean War.

I hired out as a brakeman. Matter of fact my first job as a brakeman was the best job that the GNRR had out of Seattle. It was that old extra north that made the turn to Vancouver BC on Saturday, up and back. You'd race like heck to get up there and do all the work in the little towns and if you had four or more hours they'd let you come back caboose hopping all the way. You worked sixteen hours and you made three days pay out of it. My first New Years was January first of 1963. We'd taken an east bound train to Wenatchee. The call boy was right there, he said, "Well you guys are going to get four hours rest and come back on the mail train. I think it was Number Five. It was passenger train speed so the whole crew went to the bar and I slept there in the locker room at Wenatchee, I was only seventeen. I tell you I was in the best shape of all of them.

You worked the extra board till you could hold a regular job. My first regular job, we made two round trips from Interbay to Tacoma and back. I was only cut off once in forty three years and that was February of 1964 and I was cut off a week. The yardmaster down at Tacoma, Charlie Mitchell drove every night from Everett to Tacoma to be the night yardmaster. He says if you want to come down here and work I'll put you to work switching. I had a new car and a pocketful of money, I was only nineteen I wasn't driving a hundred-and-fifty miles a night for twenty-five dollars. That's about what a switchman made.

I got some seniority and I worked out of Everett when I could. Worked out of Burlington, Bellingham, places like that. I worked out of Everett a lot cause that's where I was born and raised. Then in the seventies I was a helper pilot up here. Then they pulled the helpers from Skykomish and they went to Wenatchee. I was going to go over there and work for a while, but I decided to stay and we lived over there five years. At that time Wenatchee was an expensive place to live. You had Seattle and you had Spokane. Now if you wanted to drive to either one of those places you could get a deal on your washing machine. If you didn't want to spend the time and he money to drive to either one of those places you paid Wenatchee prices. It was the same way with everything We lived in Wenatchee before the McDonalds restaurant.

I came back to Seattle in 1978 and had pretty good seniority so I had my choice of jobs. I got itchy feet again so in 1984 I went to Spokane for fifteen years. I worked some of the locals over there, some of the work trains. Then I spent almost eleven years on the work train doing all kinds of different jobs on maintenance. I've been on every piece of track in the state of Washington. And a lot of Oregon, Idaho, part of Montana, British Columbia. For four or five years I had the rail pick-up train, we'd pick up used rail. We'd pull up old abandoned track. We pulled up the old Spokane Portland and Seattle Railway from Pasco to Spokane.

We did a branch of the NP from Pe Ell to Chehalis. We pulled up the old Milwaukee from Cedar Falls to Renton. Towards the end of my career I decided it was time to settle down. I took a regular job between Everett and Seattle. For the last three years I worked in the yard at Everett. Kind of toned down from the long hours and worked as a switchman. I had about two days left when I was going to retire. My knees hurt I'd been working about an hour I came up out of the yard and I sat down on the bench and I took my shoes and my gloves and threw them up on the roof of the yard office and said I quit. That's how I walked out.

There is a story about me and Duke on the local. There was a man that a lot of people didn't like because if there was work to do he did it. He'd volunteer to do it, but on the other hand it wasn't "Yea we'll do it". Okay guys here go do it and he'd sit in the depot or the caboose. He'd be right out there next to you working. I had a lot of respect for him. We were on the Burlington turn. We were sitting in the depot in Mt. Vernon one night, that's when there was a lot of work at Mt. Vernon. So we're sitting there going through the list and the phone rings. The clerk picks it up and you hear one side of a conversation. Pretty soon he says, "Here Duke its Delta they want to talk to you." I hear Duke and pretty soon he says, "I don't know, just a minute" He put his hand over the mouthpiece and said,

"Do you know anybody who drives a black Ford? They left their lights on there at Delta." Then the light came on in Duke's head. He drove the black Ford! A lot of the guys didn't like him but if he volunteered to do it he practically ran over you getting out the door to do it. I had a lot of respect for that guy.

I spent a lot of time at Mt Vernon on that job, I've been by several times on Amtrak since I retired. I've been thinking a lot about the jobs. Marysville had two mills, nothing there anymore. Stanwood had a gasoline outfit, a feed mill and two frozen food plants. The feed mill is still there Mt Vernon had fifty-two spots on the team track you were there for hours lining it up. That's all gone. Carnation is gone. Just north of the depot was that little two car Pacific Fruit express, that's gone. You went about half way towards north Mt Vernon and Fisher Flour Mill, that's gone. North Mt. Vernon is just about gone. Except they have some propane business over there. And Burlington, five track is the main line now. Think that it is sixty mile an hour track through there now.

I did work passenger for a while back in the sixties in my snazzy blue uniform. We worked east on the Empire Builder #32. Then we came west on the Western Star #27. That was the one that had about fifteen cars of mail on the back. Plus that rider car, 'course no air conditioning in it. Coming across that eastern Washington going about eighty miles an hour you don't get much of a cool breeze. That car is where you rode all the way back. I didn't much care for passenger service. It was the passengers, they treated you like you were a servant.

We worked all the passenger trains south. There were three passenger trains to Vancouver a day. Then I was baggage qualified to work as a baggage man. That was a good job. You didn't have to deal with the public. You were back there all by yourself. You had Edmonds, Everett, Wenatchee, Ephrata was all you had to do. The only bad thing about it you were on the same extra board as everybody else. You'd be about fifteen or sixteen times out on the board on Friday night.

And I'd be in uptown Everett. Here would come my dad, "You're called." "I can't, I'm sixteen times out!" "No," my dad said, "but you're first out baggage." There would go the week-end.

If you went up to Vancouver BC on #358, the morning passenger train, you'd go up and turn around and you were back in Seattle about five o'clock or so in the afternoon. Somebody would be there to hand you a message. "Yea, we want you to double back up on #360, the night layover job. Or #28 to Spokane. There are no hours of service on baggage. They could bounce you around forever. So there was lots of days I made a round trip to Vancouver BC and back and of course I didn't have clothes or nothing. It was a turn around. There would be my mom at the depot at Everett when #28 pulled in with a suitcase with clean clothes and a lunch.

There were a lot of good people that I worked with and there were people that I didn't care to work with, I think you find that most every place. I often wondered when I was a young lad up at Ferndale where the wind blew ninety miles an hour, it was three o'clock in the morning its raining sideways and we're switching cars and I'm wondering, WHAT AM I DOING HERE? But as you get older, you put food on the table, put a roof over your head, it paid the bills and everything.

When I was growing up we lived next door to a butcher, we had a policeman up the street, a fireman lived at the end of the street. There was a barber across the street a commercial fisherman and I don't remember what else. I think we lived a little bit better than most people did 'cause dad made more money. But it was one of those deals that if you wanted to work you could make all kinds of money. When I retired I had a conductor's and brakeman's seniority date. A switchman's seniority date. A yardmaster's date and I was RCO, Remote Control Qualified. I was a jack of all trades. I often wondered when I got close to retirement how I was going to handle it, being as how I started working when I was seventeen. I think that the last three years that I spent in Everett Yard was the best thing that I ever did. Knowing that you are only working five days a week and there was a hell of a good group of people at Everett.

Its funny when the merger came along there were two different philosophies. I can point out two fairly distinct ones. After the merger you had NP crews and GN crews that were intermingled. Going to Portland, you'd go over to the round-house and you'd get on the engine, and lots of new faces because everybody had just merged. You introduced yourself and you were asked are you NP or GN? Well if you were GN they were happy to see you but you weren't happy because they were NP guys. When an NP crew came over to get on a GN engine they weren't happy.

Another good example was Interbay and Stacy Street. Separated by about five miles.. At Interbay after you came out from lunch they handed you your list and when that was done you went home. There were times when something happened that it didn't work out that way. Ninety-nine per cent of the time that's the way it worked. At Stacy Street the yardmaster would be standing out there on the back porch about quitting time. If he saw the engine coming up the lead too early he'd walk out and hand them another list. Just a totally different philosophy.

And Everett was totally different. I had no idea whether it existed any place else on the GN. They handed you the list when you went to work and you went home when it was done. One thing the older you got, you could pick your jobs and the guys you wanted to work with. If you find somebody you like to work with it makes a big difference. The other thing was, everybody had twenty-five or thirty years seniority. Now as we sit here I look over there, I see a train sitting over there and I betcha if you went up there there's probably between the two guys, probably five years of seniority. Its sad for them because when we went to work we had six guys on a crew and there was always somebody that, if you were willing, would teach you, But if you don't know yourself how can you teach somebody else?

Fact, I was telling a story the other day, somebody was asking me about going to work for the railroad. I said, "Well they're looking for structure in their employees they're looking for people that are a little bit older." My son in law was six years in the service, was an OSHA certified crane inspector when he came out. He was forty years old when he hired out. He didn't know the old way. He knew what they taught him in the new way. He took to it like a duck to water. These kids don't know any better if they make Wenatchee in twelve hours, man they're just about ready to party.

The thing of it is nowadays with the few locals we got left. the turn over on the locals is common. Nobody stays on them. I remember the Concrete Local, the Anacortes Local, the Burlington Turn and the Oiler, some of those guys were on there for it seemed like a hundred years. They got on there and stayed. Nowadays these guys get on and all of a sudden they have a couple of bad days and they go some place else. They think they're getting abused. These guys are complaining about the crew line-ups and stuff like that. I said, "You know something, when I worked, you sat home and you sat by the phone, if you were on the extra board you didn't even go outside to mow the lawn, you didn't have cell phones, didn't have pagers, you didn't have any of this."

I can remember I got my first pager from Kelly's Answering Service in Lynnwood when Barb was working in the crew office. I called her up. It's like eleven o'clock in the morning. I said, "Barb I've got a pager" and I gave her the number. I said, "What's it look like for us? I was in the east pool. She said, "you're four times out, you'll get to sleep tonight" So I finished up my paperwork with the paging outfit and I walked a short distance and that pager goes off. I thought she's testing. So I walked back in and asked to use their phone. I called her up and she said, "Yea you're called for one-thirty. I said, "I'm four times out". She said, "they just deadheaded three crews in front of you." So right there that round trip to Wenatchee paid for that pager rental for months.

My dad put in a toggle switch downstairs in our house where the phone line was and when he'd come home from work in the morning he'd go downstairs and shut the phone off. so that he could sleep. It was criminal, he'd go to work at one o'clock in the afternoon and work sixteen hours come home at five o'clock some mornings. He'd sit there maybe reading the newspaper 'til my sister and I got up for school. Spend fifteen or twenty minutes with us and then he'd have to go to bed because he was back up again at eleven thirty to eat and go back to work. You do not wake your dad! You do not ride your bicycles around the house. You do not invite friends over to the house. It was hard for other kids to understand. My dad was working on probably six hours of sleep.

Then you get home Saturday morning and you think do I want to go to bed, waste most of the day, then be awake at night? You had to adjust to that, cause the lawn had to be mowed, you wanted to spend time with your family. Sixteen hours working don't leave you a lot of time. My dad was a conductor. We only had one black sheep in the family who was an engineer, my Uncle Buster, but he was on my mother's side.

One story my dad told me about him and my grandfather. My dad was braking for my grandfather on the Sky Logger. Grampa didn't believe in derby days, (working less than sixteen hours.)

So they go down this one day and they got like six hours left to work and they headed into Snohomish for no reason whatsoever and there they sat. Well my dad, he's chomping at the bit cause he wants to get back to Delta to drive back to Sky to see my mother. He said to grampa, "Any chance we could go in early today?" My grampa said, "Son, if you want an early quit, lay off." My grandfather was funny like that.

My grandfather would pull up to the depot there at Goldbar and he'd come out with the switch list that had one car number on it and he'd say to the brakeman, "I want you to go down to the west end and pick this car out, turn it on the Y and cut it in from the east end." Now this is an empty grain box one of among four or five hundred cars. There were eight tracks there. But anyway being as how they were all wood they'd have them in blocks of about twenty-five so that the whole track didn't burn up if there was a fire. You'd have to go and gather them all up, set all the hand brakes, pull fifty or sixty cars out of there. Set that car over. Put all that stuff back in there, space them, block them, tie them down, take it around the Y, go down to the other end and do the exact same thing again. He did that just in order to make sixteen hours!

I almost flunked being a senior in high school because I was studying the rule book to get my hiring date, but I'd gone out to the Junior College and registered for fall classes. Cost me five bucks. But in 1963 you could pick and choose where you wanted to teach, four years later that sheep skin wasn't worth anything, so I have no regrets about not ever going back to school.

Always had money in my pocket and a roof over my head. I had a good career and I figured that I did alright for myself. Being a third generation railroader, I cannot think of anything else that I probably would have ever stuck with. I was riding trains when I was six or seven years old. For the life of me I can't think of anything else that I wanted to do. So I guess I can say I had a satisfying career on the railroad. Like everybody else we retired, got old and I see a train going by here right now so I know that my pension check is good this month. I always wait for the first train after the first of the month then I figure my check is going to be good. The only thing bad, there is one drawback about retirement and that's you only get one check a month. For a while I kept waiting for that one on the fifteenth of the month.to show up. So I've learned to live on the one check a month.

I wouldn't want to work for the railroad today with the philosophy and the frustration, sitting in a siding watching the trains. In twelve hours you might only make seventy miles. My dad always told me that I was one generation too late. The big transition was in the late fifties with the steam to the diesel and everything. Mine was the last of the good generations.

I look back in my grandfather's time 1910-1911. I look back to what you had for rain gear, what you had for a winter jacket, what you had for gloves, eye protection, head protection, and especially your feet. If you can't keep your feet warm you're all through. There was nothing in those days that would keep your feet warm. And then face shoveling thirty plus feet of snow with a number ten idiot stick. Basically I can remember my old rain clothes when I first hired out. I was wetter inside from sweating than I was outside. To get up in the morning and eat whatever there was available, which could be good bad or indifferent and then go out there and work sixteen, eighteen hours a day shoveling snow. Not interested, thank you.

One last story and then we'll end it. The winter of 1973 I was braking for my dad on the snow plow. The company sent somebody up here to film some winter scenes with the snow plow and everything, Paul George was the roadmaster. They even had the section out polishing up that engine a little bit. So anyway we load these two camera guys and they got a great big tripod sitting in the middle of the cab. 'Course its raining on this side. We go up to the other side we go down around to that great big curve below Berne.

Orville Holmes was the other brakeman. So Orville and I got off with them and they backed up the hill and came down the hill by them. We loaded them up and we go down and head into the siding at Merritt. There is about eighteen inches of snow slop. They went down through the siding just fast enough to lay that eighteen inches over on top of the main line. The main had been plowed with trains but there was still some left. They backed up and they went around the wye and Jim George had a motor car sitting there next to the depot.

These guys said, "Can we get out and set up here?" Paul George said yea. They set up their camera beside the motor car and they leave the poor old rookie, "ME" with them. With a portable radio. They said, "Now we're going to go out the east end of the siding and back all the way up to Colter Creek." "You let me know when they are ready." So these guys are sitting in Jimmy's motor car and they've got their camera doing this and doing that. Finally they said okay. So I called them on the radio and said they were ready.

Joni Patterson was the hoghead. The engine went from dead silence to full throttle. You could hear them coming and pretty soon you see them crossing the east switch at Merritt. And I'm peeking out alongside the fuel shed there and I'm looking at these guys and they're still twisting all this stuff and I'm looking down there and I'm looking where that snow is landing and it ain't going to land in a good spot. They went by and they packed that motor car just like you'd put a container underneath an ice cream machine and fill it up I had to dig them out of there.

I can still see it, my dad standing there running the wing and Paul George is at the door right behind him and both of them have shit eating grins about that wide. He did it deliberately.

Joni said he was doing sixty plus when he hit the east switch at Merritt. When they got down into that wet stuff it dropped him right down to about thirty-five. I can still see it. I'm on the west end of the fuel shed. I didn't get any of it, but I watched till I couldn't watch anymore and I ducked out of the way. You couldn't have put another ounce of snow in there. I can still see that smile on my dad's face.

# BOB PIERCE

**Birthplace: Seattle, WA 1944**
**Dates of Service: Braking:1963 Track Department, 1972**
**Positions Held: Brakeman, Track Department**

*I worked in the sixties on the snowplow on the east side. It would have been the winter of 1965, right around Christmas time We worked sixteen hours a day. You don't see winters like that anymore. I missed a lot of New Years because of derailments. It seemed that we had one every New Year's.*

I came from a railroad family. All of the males on the Pierce side of the family for three generations worked for the Great Northern. My grandfather, my uncle and my dad. My granddaughter put together a heritage project and from that we figured that there was over two-hundred years of Pierces on the Great Northern.

As a kid getting together at Easter time at my grandfather's house in Everett, I can remember the family sitting around. There would be Sid Senior and Sid Junior and my dad and they would be talking railroad about "Sky" up there in "Sky." Of course I had never been to Sky but it was in my mind all the time because they were always talking about Sky.

In 1963 and 1964 when I started going to college, I was braking. I was working at Christmas time, we got on the train and it was cold. It was during the mid sixties. The conductor was Bob Crabbe. We got stuck! Stuck in Sky! The train line froze up. It was real cold. It got colder in those days. They kept us here for a couple of days, through a couple of melts. If you are tied up on the road for twenty-four hours you get paid for eight hours. This keeps the company from holding you there for longer periods of time.

I can remember going over to a place which is now the Deli and playing the pin ball machines. "Peg of my Heart" by the Harmonicats was on the jukebox. That always stuck with me and then of course I got to see Sky.

Little did I know that I would not complete school. That bad recession came where Nixon wanted to create ten percent unemployment to combat inflation. Ten percent unemployment would solve the problem of inflation. Remember "The last one out of Seattle turn out the lights?"

I was working in construction as a laborer. That summer I didn't get out through the union at all. If you were on unemployment they had you go to these classes on how to get a job. The guy gave a spiel for about fifteen or twenty minutes on how to apply for a job. When he was all done he said, "Really the truth is, your best bet is to find a relative."

That's what happened to me. My uncle talked to the roadmaster up in Skykomish and that's how I ended up coming up to Skykomish. Best day of my life. I got out of the city. At that time I thought that Seattle was huge. I enjoyed coming up here to the peace and quiet. A lot of hard work but it was worth it.

Originally I worked with Henry Cox. He was old school, hollered at you all the time. And the roadmaster, they had a name for him, called him the "Screamer."

It was alright with me. I had a little bit of long hair at the time. It wasn't real long but it was right down my neck. It was maybe a month or so and the crew and I are sitting in the depot having lunch and staying warm. The roadmaster comes in. He says, "Hey Pierce, how do you like Skykomish? How do you like working for the railroad?" I said. "I like it, I like it a lot." The next thing that he said was, "well get a haircut!" Just like that.

So I could care less. I went and got a haircut. I was enjoying myself. I wanted the job. About three months go by. Here comes a surfacing crew into town. This guy gets off of the tamper to throw a switch and he's got hair down his back. I said, "Who's that?" They said, "Oh that's the roadmaster's kid." Same guy that told me to get a haircut, that's his boy! I always thought that that was kind of humorous.

Back then we had a lot of problems with the track. Derailments. It was the ties mostly. They were worn out. One time the big guys came in. We had the ties up on the hill up for replacement. They came and looked at them and said, "this doesn't need any ties." They looked good, but in gauge track up there, in big curves they were worn out, but still looked good.

One thing about the railroad today, their maintenance is way up to snuff compared to what it was. I don't think that they have had a derailment since they put the concrete ties in. We used to have them all the time. It wasn't unheard of to have two in one week. We took a lot of pride in getting the track open as fast as we could. The longest that I ever worked steady was thirty-six hours. That was hard physical work.

It got worse as far as manpower, they were really short-handed up here. I was the only one here the night of the nineties flood. Everything washed out and there was nobody working here but me. Eventually we lost the track between every station. It was getting really bad. We didn't have anybody to call out to help. But we lived through it.

I remember when they took the walkway off the bridge at Money Creek. A train came down and pulled across the bridge and they broke in two. So they called me out and it was just a knuckle bypass. I just put it back together and sent them on their way.

They called the dispatcher, a gal, at that time there weren't many gal dispatchers. They called her and said that they were on their way. She said, "That was awfully fast." They told her the track guy had put us together, it was just a knuckle bypass. She says, "Did you thank him?" First time I ever heard that. Different with a woman on the job.

There were some fun times. I'm remembering one story, I was up at Scenic working on the work train. We were in the hole, waiting for a train to go by until we could get back out and do whatever we were doing. We had a pretty good sized crew, so a few of us were in the caboose.

The conductor, the brakeman and two track foremen were playing poker. One of our guys, an old timer on the crew (he was an old timer when I came up here in '72), he got in the game. They're playing along. It was a really miserable day.

Anyway the train that we're waiting on goes by. Well by that time the game is pretty hot and heavy. I'm standing behind this guy, watching him. He's got himself a full house. Everybody is betting big. There is a big pot. He throws his cards in, he folds. We're out working on the track and I says, "Martin what's behind throwing that full house away. Didn't you see it?" He said, "Oh yea I saw it, but all the bosses had their money in and if I'd taken that pot we'd have had to go back to work."

My dad worked the south end almost all of his years. My uncle worked the work train up here. My grandfather had the Sky Local for years.

I talked with Doug Stuart. He was the young brakeman for my grandfather. They'd get mad at my grandfather because he'd do the fifteen fifty-five thing every day. (If you tie up at fifteen fifty-five hours, by federal law you get eight hours of rest. If you would tie up at sixteen hours on the job you are required to have ten hours of rest. That means that you would be two hours late the next day switching out the businesses.)

He had them switching out boxcars at Gold Bar putting the even ones on one track and the odd ones on another track. Just to stay busy. He'd come up with any idea to keep them working.

I never did work much with my cousin Mike. Of course I wasn't a trainman. The railroad was definitely our family. What I did was what I wanted to do. It was harder work and less money but what I wanted to do.

When I came up I had applied for several CETA jobs The government was putting some jobs together because the unemployment problem was so bad. One that I applied for was a bus driver for King County. After I was here for a month or two they sent me a letter accepting me as a bus driver. We were making like $2.50 an hour here and it was going to be like fifty cents an hour more down there, but I didn't want to go back to Seattle. I wanted to work for the railroad. It was like a new beginning, it was like the old west up here. It was a lot different than what I saw in the city that is for sure.

I was making around $2.50 and hour and when I was in the laborers union in Seattle I was making around $5.00 an hour. We were forty hours a week up here but we worked so much overtime. That's how we were really able to make a decent living with the hours of overtime.

As soon as I could I got my foreman's date. At times I was a machine operator, bus driver, truck driver. I didn't like working the machines so I went the foreman route. My claim to fame is that I was the last guy to run a speeder over the hill as a track inspector.

Going over there in the wintertime all you had was one of those lunchbox radios. And sometimes they didn't work so well. I got stuck up there a few times waiting for trains on those spur tracks. Had to wait one time for six trains before they would let me go. Colder than hell sitting on that speeder. Later on I thought: "You did that?" At the time it didn't bother me a bit. It was my job, it didn't seem all that bad. They had curtains on them but you know it was still cold.

I remember one time I came out of the tunnel and I was late. I was going east. I came down and there hadn't been any trains but I was out of track time so I was in a hurry and I had to shovel my way into the siding. There were about eight or ten inches of ice and snow on the track. So I just scraped it down, I worked as hard as I could. I got in the clear just past the insulated joints, so they could run a train by. Then I get over to the phone box to call the dispatcher and the phone box is all froze up. I'm banging on it. I took a fusee and lit it to try and warm it up and open it. I got it open finally. I said, "Dispatcher Berne." No answer. So I say, "Dispatcher Berne," Silence no answer. So now I don't know if the phone is working or not. So again I say, "Dispatcher Berne." She came on and she said, "Show some patience." All I wanted to know is the phone working or am I wasting my time here.

Never served any time. I have a clean record. I remember one time my boss brings the federal inspector up here. My crew on the section, we were up here at the wye. My boss looked at the federal inspector and said, "here's my A team." The inspector says, "A team, what does that stand for?" My boss says "Obnoxious." He thought it started with an A I guess. I always had a conscience about wanting to do a good job. We're getting paid to do a day's work.

I remember one day I was up there on the hill with a surfacing crew and we were changing rails when a protector car came through. We still had some rails to change. We had one on the hill and one up at Scenic that I wanted to do but the surfacing crew was in my way. So I talked to the foreman of the surfacing crew and told him what my plans were. He said that when I got the one done he would move up to the east switch and let us go ahead. I called him and told him we're ready to go, but the boss down here say's "You leave him out here surfacing." So he wouldn't allow us to make that move.

We came down to Sky and were going to have lunch. I'm flying down the road because I'm mad. I'm zipping around up there by Profitts Point and here's a state cop sitting there. I'm doing like seventy-five. I'm not thinking, I'm mad. So the state cop pulls me over. He says, "What do you think your doing?" I said, "I had a plan and the boss screwed it up." I said to him, "You got any bosses like that?" The state cop said, "A couple." He didn't give me a ticket.

We had all kinds of guys to work with. We had guys that didn't mind working hard and we had guys that were trying to hide from work. A mixture of both. We had good bosses. And we had one we didn't like so good.

It was the roadmasters they changed so much. Every three or four years you would have a new boss. I always thought that the Peter Principal worked real well on the railroad. That's where you promote people till they get to a level where they aren't capable then they leave them there. We had some great guys, one of them went clear up to vice president. He was out here about a year.

I worked in the sixties on the snowplow on the east side. It would have been the winter of 1965, right around Christmas time We worked sixteen hours a day. You don't see winters like that anymore. I missed a lot of New Year's because of derailments. It seemed that we had one every New Year's.

I went on a steel gang as assistant foreman in order to get my dates. I didn't have to go very far like a lot of people did on lines west. When I was here it was pretty short distances that we had to go. It was Wenatchee, Centralia and Longview, and up to Canada, but we didn't have to go any further than that. Did a little of that with the steel gang. Stayed away from the tie gangs. You'd just get filthy when you worked the tie gangs. Steel work was a lot cleaner.

I remember the rail grinder. One time they were moving the grinding trains from Everett to Wenatchee. It was on a Sunday and the guy that was the foreman flagging them through, called me and said, "any chance you'd take it through from Skykomish to Wenatchee?" I said, "Sure, why not." So I get on here at Sky. They had a crummy that they would drive everybody back in, a dual seat pickup truck. It's snowing in the mountains and I'm talking to them and I say, "What kind of tires have you got?" the guy said, "Oh we're from Minnesota, we know how to drive in the snow." I said, "Well you know this is kind of wet snow here."

We get over to Wenatchee and we're on our way back and I'm sitting in the middle in the front seat and the wiper blades are starting to get all iced up, and the defroster isn't working enough and the window is starting to get all foggy. It was just an old beater truck. We get almost to the top and I'm trying to get the window wiped off. I tell them, "Man don't stop or we'll never get going again." We get to the top and stop. We're barely on a hump and we still have to push it to get over the hump.

We come down the other side and we're right there at Tunnel Creek. Believe it or not there are two cars in front of us that are going around in circles. We went right between them! I was scared to death. They didn't have snow tires, they didn't have nothing on that damn thing.

I drove the pass when I was foreman at Merritt. Boy you saw a lot of stuff, people not prepared. Laying out in the road with their legs sticking out putting on chains. I remember driving to Merritt one time right there at Tunnel Creek. A woman waving me down. Course I'm going to work. She sure had a funny look on her face when I just kept going. I'm usually a gentleman but I was on my way to work.

In the early seventies I had a dog name Arlo, you know "Arlo Guthrie". He was a big hulk of a dog. He would walk around town and there would be like five places they would feed him. There was no leash law at that time. He would visit Eileen Kinscherf, Joyce Timpe different places on his route every morning. He was kind of a railroad dog you know. On a cold day he would lay next to the radiator at the depot. I remember working here at Sky on the main street crossing. It was summertime and the work train came down. The conductor was Roy Austin. They came down the back lead and stopped. Here Arlo climbs off the caboose! Arlo had gone to work that day and I didn't even know it.

I'd walk down the street in Skykomish some days and there would be a couple of people I didn't even know and they would say, "Hi Arlo!" They didn't even know me but everybody knew Arlo. He was a great dog.

Those were great times.

**Arlo at the Skykomish depot**

# LISA KENNEDY

Birthplace: Seattle, WA 1947
Date of Service: 1968-1972
Position Held: Operator

*...how did those engineers get their orders? I would roll them up and tie*
*them to a string which was strung between to points of light wood and held*
*on a long handle. Just picture a super enlarged slingshot with a long, long*
*handle. I would be outside waiting for the train to go by, sometimes slowly,*
*sometimes quite fast and reach my arm up so the engineer could reach*
*his arm out the window and grab the string. Rarely did we ever miss.*

I was always in love with the railroad. My father's home was just a few miles up a hill from the tracks which provided the soundscape of my childhood. The whistles blew night and day and I could even hear the rhythmic pounding of the steel wheels every time they crossed a railroad tie. The kids from my neighborhood could walk a mile on pavement and then down a trail on a bluff over the tracks. We'd walk on the rails and wave to engineers. From there we climbed down huge boulders and massive chunks of cement forming the bulkhead that formed the roadbed for the tracks, and suddenly we were on a sandy beach with Puget Sound at our feet.

When I was much younger sometimes my dad would accompany me and let me walk on the rails and of course he'd repeat the ritual of putting the proverbial penny down for a train to flatten. Milkshakes always followed at nearby Love's Drug Store where you not only got a huge wide glass gull of chocolate ice cream but the big silver mixing container with the rest of it too. How cool was that?

The trains left Seattle and traveled along the Puget Sound shoreline until reaching Everett where they hooked into to the eastbound line that stretched all the way to Minneapolis, St. Paul, Minnesota and of course branched off to many other lines owned by many other companies.

I was lucky enough to get hired onto the Great Northern Railway when I was twenty-one years old, thanks to the good fortune of knowing a retired telegrapher who knew the Chief Dispatcher in Seattle, Washington. So I arranged for an appointment with Ed Khalain, a youngish and handsome man who had worked his way to the top, as so many were able to do in a company that was as much a family as a business before the merge with the Burlington Northern came and the new age of great mergers was entered.

I was hired on the spot and sent to Edmonds for hands-on training at a tiny depot on the beach bordering Puget Sound, north of Seattle. The office opened onto a cement platform in front of two main-line tracks and one spur for setting out a car or more for a later shipping date or that may have been destined for Edmonds. The ferry docks were on the same stretch of road not more than a quarter mile away or less. A real hub of transportation for a tiny little tourist town in 1968 and quite a bit larger and still thriving today. Lucky again for me, my father's home was less than five miles away and provided me with a free place to stay.

❧

The operator in this view has just handed up orders to the engineer of a moving locomotive using his left hand. Notice he has orders in his right hand that will be handed up to the conductor in the caboose as it passes by. The device used to hold the orders was called a "hoop." The process was called "hooping up" orders. W. J. Pontin photo, Walter Ainsworth collection, pnrarchive.org

The station was manned by two lightly grayed but youngish-looking men named Randy and Walt. Randy was the station manager and Walt was a telegrapher who still used the key. The key was a little brass lever on a pad bolted to an oblong narrow table crammed with communication equipment. I was actually hired for the position of telegrapher though at that time Morse code was no longer required and eventually the title of the job became "train order operator" or just "operator," which had little of the romance that "telegrapher" exuded. A little finger-sized flat spot on top of the key served as the means of activating the key which made a metal clicking or tapping noise when depressed. My primary job consisted of wearing a headset and listening to a dispatcher in Seattle somewhere, rattle off orders that I typed and sometimes had to repeat through a separate microphone that could be moved to match the position of my body at the table.

All of the operators from Western Washington to Eastern Washington were usually on the radio when train orders were being dictated—amounting to about seven or eight people. Some of the dispatchers spoke so fast that I couldn't even keep up on the typewriter and had to hand write many of them until I got the lingo down. The railroad has a special language of it's own.

The information imparted by the dispatcher on duty was critical to the engineer and conductor responsible for the train as it was their only form of communication, besides train signals of course. There were certainly no cell phones in that era. The orders referred to a particular train by it's engine number directing an engineer and conductor that a specific length of track they would soon be crossing would be out of service for a certain period of time, between a specific milepost and another milepost until a certain time, whether for fifteen minutes or forty minutes. The freight train would either wait at a signal or be sidelined on a siding out of the way of any equipment that might need access to the area of track out of service. It's even possible that an eastbound passenger might be sent up a section of westbound track and the equipment might be directed to leave the out-of-service track at the other end of the out-of-service section with the passenger train being allowed to cross that section ahead of the freight train and before the track workers were finished with their project.

And how did those engineers get their orders? I would roll them up and tie them to a string which was strung between two points of light wood and held on a long handle. Just picture a super enlarged slingshot with a long, long handle. I would be outside waiting for the train to go by, sometimes slowly, sometimes quite fast and reach my arm up so the engineer could reach his arm out the window and grab the string. Rarely did we ever miss. And when it was last minute info and I just got out in time to meet the train as it sped by, it was quite exciting.

Other jobs that I had at the Edmonds depot included selling tickets which I didn't care for and loading and unloading baggage onto huge baggage carts whenever a passenger train passed through. I trained three to six months and was moved to Everett to become a relief operator, working a strange concoction of hours encompassing all shifts until eventually taking a night shift position which suited me because I didn't have to work with the public.

The yard in Everett had a lot more switch engines making up trains to go east. Everett was also a port city though nothing near the size of Seattle. Train orders had to go to switch engines as well as freight trains and there were a few of them buzzing about to keep me busy. The strangest thing was having to go down two flights of cement stairs to a lower level where another track went by. It was dark, scary, empty and damp except for the occasional bum or drunk sleeping it off, slumped on the steps. My world was definitely broadening.

It was there that I began to meet the occasional train crew and made a lifelong friend of an engineer named Ted Cleveland. He introduced me to his large family and I became fast friends with everyone, especially his two oldest children. Forty years later I'm still part of the family and Ted and his wife Nancy are my best friends.

I also substituted at a little place called Bridge 10 located near a slough somewhere along the curve where the railway turned east toward the Cascade mountain range. It seemed I was always there in the dark and quite often it was foggy.

I had to raise the bridge for boats I could hardly see and lower it for trains I was sure were going to sink the whole bridge because everything was always vibrating.

I was more than happy to get out of there when I was offered a position again as a relief operator working all shifts just north of downtown Seattle. That was my favorite place to work yet. The place was called Interbay and it laid in a small stretch of land between Magnolia Bluff and Queen Anne Hill. It was a little bit separated from Puget Sound a half mile further south. There was very good size rail yard below the highway and a large building that housed a good many if not all of the paper pushers located at the west end of the Great Northern Rail Line. At least the ones involved in keeping track of every piece of cargo on every car. Where it came from, who shipped it, where and to whom it was destined and what it weighed, cost and was insured for. Besides any number of other things that I can't possibly imagine. Just another mile south lay Seattle, built at the edge of the Sound over seven hills. Lying below, a port full of ships and ferries and the famous Public Market.

This is where I lived and worked for the next several years. This is where the "pro's" worked. I became quite accomplished! I was in my element! "Transportation and Communication."

The operator was situated in a small room shared with a couple of banks of electrical equipment, separated by a wall and a door, which I usually kept open because there were no windows. Directly outside was the yard, but I never got to see the trains move under my authority.

There was a sliding window behind my desk next to the wall with the CTC board, where engineers and mostly conductors would come by and pick up their train list and shipping papers from a rack on the outside wall and their train orders from me.

The CTC board short for Centralized Traffic Control was a large black panel with grooves and painted white that included tiny red, amber and green lights with tiny metal switches, each selectively placed. The lines represented the tracks of the two main lines as they arrived from the north and branched out into a bunch of lines from the top of the black panel to the bottom.

For those old enough to remember, think of a diagrammed sentence in English class, just the lines without the words. This board gave me control over seven miles of track and the power to make autonomous decisions for when I would let a switch engine move a long train across the width of the yard ahead of a passenger train due to be fast-tracked through the yard with no delays. No yellow signals to slow down and definitely no reds. Inevitably I would be asked to do this just about every day. There were only two scheduled passenger trains but in the late afternoon one must have been close to shift change in the yard because someone was always in a hurry to get somewhere ahead of the passenger train.

I nearly always had a headset on and a large free standing microphone to speak into that moved from the two desks that I managed and was available to me if I was standing by the window or back from the CTC board watching each signal trip as the freight train made its way along the yard. Today the powers that be say humans don't multi-task very well, but I was quite satisfied with my performance and felt on top of the world while working there.

There were three other women rotating shifts around the clock with me filling in on their days off. One woman was nearly as young as myself and would eventually move into the dispatcher's job in Seattle. I would have been more than happy to move into her slot until retirement, that's how much I loved it!

I actually got a glimpse of the of the dispatcher's workplace one time. There were three black panels the size of classroom blackboards with lights and levers and white lines depicting the rails and train yards from Seattle to Minnesota. When talk began of me moving into that position it scared me to death. There is such a thing as moving beyond your capabilities and as far as I was concerned then that was one step too far for me.

And before too long I was moved to three other locations as the rumors solidified that my job was ultimately heading for the chopping block. I was witnessing the end of an era but I also hadn't fully realized it was the end of my career that was also looming and so I continued to enjoy my life working on the railroad.

The next location where I worked was the telegraph office at King Street Station it was called UD, it was actually underground. It was somewhere that I could access from a parking area or did I actually go downstairs from within the King Street Station? Well either way, it was underground in very tight, cramped quarters. It seemed to me that the trains that passed through came out of a tunnel and disappeared very quickly due to a bend that they went around. Meaning, I never saw more than two or three cars move by at a time. As usual there were orders to type and deliver but I had very limited contact with human beings.

Fortunately I only had to be there for a short period and I escaped the dungeon to go to my next location which was a tower called North Portal along the waterfront, north of Seattle. The office there was up a flight of outside stairs and provided me with a view of several tracks. Switch engines had to ask my permission to cross the main lines and I had to know exactly when a train left downtown Seattle going north or how long it had been since a train had passed Interbay going south, so that I could time the crossings right. With little actual control and not knowing the speed of the train or its exact location during the three to five mile distance, it was a situation ripe for confusion if there was any miscommunication between me, UD or the dispatcher. There were traffic jams with trains and cars and traffic lights. No fun at all. I got out of there as quickly as possible.

The last location that I was sent to was Skykomish, which was situated in the middle of the beautiful Cascade Mountain range. It is a town located on the

Skykomish River going east on Highway 2 on the way up to Stevens Pass. Skykomish was then, and still remains a very old and quaint little town that the railroad runs through.

A helper pool was established in Skykomish to help the trains over the 2.2 grade from Skykomish to Merritt. There were two hotels and cafes in town, that mostly housed railroad workers. They were originally built back in the early days when the railroad was being constructed over the pass.

There was little for me to do at the Skykomish Depot. I'm not sure that the passenger trains stopped there anymore as the population was so small. I think that one train a day would pick up the mail and packages. It was summer and the weather was nice. I wore slacks, a tank top and flip flops and spent time talking on the phone with one of the downtown Seattle dispatchers.

Compared to the rest of the operators that I knew, who were older people, I was the new face of what would become the Burlington Northern Railroad. In the peak of my youth and not afraid to be myself. This was the dawning of the flower power generation and the rest of my life was before me.

# ED POTTER

Birthplace: Ritzville, WA 1947
Date of Service: October 29, 1968
Position Held: Brakeman, Conductor

*...he used to get the train magazines like* Modern Railroads *and* Railway Age. *After he was through reading those magazines he'd give them to my dad and my dad would bring them home. I was about three years old when I started looking at all the railroad pictures. This is probably where I got started on the railroad.*

Starting in the beginning there in the town of Sprague, Washington, my father was the manager of the Sprague Grange Supply. Across the street was the rail depot. The section foreman there, I can't remember his name, went on to become the vice president of Maintenance-of-way for the Burlington Northern. Anyway he used to get the train magazines like Modern Railroads and Railway Age. After he was through reading those magazines he'd give them to my dad and my dad would bring them home. I was about three years old when I started looking at all the railroad pictures. This is probably where I got started on the railroad. From Sprague we moved to Spokane for a while, then my dad decided to move to Seattle.

As far as railroad connections go with families, I have two uncles. One was an engineer and one was a switchman. Both uncles hired out in 1939 on the SP&S (Spokane, Portland and Seattle Railway). One of the interesting things was the uncle who was the engineer worked during the Depression for the Deer Park Logging Company, between Deer Park and Ford. His wedding day was during the Depression so he didn't dare ask for a day off. It was supposed to be a real short day. They were supposed to take the empties up to the reload at Ford and come back cab hop and tie up at Springdale for the day. Well, the engine broke down at Ford so he was twelve hours late getting to his wedding.

My other uncle, John, was a switchman. John first hired out as a brakeman and he had the shortest career of any brakeman on the SP&S. The first thing he caught was a ten day hold down on the Wishram extra board. So he deadheaded on the train from Vancouver to Wishram, got off the train, took one look at Wishram, got on the next westbound train, quit and hired out as a switchman. Where he stayed till 1962 when he passed away.

After the war was over my father graduated from Annapolis with a degree in diesel engineering. The railroad had offered him a job as road foreman because they were making the big transition from steam to diesel and he turned down that road foreman's job in 1946 because he didn't think that the railroads would be around another ten years. I think that my mother thought that he had done enough traveling in the navy.

I hired out on the railroad in 1968. I graduated from high school in 1965 and worked for the highway department until I was drafted into the army in October of 1966. I was in the army for two years.

I was always interested in trains. I'd be sitting there at my desk doing homework and drawing pictures of trains, something I shouldn't have been doing. I missed the big transition from steam to diesel but fortunately when I was in the army they sent me to Schweinfurt, Germany, where in 1967 and 1968 it was practically all still steam. That was beautiful for me. I loved that. When I got out of the army I went to Interbay. They didn't have a fireman, so there was a spare seat on the switch engine and I rode for a couple of days. There was a switch foreman named Vito Tenerelli he dropped me off at the yard and he said, "well if you're going to hang around here all the time you better get paid for it. So I filled out all the paperwork and that's how I got to work for the railroad until October 2006.

I thought that I knew quite a bit about railroads but what really shocked me the first few days was that I didn't realize how much picking up and setting out trains did. The other thing I didn't realize was when the crew caller said we'll probably call you early in the morning, I thought early in the morning was five or six a.m. To the railroad, "early" was anything after twelve or one a.m. Everything ran at night and for some reason they had a train called the hi-ball that went to work about one o'clock in the morning. Sixteen hours you had to scratch into Portland. You might have a nice trip until you got to Vancouver, Washington, and then spend six hours just from Vancouver to Portland.

It was interesting. I worked the extra board at Interbay, freight and passenger brakeman and baggage man. I was also active at the Snoqualmie Railroad Museum when I was working on the west side.

I went to Wenatchee in 1970. I caught a local called the Merritt Local off the extra board. At that time I went to downtown Leavenworth for the lunch break. There was a girl working at Shelton's Café, that I just got an overpowering crush on. It was like I was back in high school.

She made the remark, "I'm impressed when people own real estate." Well, the rock pile had a for sale sign on it. I bought the rock pile and the girl went off and married somebody else! So I owned real estate, "the rock pile" and I pretty much became a resident of Leavenworth.

I was on the Merritt Local as a brakeman. Then went to the Wenatchee to Skykomish Helpers for quite a while. Then the Wenatchee to Oroville Local which is a six-day-a-week job and then they put on a Omak to Oroville Local. I was the conductor on that job.

That line was sold to Rail America. When that happened I went on the Merritt-Alcoa Local. That was pulled off when the Alcoa Plant went dormant. Then I went on the Wenatchee to Quincy Local and that's where I stayed until I retired. I also worked the helpers between Wenatchee and Skykomish.

When I worked the helpers from Wenatchee to Skykomish I had a little dog named "Boxcar". He rode in the cab of the engine all the way over, just wide alert "Casey Jones special", his head out the window watching everything. He'd get over here to Skykomish and he'd run around with all the local dogs for about two hours. When it came train time he'd get back on the helpers and just sleep all the way back. He must have been a railroader in his earlier life.

I never lost a car down the hill into Leavenworth but we were going to make a drop and the conductor, Bill Hartly, would not let me ride the brake on the car, he wanted me to make sure I got the switch instead of the car. He said if I tried to do that I would probably try to ride the thing right to the spot. How'd he know that?

We had two serious derailments. We had one about ten cars in the middle of the train piled up on one of the drags there. Another time the engine broke away in the middle of the tunnel and we had a dynamiter in the train. We were about eighty-two in the helpers. We set the air, went into emergency and we waited. And waited. The air didn't come up and the crew on the head-end said, "We hear something blowing." So they get off the engine and the engine started to roll away. We went off at the west switch at Scenic, had to use a house moving outfit to get it back, to get it re-railed.

So anyway, I wondered how long it took to get everything coordinated on the railroad. I didn't know how badly hurt they were because the crew had to jump off. So I tied down the train and uncoupled the lead unit and went down about two bays and picked them up and took them out to the aid car. It might take hours and if someone is hurt you need to get them out of there now!

I did try to drop a caboose by myself. We had to go from Wenatchee into Quincy and set out a big block of cars and come back cab hop. The brakeman had got hurt and I said I could take care of it myself. I dropped that caboose there at the caboose spur in Wenatchee went to get on it when it was rolling by and I got knocked on the ground. Fortunately the helper engine was there or it would have gone in the street there at Thurston. I was off a few days on that one.

When I was working the baggage job I didn't realize that when the weather was bad, a lot of air mail traveled by train. The U.S. Surface Mail came in heavy canvas bags with a fairly heavy patina of dirt on them. The airmail came in nice freshly washed nylon coated bags.

One night we had a dog and they had given him a tranquilizer and they just put him in a cardboard box. Well he woke up and decided he wanted out and he chewed his way out, Here we get to Spokane and here's a dog on a leash sitting by the baggage door. I said, "Is that checked off, where's his cage?" Oh chewed up over there. He wasn't part of the airmail.

There is probably more mail now on the Z trains (hot piggyback trains), UPS, FedEx and such, that the passenger trains used to haul. The internet opened up the amount of parcel post, cut way back on the first class mail but it made a huge increase on the parcel post.

One of my pet peeves is that if you just consider Amtrak something to haul people with it is very efficient. But if you would consider it a research and development tool in the real world for transportation problems, it could be a huge redevelopment tool. Look at passenger trains. That's where you first had the diesels, that's where you first had the roller bearings, that's where you first had the steel cars. You didn't have to have something that would interface with Civil War era freight equipment. You could have a separate train set.

In the 1930's they found out that stainless steel was the best thing to make trains out of and aluminum was a great material to make airplanes out of. To me, Amtrak should be in research and development to get better long-time performance. In engineering, you're solving real life problems, stuff like that. I'd like to see them put Passenger Number Five and Six back on. That way they can have stops at Edmonds, Everett, Monroe, Skykomish, Leavenworth, Wenatchee, Quincy, Wilson Creek, Odessa, Harrington, Fairchild and Spokane.

I can remember riding Number Six to my gramma's place, they had an open platform observation car on it. For some reason I can visually remember that. The brakeman lining the switch up and getting back on. That shows you how hard the mountain was there. The fact that both trains left Spokane and Seattle simultaneously at eight o'clock and the meeting point mathematically would be the Columbia River. Instead it was the mountain territory. You had to stop at Wenatchee and take the steam or diesel engine off and put on an electric engine.

I went to the Boy Scout jamboree in 1960 and 1964. We traveled by train. The one in 1960 was at Colorado Springs and the one in 1964 was at Valley Forge and for me the train trip was almost more fun than the Boy Scouts.

On the 1964 one we were probably one of the first passenger excursion to go through the Kootenai River Canyon after the big flood. I remember seeing miles of track, wood ties on steel rails flipped upside down. They were rebuilding tunnel portals. They were starting to get short of extra dining cars. The Boy Scouts had to get some army kitchen cars and used a full length picnic table in a baggage car for seating.

There was one cook on that army dining car. I remember him because he had my grandfather's middle name, "Dewey". When I started working and catching a passenger once in a while on train #32 and #27, here he was. In four years he had enough seniority to hold a regular job. I asked him what it was like cooking over anthracite instead of propane? He said, "Not too bad because once you have the temperature right it holds just about as good as propane." Kind of interesting to make that transition, going from a modern dining car to WW2 vintage kitchen car and back to a modern dining car. That was quite a trip.

For the 1960 Jamboree we had what they called a "twelve and one" Pullman car. Twelve berths, one scout in the top berth, two scouts in the bottom berth so thirty-six scouts from the Seattle Council to the jamboree. The one we had in 1964 was about the same thing only they were more streamlined cars

My brother was a sign painter at the time, he painted a sign on the one we had in 1960. It was supposed to be washable tempera paint. It said "Troupe 24, Section 11, Seattle, Washington" on the side of the Pennsylvania car. Well, while we were at Colorado Springs they deadheaded all the equipment to Denver and ran it through the car washer and apparently it was permanent paint he put on there because it was just as fresh and it probably wore that lettering of his until the day they scrapped the car.

A couple of stories I heard from my thirty-nine years on the railroad: I don't know if this is a good story or a true story, but one time a hostler was sleeping in the cab of a GP7 his foot went over and kicked off the air brakes, the engine rolled back and dropped into the turntable pit. When asked what happened he said, "I guess I was sleeping and kicked the air off." So they called the Interbay hook over to get the engine out of the pit. Somebody didn't take the time to put the outriggers out on the hook and the hook tipped over and went in the pit. So they called up the superintendent and said, "I think we need the hook from Spokane." The superintendent, he knew what had happened. He asked, "Is there room in the pit for it?"

Sid Pierce told me this story years ago: They had a derailment and they got the track back in service but it was pretty rough with the mud and the dirt and everything. It so happened that John Budd, the president of the railroad was out in his private car inspecting the derailment area. Someone said, "There's a car of those real fine rock chips down in the pit, the kind that looks like crushed brick that comes from Montana, like five-eights minus. If we can just give a dusting of it along the derailment site, they can clean up along there." So they ran the work train down there and grabbed the car. Normally when you unload a ballast car you do it at walking speed so the section crew can open and close the doors to regulate the amount of material coming out. With one car to cover a little over a thousand feet they didn't have enough for that so they decided to crack the doors open. We'll give a hi-ball sign and the engineer on the work train can take it ahead about fifteen or twenty miles an hour and make a nice dusting of these rock chips make everything nice and pretty. So they did that, but as Paul Harvey used to say, "the rest of the story is." As soon as they did that here comes an almost intolerable stench, it was all but stifling the air.

What happened was a car of sugar beets had been delayed in transit, it had frozen and the claims department had to buy it. They didn't know what to do with it so they decided to dump it in one of the played out areas of the pit. But it started to stink so bad that in order to keep the stench down somebody decided we needed to cover it with about six inches of these fine rocks. So that's how they spread one car load of rotted sugar beets over a quarter of mile just before John Budd came through to examine the area.

This is another railroad story. I heard this from my father who heard it from an uncle who worked for the SP&S: Back some years ago, a doctor in Portland had ordered an expensive Maine Coon cat. It was being shipped by rail by the breeder to the doctor's home in Portland, Oregon. At Spokane it was necessary for the baggage to be transferred from the Seattle train to the Portland section. Baggage and such was hauled into the baggage room. The baggage men felt sorry for this poor cat. They decided to let it run around the baggage room for about an hour or so until train time, then put it back in the cage. As soon as they opened the cage, the cat took off like a streak of lightning for downtown Spokane, never to be seen again. So they had a problem. They had a train that was due to leave in about an hour. They had an empty cage that was supposed to have an expensive cat in it for a doctor in Portland. Not only that but with all of these men, there with probably a combined seniority of several hundred years that was at risk.

One of the men had a bright idea. He remembered the stray cat that hung around there that had been living off lunch boxes leftovers and such. So one of the guys just grabbed that cat and threw it in the cage put it on the train for Portland and they never heard another word! End of story.

The two old heads when I hired out were Claude Witt and Earl Hilling. George Leu, another old head's comment one day was, "Well I went to the Skykomish Old Timers Picnic to talk to the Old Timers, I sat there and suddenly realized, I was one!"

I worked for the railroad for thirty nine years.

# VICK POLLOW

Birthplace: Everett, Washington, 1953
Date of Service: December 18, 1975
Positions Held: Steel Bridge Mechanic, First Class Carpenter B&B

*...I'm way up there at the switch, cleaning my switch of snow. I look down and Amtrak is supposed to pop out of the tunnel at anytime. I look down and here's this front-end loader over one track and backed up to the other track is a cement truck. I know because I'm listening to the radio that Amtrak is going to jump out of the tunnel at anytime. They don't have a radio, so here I am running like hell, yelling and screaming. "What did I tell you guys?"*

I went to work for the railroad because I came out of the service and needed a job. Dad was tired of me hanging around the house.

First of all I went to work for the steel gang. Steel Erection Crew Number One. I worked there for thirteen years. Everybody kept telling me to get into the B&B (bridge and building crew) to get my date. I wasn't a carpenter, didn't know nothing about it. Then when they got rid of the steel crew I was forced into the B&B and I realized half of those guys weren't carpenters. They'd been there for years. So I should have got my date a lot earlier. That was something I couldn't believe. I've seen guys put in windows that didn't fit. They'd get a ten or twelve pound maul and start beating on the frame to get that window to fit. What! Who does that?

When I was on the steel crew they wouldn't give us a chain saw, we had those old misery whips (a misery whip was the old cross cut saws that the loggers used before chain saws). They didn't trust us with a chain saw, so they'd give us the misery whip to cut beams with. What? That's antique stuff you know. Those whips were sharp, but being young guys we thought it was crazy. They didn't trust us with a chain saw.

One guy I remember was named Harold, I called him the bulldog. He was just this short stocky guy and he went all day long. He'd outwork any of the guys. And he knew anything you needed to know about steel bridges. We were working on a bridge in Olympia, we had to jack it up to reduce the steel underneath it. You had to go up more than ten feet before you could get a jack underneath it. The engineer was trying to tell Harold how it was going to be done. Harold goes, "No, no, we're not going to be doing it that way." He says, "Get a goddang beam, stick it up there and wire it in tight so it won't split. Jack it up, split that thing off, slip another one in and get the hell out of here." It worked just like Harold said. He made it look easy, but he was telling the supervisor how to do it.

He got into some trouble flagging the bridges. I got laid off for a couple of weeks and while I was gone he was flagging the bridges. He told the one guy to pull up the reds and yellows. For some reason he told the other guy to leave the reds out there, pull the yellows, leave the reds. Well, Amtrak comes down that way, sees the reds and dynamites the brakes and went right onto the bridge.

The yellow reds are your warning signs that you've got something coming up a few miles ahead. Then you've got the reds. They'll stop you and they'll use a radio to tell you whether you need to stop at the reds or continue on through at twenty miles an hour or twenty-five miles an hour or whatever. It's just a steel flag that you pound into the ground next to where you are working. You are supposed to pull the red first. Then go after the yellow red because that's just a warning sign. But the red is what stops you if you don't get ahold of anyone on the railroad. You got to stop for it.

He got canned for it, he got back but not as a foreman just as a mechanic. He was the one that had all the knowledge. Harold didn't get along with the next guy who was young and didn't know nothing So they kind of squabbled all the time. He finally got tired of it after a couple of years and transferred into the track department in Wenatchee. This is in the seventies or early eighties, they had layoffs every year. He got laid off and went to the lumber mill in Cashmere as a millwright. He was one of the best guys the railroad had, he was a working fool and knew everything there was to know about steel bridges. He never came back to work on the railroad.

He saved my life one time down there at Olympia. Back then you worked off of the side of a bridge you just kind of put a plank up there and walked up and down that plank with your tools and bolts. You know a plank is only twelve inches wide. Harold and me were up there pounding rivets out with hammers. You got to swing as hard as you can to get those rivets out. I swung a couple of times and I was doing good. Then I swung and I hit another one and lost my balance, it was about forty feet down to the river, Harold grabbed my shirt and held onto me. He was hard to work for but I had a lot of respect for him because he knew his business.

One time I was helping Harold, I was a bridge mechanic helper. Back then all the bridge mechanics had a helper. I was the dog, I was the guy that ran after the bolts he needed and the hammer. Anyway I was helping him and we were doing some cross bracing beams, (lattice) work. I was just waiting for him to do his thing and I'd hand him the bolts and stuff. Well I'm bored you know so I've got some bolts here and some washers over there and I thought why not just hand him the whole thing? So anyway I handed him the first one all put together and he's all upset, he says, "Damn it, what's this?" I thought it would be easier. So I'm scrambling to calm him down. Those old guys, once they get on you they can rip on you for five minutes or more.

Another time I was down there by Tacoma, at Puyallup. We were working on a bridge and I didn't know nothing about the torch set up, the oxygen, acetylene. Usually my job in the afternoon was to tear it down. Sometimes those caps on the tanks they'd get rusted up a little bit, harder than hell to get on. You'd tap on them and nothing happened, so I thought, oil! Oil helps everything, I thought. This was in he afternoon, then we go home you know.

Me and Bill Steel was out there loading up this car to take everything out to the bridge for the next morning. Harold went out there and was looking around. He's coming back and and we can hear him yelling and we think what's wrong with him? What the hell's his problem? I called him the bulldog you know. He's coming at us with a full head of steam and he gets up to us, "Who's the guy that put that oil on that tank out there?" "It could have blown up you know?" Any kind of oil or containment on acetylene or oxygen and it can blow. Just a speck of oil can blow them up. I said, "Hey, I've never been around this kind of stuff before." To which Harold said, "you get some soap and water and you scrub those tanks." Then he apologized about an hour later. He was scared. Anyway you just don't do stuff like that. I didn't have a clue. I thought, put a little oil on it and it worked great. I never did it again,

Further on in my career when I was working on the B&B, you'd get bounced around quite a bit. You'd go wherever you can stay working and not get laid off. There were some crews nobody wanted to work for and that's what the guy with no time got stuck with. The only job I never took was the truck driver job. You're sitting around too much. Otherwise I did everything.

I worked on all the jobs on the Skagit River. Every time it flooded we'd be out there sawing all those logs up by hand. The ones that choked the river by the bridges. One time the logs were piled to the top of the bridge, that's like thirty feet. Anyway we just got a crew and the saws and started cutting.

One time we just stepped right off the bridge onto the logs and started cutting, throwing them over the side. One guy, usually the foreman, had a ten or twelve foot Livingston. He'd get them out of the way so we'd have more room to throw logs down. One day he started getting the bright idea of hooking a rope to them, and yanking some of them out of there. Worked pretty good for I don't know how many years. Once in a while we'd get lucky, he'd pull the right log and the whole works would come down.

We had a crew cab International that we took from job to job. If we had too many people, me and another guy had to jump in back, in the old doghouse. No heat no nothing, from Tacoma down past Fort Lewis, middle of winter, oh god it was cold. Somebody had to come up with a better idea, drive their own car or something. Just sitting there was like freezing to death. The doghouse held the tools and the wind just came through there.

We were working on that Sandpoint Bridge over there in Idaho. First thing in the morning we were working on the far end when here comes this boat around the corner. About a week or so before we got there they were throwing ties off onto the beach there. The tie gang was coming through later on to put them in.

That boat came around pulled in real slow, he was right below us, only about thirty feet down. Got his rope nailed on some kind of a spike and started tugging on it. The foreman yelled, "What the hell do you think you're doing, that's Burlington Northern property." The guy just looked up at him and Vroooom! just took off. What can you do? Brand new ties and he had two of them.

They would send me up here to Sky often. When the snowplow would plow out the yard, they'd shoot that snow out and it would break out the windows above the door in the depot. Then they'd call down to Delta where I worked.

They'd say. "You got to send someone up here to fix these windows." "Well, Vick you'd better get going." I'd get an early off and come up and fix the windows. I did any little job that was up here, like the toilets when those big gangs were up here, "Oh no not me, I don't want to do that!" Steel gangs, tie gangs any big gangs, like thirty, forty men would come through every so often.

Our outfit cars were the old Pullman cars. We had a gal to cook for us. It was just like eating at home. Every Monday morning when she'd show up we'd have to go down there to her car and pack this big old TV up to her room, cause she lived in the cook car by herself. On one end she had her bedroom, then the kitchen with this big old long table and stuff. We'd pack this TV there for her. On Friday morning she'd make us breakfast and fix us a box lunch then she was free to go. So every Friday morning we got to pack that TV back into her car. Took it home with her every weekend because back then you didn't have two TV's. If there was a good movie on or something she'd come over, "Hey there's a good movie on, you guys want to come over?" Then she'd make us popcorn. She'd usually buy ice cream by the tub and she'd give us ice cream too.

During the summer when there was watermelon, we'd have it for dinner, then later on she'd bring it in and set it on the table in our car so we could snack on it. She was good. Then she retired and we got some guy out of the military, he was a cook in the navy. Just grease, everything floated in grease. He was bad. If you mentioned something that you wanted in your sandwich, that's what you got every day.

We slept in the Pullman cars. We had them all sectioned off. Two to four bunks per little section or room. After those old guys left, I was usually the only one that stuck around on a regular basis. Everyone else was coming and going, all the way from Spokane and down south even. They'd get laid off from their B&B jobs then they'd come to us because we were working year around.

Once all the old guys left I moved down to the end because it had a stove in there. I put in a stereo and stripped the windows because they had the oak and brass fittings. I loved them. I didn't want them to get rid of them when they got the univans, (which is a trailer on a car). They were cramped and everybody was in there. You had your own cooking and stuff so they eventually got rid of the cook. I tried to talk the supervisor out of that, but he said, "You just got to go with the times." You had to go into another car to shower. Half of it was a shower car and I put an old wringer washer in there because our clothes—gosh were just greasy and oily. On the other end of the car was the foreman's office. This was one of the cars that had the big window and the deck out the back. All brass railings. Up in the car was a stained glass window you know, like a half moon.

Every so often some old guy would be out there taking pictures. He'd say you know I'm from such and such historical society and when you retire these let us know we'd be interested.

I remember when we hit this gas pipe with a rail while driving it in for a bulkhead. The foreman hit this gas pipe. I was three hundred yards down the track. I was cutting off the top of the rails for height, to put our beams in for the bulkhead. We had to cut off the excess, let them flop and we'd pick them up later. I had been doing that all day, I hadn't been down by the crew at all. Anyway they come running down there and I thought, what the hell, what's their problem? They acted like they were scared, then I looked down in the ditch and it looked like water running. It was jet fuel, about two feet deep. It was coming down behind those guys. They yelled, "Shut your torch off, shut it off!" I thought it was water. They had hit the gas line. The guys from the gas company had come over there, marked where to go. "Don't go near this spot, don't go by that spot. You can drive over here, you can drive a rail over there, but don't do it here". So the guys are moving the rail with the pile driver, the foreman comes up, "Put it right here!" Those two guys say no. "No, he says not to do it there". The foreman says, "Put the damn thing right here, or I'll do it myself." They drove it in and they felt it when it first hit, then the hammer hit it again. It felt like an earthquake. The ground just started shaking. Then they started running.

We finely got a boring machine, for pushing pipes in the same time you were boring the culverts in. You could do up to twelve inches I think. It was nice.

We were over at Stampede one time to clean out a three foot pipe. It would take a week with a crew, dragging out five gallon buckets. I said, we got that auger, why don't we just stick that auger in there and drag it out? We had a backhoe there and we could dig. It worked slicker than heck. The only time that it didn't was if you had a big chunk of wood in there, then it would get jammed. You'd have to stop and send a guy in there to drag it out. Otherwise it saved us a lot of time crawling around in there.

As long as you had the extensions you could do thirty feet, maybe even more. It had a hydraulic that pushed it forward as you went in. Then you'd pull it back and hook up another set and start pushing again. Any dirt or gravel, it would just drag it right out. It had a carbide head. It was powered with a Wisconsin motor probably a twenty or thirty horse power. It had a little three-speed transmission on it. We'd just stand next to it and shift the clutch. Wasn't very big, worked really slick, pretty simple.

They were trying to take that auger machine to Wenatchee because they didn't want us doing that job, they wanted contractors in there doing it. Anyway we took it to Wenatchee and kind of hid it out where nobody knew. Even though nobody used it, it just seemed like they'd forget about it after they didn't see it again.

"The Tunnel!" Yea, I worked a lot in the tunnel. We had the one big job that we always had. We were part of the crew that watched the contractors, (we called it babysitting) cutting notches in the crown of the tunnel I was in there every day for over a year. That was pretty exciting. At one point I told those guys if the car moves (we had a little train set up), I said, "If those cars are moving or switching or whatever, do not get on, do not get off. Wait until it stops.

A lot of times I wasn't down there watching because I had to keep the switches open, so I was away from the machinery. Well one time I was up there cleaning a switch. I heard some yelling below and I looked, I could see this guy hanging off the car and the car was moving and his feet were down by the wheels. He was screaming. I thought, "Oh my god, I'm going to have to go down there and pick up this guy's toes". Well I went down there and everything was so frozen, right up to the top of the rail that it just slid his feet under the wheel. It didn't clip them off it just kind of crushed them a little bit, just lucky!

I'd tell the guys just about weekly not to get on and off the car. I'll stop it or the machine operator will stop it, but they wouldn't listen. I'd tell them to stay away from the crossing with your big front-end loader, cause we got Amtrak or some train coming through. We're not sure when.

Anyway I'm way up there at the switch, cleaning my switch of snow. I look down and Amtrak is supposed to pop out of the tunnel at anytime. I look down and here's this front-end loader over one track and backed up to the other track is a cement truck. I know because I'm listening to the radio that Amtrak is going to jump out of the tunnel at anytime. They don't have a radio, so here I am running like hell, yelling and screaming. "What did I tell you guys?" They say, "what's the big deal?" It wasn't five or ten seconds later, here comes Amtrak. It's a big joke, but if you guys wreck Amtrak, it's a big big thing. These contractor guys didn't understand that. They had never been around the railroad before, so they didn't understand the danger. They didn't seem to care. Listen guys, people get killed out here.

One time we were in the tunnel and this guy was on what we called "the drill truck." He wanted to go out early. He didn't have anything to do so he was just

**Amtrak's Empire Builder passenger train crosses the Foss River bridge.**

178

going to go and sit out there. Okay, but be there when we get out, so I can switch you in, because we have to account for everybody. So we have my end and a whole new set-up on the other end. Anyway I get out there and there is no drill truck. I can't release the track without finding this guy. He's got a radio on, so I call him up. No answer, my boss on the other side, Paul Miller, says, "Vick where's this guy at?" I don't know, maybe he's on his way to your side? So he talks to the guys foreman and he doesn't know where he is. Finally I walk down the tracks and there he is sitting there sleeping along the track. "What are you doing man, everybody's waiting on you, we got trains waiting on you." Back in the hole we go, but he didn't care, he got his nap in.

Same guy, I was switching him in, they were going to come back out so I had to switch him back out. Anyway I switched him in but I hadn't gone up there and switched him back. We see him start moving and know backing up. He's getting closer, he's seen me throw the switch enough times to know he can't make it through there. No, I think, "he's going to keep coming. Yea, he's going to go through it!" DERAIL you know! I go up to him and say, "Didn't you see the red sign, that sign means stop, green means go!"

So then we got to call Jimmy George to come to inspect it because I'm not qualified to inspect it. So the train is waiting on us for another extra hour. Jimmy isn't even working because it's after hours. You had to watch those guys like a hawk, and still do your work. After a while I just hated those guys. They had me so stressed out.

After a while you get to the second half of the job and you have to pump cement up into the crown to rebuild some of the cuts and stuff, to fill up voids in there. They pump it up there, sometimes they pump in one hole for a week, it is that big. But anyway at the end of the day they slide the hose down and put a cork in it. Meantime its gushing out cement because there is nothing to hold it. So there's cement all over everything. So the next morning I have to go out there and chip all that stuff off the hand brake, to release the hand brake. I tell their foreman you got anyone to come out here and chip this stuff? I've got to keep those switches open.

Nobody came, I was down there with my hammer, chisel and screwdriver trying to keep them free so when we get time we can get the heck out. They mark your time down every minute. You get track time from the minute you get to that switch to the minute you get to the opening of the tunnel. This went on for a month and it's getting tougher and tougher to get this brake released. Finally the one morning I didn't have time, I had to go shovel snow. I told that foreman, hey, I'm not touching that brake. From now on that's your responsibility. You put the stuff on it, you clean it off.

I get the switch cleaned up, we get track time, the train can't move, the brake won't release. That foreman is yelling, why ain't we moving? I said, "You get that brake?" NO! well there you go! What did I tell you?" From then on I never had any more trouble.

Another time up in the tunnel: we used to walk through the Pioneer Tunnel, right next to the main tunnel. Every year Scott, the supervisor would come up to inspect it. Scott would get me to go with him because I lived here. We'd walk through it. Sometimes we'd go out the side door, he'd call the first train coming through and have them stop and we'd jump on and ride out. You couldn't do that now. It was kind of like an adventure. But after a few years I thought I don't want to go in that dirty old hole again.

The Foss River bridge is a bridge within a bridge. They built a bridge around a bridge. It is one of the strongest ones I've ever seen, twice as much steel. We'd been running up and down over the Foss River Bridge in the motor car doing some work at Carroll Creek. Anyway we got this new guy on the job. Going up it wasn't too bad, going over the bridge, but then coming down (that was when they still had the jointed rail) everybody was used to it. Coming back down in the afternoon this new guy was on the upriver side with his back turned to the Foss River bridge. Everybody kind of looked at each other smiling We were bouncing like hell and the next thing you know the guy is on that side and there is nothing out there. When you come on that bridge, you come around that corner and its like you are in thin air. He was yelling, "Slow this thing down." A minute ago he had ground under him and now there is a hundred feet of nothing. He was scared and we were all laughing like hell.

Once in a while I'd take over as the foreman, when the regular guy was on vacation. I'd have to tell these guys, okay you do this and you do that. We had this one great big young guy. He was from Spokane. He was like six foot five tall and for some reason every time I told that guy to do something he'd be arguing and moaning. I'd say, "It isn't that big of a deal, just go over there and get it done."

One morning I go: "Okay, I got five jobs here, I got five of you guys. This is what we got to do today, what one would you like there big guy?" He says, " I don't know." I go okay you do this one then. I start at the other end of the line and told the other ones what to do. When I come to the big guy he had to go see if he could get this motor car going, tune up the carburetor. Here he is, "Why do I gotta do that?" I said, "Just get going, just do it." He came back about ten or fifteen minutes later, "Okay I got that job done". I said, "Don't you feel bad about all your bitching then." He said, "No, not really."

This big guy came to work with another guy from Spokane. This was just a little guy. After working with them for a two or three months I noticed every time that little guy told this big guy to go do something, he'd just go do it, no bitching, no nothing. I asked the little guy, "What have you got on that guy? When I tell him to do something he flares up and doesn't want to do it. But I noticed when you tell him he just goes and does it". He kind of got a little smile on his face and said, we just get along good you know. From then on when I had a job for the big guy, I'd just go over to the little guy and say, "Hey, will you tell him to go do this?" It took me a couple of months to figure that whole thing out.

One time I was bitching at the big guy, he said something and I started getting smart with him. I turned around and someone said watch out! The big guy was running at me. So I started running figuring a guy that big, he can't catch me. I turned around and a big old hand was about ready to grab me. I said, "Man why aren't you playing football?" It turned out he had bad knees.

I'm real happy to be retired.

# MIKE SHAWVER

Birthplace: Boise, Idaho 1957
Date of Service: April 4, 1977
Position Held: Skykomish Section Foreman

*One day a train was leaving Balmer Yard going south and I'm giv-ing a roll by, I always give trains roll bys. A roll by is when you stand and watch the train go by, inspecting it. That's a rule we have in our rulebook. We're supposed to give them a roll by.*

I started working my job here in Skykomish on the section in April of 1977. Marv was the roadmaster. Gary was the section foreman and Brad Pollow, Bob Pierce, Rudy Jonus, and Bill Christman were on the section when I hired out. I worked here in Skykomish on the section (district). Then I went to a steel gang. They were done with all the projects that they'd hired all the people for in Skykomish. I think they hired forty people for the work here. I think that there are only two of us left. Everybody else has since retired, quit or got fired. There was a lot of transi-tion back then because people tramped around the jobs instead of sticking to it.

I was hired because of who I knew. This is a weird story, how I wound up being hired on the railroad. The Gilmere family owned the Cascadia Restaurant. Rick Gilmere was good friends with the roadmaster up here. Rick's son Ronnie was supposed to get hired on the railroad in 1977 but on December 25, 1976

Mike Shawver with his 1932 Chevy truck on Railroad Avenue in Skykomish. Lindsay Korst photo

Ronnie Gilmere got killed on the highway down below Baring. I came up because I was really good friends with Ronnie and because I was a pallbearer at his funeral. Afterwards Rick approached me and asked me if I'd ever thought about going to work for the railroad? I was working in the woods in California with my brother at the time. I never even thought I'd go to work for the railroad. Rick, said, "Come back in March and I'll see that you get a job on the railroad". So I came back, went over to the depot and met the roadmaster. That's how I got hired on the railroad, purely a bad circumstance. It was unfortunate that it happened the way that it did.

The job they hired us for here in Skykomish was to sled the hill. The sled was a piece of equipment they stuck underneath the tracks and they pulled it with a couple of locomotives and it raised the track up. As it raised the track up you had a couple of guys with sledge hammers walking behind it and they knocked the bad ties off. Somebody was standing there with tie tongs pulling the bad ties out when they knocked them down on the ground. Then the sled let the track back down and all of the ballast was plowed out of the track. It was just regular ties and rail sitting there. Then you had guys behind putting ties back in. Then there were guys spiking them up and then one of jobs I had everyday was lining track. We lined the track by hand. There were seven guys on each side of the rail and you'd throw the rail one way or the other. You had somebody telling you which way to throw the rail, that was the job we had on the sled gang, was lining the track. I think I got stuck on that job because I was one of the younger kids. They didn't hire us for our brains, they hired us for our strength.

Then I went to the steel gang that was worse. Did a lot more hand work and it was really back breaking work there. I did that till September 26, 1977. Then I got laid off. I got called back to work in March of 1978 to a tie gang at Cashmere, putting in ties. Paul George was the foreman on that crew.

I got a ticket for "minor consumption" over at Cashmere when I was on the gang over there and living in the outfit cars. There was a lot of guys a lot older than me over there and they all had beer and they'd give me beer and one day I had a couple of beers and I walked across the railroad tracks there at Cashmere by the depot. Well the cop shop is right there. I didn't know that at the time. The Chelan County cop came over and said, "hey, let's see your ID, you're not old enough to be drinking this beer." There was a lot of that stuff back then when we had the outfit cars. Pretty wild times in those outfit cars.

I got stuck on a claw bar, they didn't have the modern equipment they have now. Now they have spike pullers that pull the spikes out hydraulically. When we did it they had a tie saw that cut the tie into three pieces but before the tie could get cut you had to pull the spikes out of it. I was assigned a claw bar. Gary

Kriewald. who was from Leavenworth had a claw bar on the other rail. We did a thousand ties a day and each guy pulled four spikes per tie, for a thousand ties. The claw bar was big and heavy. I did that for about a month then they said your doing such a good job on this we're going to put you behind a digger. The digger was like a giant rototiller. Once the tie was removed it churned up the ballast where the new tie was going to go in and somebody had to dig the hole out to stuff the tie in. So you got a number two shovel, you dug the hole for the tie to go in. One thing I remember very distinctly when I was behind that digger was this. The butt crane picked up the three pieces of tie that were cut from the tie saw and it threw them off to the side, Bill Webster was running the butt crane, I remember this, there was a dead dog laying alongside the track and it was all bloated up and that butt crane had pincher type jaws on it for picking up the ties and he reached over to grab that dog and it just popped like a balloon. I remember that. I don't know why.

I worked the tie gang most of that year then I came back here to Skykomish and worked on the section for awhile. Then I went to Monroe and worked on the section in Monroe. At Monroe you had Frenchy, I don't know what his real name was. You had Vern Wilkes, and Ruben Levi and there was another gentleman whose name I can't remember. They were called the hospital crew because all those guys were in their early sixties getting ready to retire. They were within a year or two of retirement. But they called them the hospital crew because they couldn't do a whole lot and they were close to the hospital.

I worked in Monroe till 1979 then I went back out on the steel gang. I worked steel gangs in '79, '80, '81, '82, '83, '84. and '85. I did a lot of different jobs there. I was a machine operator. Then I was on bigger machines, called pettibones. Thats the machine that moves the rail. I was on spikers, for spiking the ties as the rail was put in.. My last two years on the steel gang was assistant foreman. That job consisted of running back and forth six-thousand-four-hundred feet a day about twenty times telling the new hires what to do.

In 1986 I got on a tie gang I worked a tie gang we went over to Leonia, Idaho between Bonners Ferry, Idaho and Troy, Montana. We put in the first concrete ties that were put in on the Burlington Northern. That was quite a deal cause they do it all now with a big one piece machine called the P811. Back then we did it with regular tie gang machines and it took us forever to put the ties in. That was the first concrete ties they put in on the BN. I still have all of the paraphernalia they put out for celebrating that event.

In 1987 we came up to Scenic I got on Jimmy George's crew. We started putting in concrete ties coming down the hill from Scenic, down to Tonga. Stayed on Jimmy George's crew for quite a while. He was a good guy to work for. About the best foreman I think they ever had on the railroad. We worked in 1987 putting in ties. Then in 1988 we finished putting in ties from Tonga down to milepost 1751 which is down by Zekes. They called it the racetrack. We put in ties all the way to there. Then we went over the hill and put in ties from Bern all the way to Wenatchee. We put in a lot of concrete ties.

I bounced around quite a bit, more than I wanted to. I missed my kids growing up the first seven years. I would come home, Mayrene, my wife was telling a story the other day. I came home one week-end the kids come running in, "Mom, Mom there's a stranger at the door." It was a lot of traveling. I don't know how I raised three kids and did this job. Half the time I wasn't home. A lot of the guys I know on the railroad are divorced and married two or three times. Mayrene and I have known each other since we were kids. I was only nineteen when I hired out on the railroad. Nowadays they pay these guys to travel. We did it all on our own dime. We stayed in out-fit cars. We still had motor-cars and out-fit cars when I hired out. Now they put them up in motels and parade around in these hi-rail trucks.

These guys have no idea what it was like. You'd get on that motor car down here at Sky and you might go up the hill to a set off there and freeze your butt off all day working. No way to get back down because your stuck up there till you can get track time to come back down. You had motor-cars and outfit cars. They parked us down there at Nisqually in the outfit cars. It was on a high curve and they parked the outfit cars on the outside of the curve. Amtrak would go by about four times a night and it would just shake those outfit cars. You didn't know if they were coming in the front door or not. It was pretty interesting.

I was running the car mover that pulled the car topper around. The roadmaster asked if I could run the car topper (a material handling machine) and if I could bring a load of switch ties over, I told him not a problem I can do it. I didn't have a problem and I was getting off the machine at the end of the day and I slipped down into that car and got hurt. I was off for a year with that. I hurt my knee. Then I went back on the machines for a couple of years.

Then in 1993 I went to Seattle and worked in Seattle for two years. We built the bridge from the Art Institute across the track and down to the waterfront.

Another part of my railroad career is I was always in the right spot at the right time. One time in 1994. About January 4th of 1994 I was at my house here in Sky. I live right next to the railroad track. I could hear this godawful commotion coming down the tracks. This trains coming by and I can just hear this loud noise. I thought the whole thing was falling off the tracks. I ran to the front door and I looked out to see this boxcar, it was actually leaving the rail as it was hopping down the track because there was so much brake shoe build up on it. I had a portable radio at my house and I called them and I told them don't fear, but just stop when you can. Bob Pierce, who was the foreman at the time here in Skykomish, had his scanner on and he heard me call that train. We wouldn't of been surprised if it wasn't on the ground by the time we get down there to where they get it stopped." They got stopped about three quarters of a mile west of Skykomish. We drove down the back road to a private crossing and walked the track up to where we were looking for the car because I couldn't remember what car it was. We got up to the car and the brake shoe buildup was clear to the top of the flange of the wheel. They were literally leaving the rail as that wheel was coming around. So Bob and I got track chisels and a sledge hammer and chiseled that stuff off the wheel so they could take it back into town and set it out.

I was working in Seattle at that flagging job there at the North Portal. One day a train was leaving Balmer Yard going south and I'm giving a roll by, I always give trains roll bys. A roll by is when you stand and watch the train go by, inspecting it. That's a rule we have in our rulebook. We're supposed to give them a roll by.

While working in Edmonds this train goes by and all the hand brakes were tied on ten cars. Then when working in Seattle this empty car goes by but all the ribs were bouncing on the rail as it was going down the track. Somebody had dropped a container in it and nobody had caught it. All of the ribs were dragging on the track.

When the depot at Skykomish was still manned by Russ Kvam. I was going to work one morning, this was in1986 or early 1987. I was sitting at the crossing in my pickup watching a train go by and here goes a car by. The axle was cherry red. It had a hot box, that axle was glowing red. I backed up to the depot got in there and told them to stop that train, there was a hot box. They got it stopped and backed it into town and set the car out. Two hours later you could still fry an egg on that axle.

Mayrene and I are standing on our front porch watching. We're watching them back into the back lead here. The slack kept running in and out on the train and I no sooner said they're going to go on the ground than I see this box car bouncing on the ties. I ran back in the house and got my portable radio and told them to stop. By the time I got them to stop they had three cars on the ground It was a student engineer on the head end. The engineer was in the back watching the shove, I don't know where the conductor was They were making a rear end only pick up with the yard cleaner here at Skykomish. That track crowns right there at the crossing. Goes from pushing up to going back down on the east side. That slack was just running back and forth. They were just slamming it, sounded like they were switching in the yard.

I worked in Seattle in 1994, 1995. Bob Pierce was the section foreman here in Skykomish. Marv was the roadmaster. Marv was going to get promoted and he asked Bob if there was anything he could do for him? Bob took a lot of calls by himself because he couldn't get anyone to work up here at Skykomish. Bob said, "yea, put a job up here that Mike can hold, assistant foreman." "Mike can bid it in and I can have some relief up here." That's how I got to Skykomish in 1995. Been working at Skykomish ever since. I've been on the section for twenty years now without leaving. That's quite a stay for one time for somebody on the railroad.

About 2003 I got called at two in the morning by the dispatcher. He said, "a train had run over somebody in the Cascade Tunnel, everybody has been notified that needs to be notified, I need you to get up there." I get my boots on. The volunteer fire department in Skykomish has a siren and I never heard the siren go off. George Wahl was the Fire Chief here in Skykomish, so I called him at home. I told him, "George, the train ran over someone in the Cascade Tunnel and we need to get up there." George called Mike Janasz who was also a volunteer fireman. He also called it into his fire dispatch.

They raced up to Scenic and I met them up there. I secured track and time and George, Mike and I headed into the tunnel to look for this body that was in there.

I told them to bring a big blue tarp because we are probably going to be picking up pieces. The tunnel has twenty one bays in it. We get over half way through the tunnel twenty one being on the west end and bay one being on the east end. We get to bay nine and I see this lump in the middle of the tracks. I stopped about twenty feet away and the guy raises his head up and looks at us. His left foot was laying over the rail and it was cut off, right above the boot. So now we got to get the guy out. We've got to do a rescue on this guy.

Mike and George jump out of the truck and I have to work the doors to get him in the truck because there isn't enough room to get around the truck with the doors open. They get the guy up, they're getting ready to pack him to the truck and I hear this "Owwwww." The guy had started walking on his stump where his foot had been cut off. I said, "don't do that you'll get it to bleed. Well sure enough he got it to bleed. It wasn't bleeding really bad. The guy was drunk on his butt. He'd fallen off one train and the next train through was the one that had ran over him. He was a little skinny guy. Probably a good thing cause if he'd been a portly guy like me he wouldn't of made it. I just picked his boot up and threw it in the back of the truck with the foot in it cause there was nothing I could do with that. We got him in the truck. We got him out the east end of the tunnel, the aid car was waiting over there for us. We got him in the aid car and they gave me a garbage bag for his boot and foot, so I just put it in the aid car. They headed over the pass with him to bring him over to this side. They got to the top of the pass and the Monroe Medics met them and they transferred him and they hauled him to Monroe. They air lifted him to Harborview. The guy lived minus a foot.

I remember when we still had the motor cars we were going up the hill. We had a couple of new guys on the motor car with us, new hires. We were just below Milepost 1722. At that time the section foreman that was here was carrying a rifle because it was bear season. We were going up the tracks and sure enough there was a bear down over the bank. So he pulls on the old hand brake and stops the motor car and jumps off and he shoots this bear and it takes off down through the woods. He says, "Lets go" and I said, "I'm not leaving this motor car because I don't have a gun."

We had a welder named Bob. We had a couple of drama's below Milepost 1722. They call it the Corn Cut because that's where the they'd always dump a C-6 over Bob would go up there and sit on that rock wall, called the Bonneville Cut which was just below the Corn Cut. He'd sit up there and he'd watch for the bears going down there to feed on that corn. That happened about three times in my career where they'd dump those grain cars off in the same spot.

I remember a train we had that had a bad order car and they had to take it up to Scenic and set it out. They set the car out and then they put a fuse in the knuckle of the rear car and started backing the train down the hill there. The fuse forgot to tell them when to stop and they ran into their train and knocked three cars off the track.

I remember coming to work the work train. Roy was the conductor they were backing down the hill. There was a slid across the tracks. It was a little ways away but they were all in the caboose playing poker. I was just standing out on track watching the shove I was just a kid, I said, "Hey there's a slide across the tracks." Roy said, "Well dump the air." I said, "I'm not dumping the air this ain't my train." They dumped the air, and we didn't hit the slide.

I remember one time we were laying rail across the Foss River Bridge. Roy Keenan had a crawler crane on the flat car that was before they got all this modern machinery We were on the work train and they were working down hill putting in rail on the Foss River Bridge on the west end. We'd put in a rail then the work train would back down then we'd put in another rail and the work train would back down, well on one of the moves backing up they were told to stop and they didn't stop and the end of that flat car went off the end of the rail kerlunk! Roy was fit to be tied cause they'd run his flat car off the end of that rail. He said back up so the work train backed up and the wheels went back on the rail. Fortunately we didn't have a big disaster.

I worked on a lot of derailments up on the hill and down the hill and all over. We had one in Sultan. I don't remember what year it was A lowboy was going across the crossing at the Ben Howard Road. The lowboy hooked the rail and it tipped the rail out of the tie plates and the lowboy was gone. The hook wrecker train was coming back from a derailment in Spokane. They were coming through Sultan and they saw the track and they thought it was a track buckle which is a thermal misalignment where the sun heats up the rail and makes a kink. They thought that's what it was. But in fact it was the rail had been tipped up out of its spikes and rocked back down by that lowboy. Of course the lowboy was long gone. They didn't even know what had happened. The engineer dynamited the air and the hook (crane) ended up in the park down there in Sultan.

That's the second time I saw the hook on its side. The first time was up at Scenic in 1980. They ran an engine out of the tunnel with nobody on it. It left the tracks up here west of Scenic and hit the highway and didn't even leave a mark on the tracks when it left. No track damage. I think it was going over a hundred-and-twenty miles an hour when it left the rail. The crew had all jumped off of it in the tunnel. They were doing something to the engine in the tunnel and it started rolling on them and they couldn't get it stopped so they all jumped off and the engine just took off.

Didn't hit anyone on the highway. There was a van going by, and when the engine hit the ditch it sprayed that van with mud They said, "Oh we're going to save this engine" so they picked it up off the shoulder of the highway. I remember it sitting in the chain-up area at Scenic. Then they had to have the county in, cause that's a county road that goes in there at Scenic. Had to have the county beef up that bridge there so they could get it across the bridge to get it up to the tracks. They were going to put it back on the track. They had a big crane on the outside of the tracks and they had our railroad wrecker on the mainline on the other side of the tracks. They went to pick that engine up and they got it up in the air and for some reason it started swinging and it just flopped that railroad hook over on its roof in the ditch.

I've had a great career. I've shoveled more snow than I care to talk about. I love the railroad. I've got trains in my veins. I work for the railroad because they put the food on the table, I never turn anything down. The railroad takes care of me.

The railroad is going to miss my wife though. They aren't going to get all the cookies and pies and all that stuff she makes for the railroaders. She's always baking them something.

Mayrene says, "They swear he sleeps with his boots on, but he doesn't. He's there before they get there."

# NANCY MCLAUGHLIN DELACOUR

Birthplace: Columbus, Ohio, 1954
Date of Service: September 21, 1978
Positions Held: Carman Apprentice, September 1978 and Engineer, August 1980

*...it wasn't every trip you could appreciate the beauty of that run, but the Cascades were spectacular. I loved the towering peaks at Index and the miles of bloom-ing foxglove and daisies along the right of way. As you paralleled the Skykomish River, you could look down into deep Caribbean blue-green pools. This was a new paradise to me; mountains full of beauty and the history of old railroad stories. But I didn't much care for the Cascade Tunnel, the longest railroad tunnel in the US. It was eight miles of creepy darkness and isolation in a constant diesel haze.*

Most of my life I worked for the railroad. First for the Burlington Northern, which in 1970 had formed when the Great Northern and Northern Pacific merged, and later for the BNSF when the BN merged with the Atchison Topeka and Santa Fe.

I was born and raised in Ohio, then came out west for the adventure and mountains. When I came to Seattle in 1978 I had no job prospects, though I applied for art and teaching related jobs. I had an art degree and a secondary school teaching certification, but a teachers' strike was in effect, and substituting was not an option for me under those circumstances. While visiting a pay-what-you-can health clinic on Beacon Hill, my doctor told me about Alternatives for Women, a

Nancy McLaughlin Delacour started her railroad career as a carman doing a series of unpleasant outside jobs. After observing engineers sitting snug in a warm cab on rainy cold days she applied for engineer school. Her first day running a locomotive was in the Auburn Yard.

non-traditional job-finding service in the neighborhood. The idea of a man-sized income was very appealing to me, so I went straight there, filled out an application, and paid them five dollars.

A few days later I got a call from them saying there would be a meeting the next day with a woman "carman" from Balmer yard. There were several other women there when I arrived. We had already been scheduled for interviews and had no idea what a carman was! That same day, Nina, one of the other women at the meeting, and I drove together to King Street for our job interviews with the head of the mechanical department. I believe his name was Stuart. He asked me if I was going to go through all the training only to get married, pregnant, and then quit. He also wondered if I would be frightened in the dark when I walked through the train yard making train inspections. I had never in my life been in a train yard, but I also had never really been frightened by the dark or wanted to get married and pregnant, and I answered, "No, of course not!"

Within a week I had taken a physical exam and was driving up I-5 to Delta yard in Everett for my first day of work on the Burlington Northern railroad as a carman apprentice. There were three of us from that meeting working the day shift at Delta yard; Nina, Cindy, and I. They didn't really know what to do with us, and put Nina and me together with partners Marv and Jerry. We were doing light repairs on freight cars under a huge open shed with a metal roof, called the "rip track" or "rips". Mostly we were straightening ladders, handholds and sill steps, changing brake shoes and fixing doors. I pushed the big oxygen and acetylene torch cans around all day, and that first week my whole body was pretty sore. After breaking the handles on a couple of tenpound sledge hammers, I got them to give me an eight pounder which I could manage much better. Once we had learned a little of the routine, which for the most part was to appear very busy when the foreman came by and make whatever work we had last until quitting time, I was partnered up with Jerry, Nina with Marv, and Cindy with Tabby, a charming and funny Italian old-timer, affectionately called "Whopper".

Of course there were lots of men there who found our presence unnatural to say the least. There were also several young male "new hires" to take the pressure off. But the first few weeks we were given some tough tasks for our initiation. I was sent over to some log flats outside the coach house with a cutting torch. Those ancient cars were decked with oak that was rotted through and wet. My job was to cut the tops off the big decking bolts and pry the decking off with a bar. The torch blew bits of flaming rotten wood back at you while smoke blinded you. I learned pretty quickly, after setting my polyester pant legs on fire numerous times, that I needed one hundred percent cotton overalls!

Another initiation for us was the clean-out track. During a shortage of grain "hoppers" (grain freight cars) box cars were lined with cardboard sheets stapled to a crude wood frame inside. First the cars were hosed out and the old cardboard stripped. Then new cardboard was stacked inside and stapled to the walls of the cars. The stench of rotting grain was enough to knock you over. The cars were attached to a cable which the clean-out foreman could speed up or slowdown as needed. You would crawl into each box car as it was moving along, and he would see just how fast you could staple that cardboard as you got closer and closer to a very long jump to the ground. It was also amusing for some to see a woman's reaction to a man's idea of fun. There was a large mound of decomposing grain downhill from the clean-out track which was filled with rat tunnels. One particular jokester shoved a hose into one, and out came scampering hordes of rats!

One day Steve came up to me brandishing a hobo's battered frying pan he had found in the yard. "Take this and get back in the kitchen where you belong!" he shouted as he waved it at me, both of us laughing.

There were still friction bearing wheels in use back then, though they were being phased out and replaced by modern roller bearings. There was an oil shack which had huge vats of oil called "dope" which was added to the wheel box through a hinged door. Strips of old black rags were pulled out of the wheel boxes with a hook and tossed into a wheelbarrow, and new rags, called "waste" were crammed in. The "oiler" pushed his vat of slimy used black waste around the car shed, cursing us gals under his breath as he passed, coughing out the "c" word for emphasis. He was fairly easy to ignore, as he worked alone and rarely talked with anyone as he made his rounds.

Of course I was young and there was lots of fun to be had. Some of the most memorable times were when we gathered around the fire pots, fifty- gallon drums full of smoldering wood scrap, for work breaks. We warmed our hands, smoked cigarettes and told jokes until the foreman came by to shoo us back to work. That winter was particularly cold, and Delta yard was just above the Snohomish River. On many foggy mornings everything was covered in a thick frost when we got to work. Sometimes we would sit on top of the cars and our overalls would stick to the cold steel.

I became close friends with some of the guys my age, and occasionally we hung out after work together at the Copper Penny in Everett, where they gladly cashed our paychecks on payday. I fell in love with Ted, and in the spring of 1979 we rented a little house above Columbia beach on Whidbey Island and took the ferry to work and back every day.

In late 1979 we were furloughed. Railroad unemployment was around $50 a week, so our fun had to be cheap. We used to row out on the sound in a leaky wooden boat someone had abandoned. We caught hake and lingcod and set crab traps. At Christmas we made tree ornaments out of driftwood tied with red and green curling ribbon, and a star of cardboard and aluminum foil for a topper.

We moved back to the mainland when I got a job at ColorLab, a photo lab in Edmonds, as a retouched. I drew with dye and colored pencils directly onto the prints to whiten teeth, cover blemishes and eyeglass glare. Sometimes I painted background colors over a relative in a group photo who had lost favor. The pay was not great, but it helped a little, and Ted went back to work as a cement finisher, his default job.

I decided to apply for locomotive engineer training. Many cold and rainy days on the rip track I had watched the train crews out in the yard. The switchmen tromped around soaking wet through lake-sized puddles, while the engineer sat snug in the engine cab, and I thought, "I want THAT job." I was discouraged by my supervisor when he got my "This Way Up" application. He said I should think about becoming a car foreman if I wanted a promotion, but I thought that seemed unlikely as carmen were obviously being phased out. After the big layoffs, Delta car shop was like a ghost town. One day I had to go to the car foreman's office to pick up some paper work for my engineer application. I saw the stacks of one inch plywood we had spent a month measuring and drilling to re-side a fleet of wood-chip cars. They were left outside in the rain to warp and rot.

I called every few weeks and found I had not been included in the next class. But I kept calling, and finally in April of 1980 I discovered I was enrolled in an engineer's class, but had missed the first few weeks of hostler training at Interbay roundhouse. I was annoyed that they hadn't called me, as that set my seniority date behind everyone else in the class. But I was excited to be in engineer training. I was going to buy a real bed to replace my old mattress and box springs on the floor. My bookshelves were built from shipping crates I had scavenged from the rip track. I was more than ready for an upgrade, ready to make some money.

Our class flew to St. Paul Minnesota for training, and on the first day we were told under no circumstances were we to go down to the river at night, the "river rats" that lived there were sure to roll you for your wallet. On our first morning of class, Tom showed up an hour late with a black eye and swollen nose. We all knew what had happened. We spent a month watching unbearably dull slide shows narrated by Art, "You, as a locomotive engineer..." with Tom sniffing and snorking in the background as his sinuses drained. I had no hands on experience to help me through, but I somehow managed to pass all the preliminary tests and we headed back to Seattle for on the job training. While we were marooned in St. Paul, Mt. St. Helens had erupted in Washington, and ash was falling all over our home state. Luckily for us, it had blown mostly to the east and western Washington had escaped the heaviest fallout.

At first we were sent to different yards all over the division, ideally to familiarize ourselves with the territory for our rapidly approaching debut on the engineer's extra board. The BN was short of engineers and wanted us trained and ready to go by the end of August.

My first day with a train crew was on the Maltby Turn. We were on duty at around 6:00 a.m. at Interbay (former GN yard Seattle), got our engine out of the roundhouse and onto our train, made an air test and were on our way within the hour. I wondered what the hurry was until we parked our train on the siding at Edmonds. It was time for "coffee". We scrambled up a well-worn and steep trail to a local bar, and beers and drinks were ordered by the crew, though it was a bit early for me so I decided on breakfast instead. My engineer, John, had a noticeable limp, and I found out later that he had injured his leg in a serious train accident.

My first day at Tacoma yard was also an eye opener. On duty at 7:00 a.m., our switchman, who looked to me to be one hundred years old, had tried numerous times, unsuccessfully, to step up on the engine's front step. He finally was attached, but as we were moving along he began to sway and fell off onto the ground. He was unhurt, and looked up red-faced and bewildered, as drunk as a skunk. The switch foreman eventually shuffled him off somewhere to sleep it off, and we resumed without him.

The first time I ever ran an engine was at Auburn yard. The crew was playing pitch (the card game) in the shack and did not want to be interrupted. They were supposed to add a caboose to a train in the yard. Besides the regular crew, there was a new-hire switchman trainee who had no radio and no idea how to give hand signals, and me. They sent us out alone and we somehow found the caboose, tied it onto the train and returned without getting lost or running through any switches. It must have taken at least an hour.

I "familiarized" one day on the Oly (Olympia) Turn, a twelve hour local on duty in Centralia. My engineer, "Big Jim", let me take over running the train after we left an industry track where we had spotted some cars. Back on the main line, I was gradually increasing the throttle, just as we were instructed in the BN Air Brake and Train Handling manual. Jim came over to my side of the cab and slammed the throttle into the eighth notch, bellowing, "Don't let fear hold you back!"

There was a big push to train our class to work the "GN hill"; the Cascade Division territory between Seattle and Wenatchee. There were not enough engineers to cover the extra board, and we needed to be "mountain grade" qualified. I was assigned to train with one engineer for about four weeks, and I showed up at the Interbay round house for my first trip east over the mountains. There in the register room was Ted Cleveland, my new hoghead mentor. He looked at me like I was the last thing he wanted to see that day. I said, "I'm your student engineer," and he said, "I don't take students! I told them no students!" I had been assigned by our road foreman to his turn in the pool. He didn't seem too happy about that, but after quite a few minutes of taking notes and writing in the register he came over to me and said, "If you're going to be my student, you had better be the best damn engineer out there when I'm through with you!", which I took to mean he was giving in just a little!

He had me running the trains right away, and was a stickler for every detail. There was a lot to remember as far as learning the territory, but I also was just figuring out where all the handles were on the control stand! It was an intense time, full of mistakes and triumphs. It was midsummer, and one trip Ted suggested we get some peaches while we were laying over in Wenatchee. His wife Nancy was planning to do some canning. I love peaches, especially Red Havens, so I bought a box too. We had seven or eight boxes, and loaded them up on the lead unit when we came to work. They were stacked on the walkway in front of the engine nose, just clear of the steps on both sides.

Our trip back to Seattle was uneventful until we got to Monroe. There was a huge dump truck loaded with rock in the middle of the tracks on E. Main Street. The crossing gates both in front and behind were lowered. I had my hand on the brake handle, thinking I had better "dump the air", when before I knew it, Ted had jumped up from the other side of the cab and pulled me down to the floor, slamming the brake handle into emergency and hitting the deck himself. A few seconds seemed like eternity as we waited for impact... but nothing happened, and we came to a stop several hundred feet beyond the crossing. Thankfully the truck driver had the sense to gun it through the crossing gate in time to clear the tracks, and we all were safe! I went out the fireman's door to check on the peaches, and there they sat, while my heart raced, rosy and perfectly stacked, like nothing at all had happened!

I learned that day that this could be a dangerous job, and Ted was looking out for us both. I couldn't have asked for a better mentor, though his intensity did scare me a little from time to time.

One night we were struggling up the hill eastbound and had lost a lot of momentum, and we were still short of Scenic. We probably were underpowered for our train tonnage, with no "helpers", which was somewhat common back then. Ted went back to see if all the trailing units were working at full power. We were probably down to fifteen miles per hour at that point. I suddenly noticed a sparkling mist in the headlight beam, like nothing I had ever seen before. A few minutes later, Ted burst into the cab behind me, yelling, "Turn the damn sanders off when I'm back there, you know better than that!", to which I said, "The sanders aren't on...", and we realized we were looking at the ash fall from an eruption of Mt. St. Helens.

I was also lucky that Ted was willing to jump to my defense when needed. One trip east our conductor, Chuck, had experienced a particularly rough caboose ride. We had no idea there was any problem at all, but as I was registering our arrival at the Wenatchee yard office, Chuck came storming up to me screaming, "What in the hell were you doing up there, that was the worst ride I've ever had in my life, you nearly killed me back there!" I was really shocked for a second, as I had never had a rough ride complaint before, and had not been screamed at like that since I'd left my parents' house. I said he should have called me on the radio and told me what was happening so I could make adjustments. I couldn't do anything about it now. He kept yelling about it and Ted overheard him. He got right in Chuck's face and chewed him out good. I learned we had an empty flat car ahead of the caboose that had a long "bad order" drawbar (coupler), and if I had known that, I could have tried to bunch the train slack when we stopped and slowed, which would have softened the caboose run-ins. But if you don't know it's happening, there's not much you can do. I also learned that people on the railroad can be hot-tempered jerks, and you have to be ready to come right back at them, or they'll think they can push you around. An animosity between engineers and trainmen was part of railroad history, lots of fights, stony silence and mutual hatred to live down. That culture was gradually fading, but some traces of it remained, and engineers would take no crap from trainmen!

Many of the eastbound trains out of Seattle were called at night, to avoid daytime Amtrak trains and westbounds, and it was often very late (or very early) when the trains were switched and ready to go east from Seattle. So it wasn't every trip you could appreciate the beauty of that run, but the Cascades were spectacular. I loved the towering peaks at Index and the miles of blooming foxglove and daisies along the right of way. As you paralleled the Skykomish River, you could look down into deep Caribbean blue-green pools. This was a new paradise to me, mountains full of beauty and the history of old railroad stories. But I didn't much care for the Cascade Tunnel, the longest railroad tunnel in the US. It was eight miles of creepy darkness and isolation in a constant diesel haze. You could ask for a longer "flush" from the dispatcher if you were closely following another train into the tunnel, but you risked being held to wait for another train, or lined into a siding later in the trip if the dispatcher didn't think you were going to get "over the road". After I was promoted to engineer that fall, I worked quite a few trains east on the extra-board, but didn't have the seniority or the desire to mark to the East End pool. It was good to get the experience up there, as so many things can go wrong so quickly on a steep grade. The BN powers that be figured if you could qualify on the "hill", you could work a train anywhere on the division.

Another territory we had to qualify on was the north end, between Seattle and Vancouver BC. I was assigned to work with an engineer on the pool, though we only made about four or five round trips north before I took the final test and began working the extra board. I worked with many engineers who taught me valuable lessons I was grateful to have learned before I was on my own, and inevitably I sometimes learned what NOT to do. The engineer I was assigned to on the north end was memorable for many reasons, not the least of which was his cheap cigar habit, which filled the cab with a constant sickly sweet haze. On one of our first trips together, while we were doubling our train together and getting the air tested, we chatted. I found out he had a cabin in the mountains somewhere in eastern Washington, and some kids as well. During the conversation he was drinking numerous cups of coffee from his thermos and getting more and more adamant about those kids. "They go up there to use the place and they don't even sweep the goddamn floor!" he shouted, and I finally realized that what he was drinking from his thermos was a little stronger than coffee. Shortly after we left the yard he fell sound asleep, and didn't wake up till we got to Vancouver. I was left to run the train without his expertise, which was fine by me.

And so it was, I felt my way back and forth from Seattle to Vancouver by reading the Timetable/Special Instructions as I went. We had long stops at the border for Customs inspections, so when I wasn't trotting over to the convenience store to buy a sandwich or more cheap cigars for my engineer, I used the time to try to memorize the speed restrictions ahead. After a few trips the road foreman in charge of our engineer's class, Marty, met us at the roundhouse register room to ask how I was doing. My mouth dropped open as my engineer said, "Oh she's doing fine, but I think she needs more practice." Of course he was absolutely right, but I knew this didn't come from any observation on his part!

Before we knew it and before we were ready, our class had taken the engineer's exam and I was "set up" to the engineer's extra board. We were called the "five month wonders", not "hogheads", as you had to earn the "hogger" title with your reputation and experience. I admit I was somewhat terrified, but reassured myself that I would be cautious and learn the ropes on the job, which was exactly what I had already been doing.

My very first call was for the Kirkland Turn, on duty at Delta yard in Everett. The regular engineer was on vacation, and I was assigned to the job for at least a week. When I walked into the yard office the crew took one look at me and they were not happy. "Who are you?" the conductor demanded, and when I said I was their engineer he responded, "Are you qualified on this hill?" meaning the hill between Snohomish Junction and Woodinville. Of course at the time I had no idea this hill existed, but I told him the BN considered me qualified because I had been tested and qualified in mountain grade territory on the GN hill. He answered, "Well I'm calling the dispatcher to tell him what's going on here, and have him put the wrecker on standby..." One of the brakemen was staring at my work boots. They were heavy duty Red Wings my dad had sent me from Ohio. Back then engineers wore regular street shoes to work; they hadn't yet required engineers to wear steel-toed work boots. "You better take some of the leather off those boots and sew it on the seat of your pants!" he said laughing.

It took quite a while to get used to switching cars, as I had almost no yard experience at all. They had sent us to several switching yards during training, but with only one or two shifts, each at different locations, I never got to know the crews well enough to get much practice running the engine. Plus I had never been a switchman, so I had only the faintest idea what the crews on the ground were doing. The Kirkland Turn was a great learning experience, as we switched for many hours on that job. I wondered to myself, "What on earth are they doing, going back and forth, kicking cars right and left?!", as I could only see the head brakeman's hand signals, not where the cars were going.

There were other things to adjust to as well, such as the many different types of controls in the engine cabs. I had never run an old EMD switcher before, and the air brake valves were completely different from any I had worked with during training. I spent the time my crew was gathering up the switching lists for the day sitting on the engine, playing around with the brake valves to see how they responded. An old 6BL brake valve has no maintaining feature, this I had learned in "hoghead" school in St. Paul, so once the air brakes are applied the train air gradually leaks down. This can over-apply the brakes on the train. I had to figure out how to overcome that by making an air reduction, "lapping" the valve by bringing it back to its original position, while turning the regulating valve down to the exact same pressure. This would keep the train line charged to a consistent pressure, and avoid an unwanted air loss which would slow the train too much. It was really important to do this on a long hill, as releasing the train and resetting the brakes numerous times leaves you with little or no brakes at all, sometimes not even enough for an emergency application. I had never used a 6BL brake valve before my first day on the Kirkland Turn, nor had I ever been on that territory south of Snohomish Junction.

I was on the job for just one week, and most of that time I experienced the distressing feeling that newbies often do; that you have no idea what you are doing. There was a switch at the bottom of the hill which had to be lined for our route toward Woodinville. The first day I stopped our little train of about twenty cars too soon, about four or five car lengths from the switch. This was a fail because the brakeman had to walk too far to the switch. The second day I stopped too late. It was a facing point switch, so no damage was done except to my pride when we had to back up a few car lengths to line ourselves the right way. On the third day, and for the rest of that week, I got our train stopped right at the switch. There were no comments from the crew regarding any of these events, but I think when their regular engineer returned from vacation they were glad to have survived the week unscathed!

The winter of 1980 was a bad one for the economy, and though there had been a shortage of engineers that summer, in the fall the extra board was cut repeatedly as there were fewer and fewer jobs to fill. Eventually I was "bumped" from the extra board, but was allowed by union contract to work as a fireman during a surplus of engineers in Seattle and other terminals in our region. Some of the engineers in our class went to work in Vancouver Washington, some went to other locations, but I had enough seniority to stay in Seattle. I was still living in a little rental house in Lynnwood with Ted K, and commuting mostly to Interbay, Seattle. Working as a fireman was a cut in pay, but it was also an opportunity to learn a lot.

I ended up firing on the South End Pool, between Seattle and Portland. It was the best paying pool job in Seattle, but most of the trips were 10 hours or longer in each direction, and sometimes we expired our twelve hours of service and had to be relieved by another crew wherever we ended up. At that time a relatively new federal law required that no member of a train crew could be on duty more than twelve hours. Often we had to wait for another crew to be called and driven to where we had expired our hours of service and "died". It could make for a very long day or night. Lots of old timers talked about the good old days when you could work for sixteen hours and make much more money. Twelve or fourteen hours were plenty for me!

Thinking back on it now, this was a unique time when I got to know so many engineers, see them in action on the job, and hear their stories. Not everyone had this opportunity, as they had little or no time firing. Today, you go right from engineer training to working with a single conductor. I had the advantage of working with three trainmen on the crew as well, and had to learn the train handling that hopefully kept their coffee from spilling on the caboose!

While I worked as a fireman I saw everything from screaming-in-your-face battles between engineers and trainmen to sheepish resignation when our train broke in two on the Nisqually bridge, and once on the mainline at Auburn yard. Fortunately, that was three different engineers! I learned what was best to do and best not to do, both invaluable lessons. But even more memorable were the characters I got to know. It is impossible to describe how varied and unique railroaders are, you would have to experience it for yourself.

Many of the older Northern Pacific engineers on the South End were working as firemen toward the end of the steam era. I am sure they believed me incapable of stoking a firebox, and they may have been right. But I tried to make it a point to do any physical work that came our way, such as connecting hoses and cables when we were picking up engines enroute, or as it happened at Auburn yard, carrying a knuckle threaded on a broomstick from the yard office to the mainline with our very cranky conductor, Freddie. He was not generally warm toward engineers, but he treated me like gold after that!

I could tell a lot of stories about the "away from home terminal" life, and you can probably imagine it was a novel experience for a girl from the suburbs of

Ohio. We stayed at the Portland Travel Lodge on Burnside Street. Across the street was the Union Jack's tavern, where crews went for sandwiches, drinks, and entertainment. All the train crews knew that "after hours" you could knock on the door and you would still be served, usually along with a small crowd of rails. The first time I went there, I was told it was a great place for sandwiches. I was surprised to see a burned-out looking stripper, completely naked, dancing in a dark smoky haze beyond the tables. I didn't go there often, but the sandwiches were fantastic, several inches thick with meat and fixings, and there was always a rail at the bar to talk to. There was also a drag club up the street, so if you happened to be out at closing time, you would be treated to a parade of colorfully dressed queens sporting five inch heels and feather boas.

As a fireman on the South end pool I had made pretty good money. I was able to save enough for a down payment on a small two-bedroom house on 69th Street in Ballard, and Ted and I moved there in the fall of '81. It was great to be so close to work, only minutes away from Interbay roundhouse. Ted was working as a mechanic at Pacific Iron and Metal. Just days after we moved into the house I had an eye-opening experience. Ted was at work and I had just returned from a trip to Portland of several days. While I was in the bedroom getting unpacked, a loud bang and whoosh sound came from the kitchen. I came running out to find water shooting from the cabinet under the sink. The cold water supply had popped off and water was pouring all over

the floor. The owners had shown Ted where the water shutoff was, but not me. I ran down the basement stairs where water was already dripping through the floor and flowing toward the moving boxes that had not been unpacked. I ran from the washer and dryer to the garage looking for that shutoff. Finally I saw a valve near the front of the house beyond the downpour and our boxes, and turned it off. I wonder to this day what would have happened if I hadn't gotten home at that moment. I knew right then that being a homeowner was going to be an interesting challenge!

I loved working the road and I knew I was lucky to be working as a fireman. I usually ran the train at least half the trip, or the entire trip if the engineer wanted me to. But I began regretting all the time I was away from home, and the many hours sitting in hotel rooms seemed to be adding up. My life seemed to be passing me by; I longed for time with my friends, time to travel, hike in the mountains, and do my artwork. And I wasn't even dealing with the unpredictability of the extra board. Engineers' pool calls came somewhat regularly, and if you kept track of how many trains and crews were ahead of you, you could usually predict within a reasonable number of hours when you were going to work. Eventually the economy worsened and I couldn't hold a fireman's job on the road anywhere in the Seattle terminal. My next choice was to hire on a yard job. I thought the worst thing that could happen was to have to work in the yard!

First I marked up close to home on a day switcher at Balmer yard, Interbay. I worked mostly with old-timers who taught me a lot. I had very little experience handling cars without air brakes, especially in a yard built on a hill like Balmer. At the north end, in order to roll a car into a track it barely needed to be moving. At the south end, you had to get a good run at it to kick a car or shove a heavy cut uphill into the clear. And if you were pulling a big track out onto the south lead, you better be going slow enough to stop with just the engine brakes or you would be shoved by the weight of the cars right through a red signal on the dock lead at Galer street. I also learned to run the hump engine, which had a speed governor to keep the cars rolling at walking speed. Every day it seemed that hump control had a different personality and never worked the same way. It was all about keeping the slack bunched as each car crested the hump so the switchman could pull the "pin", or operating lever, to separate the cars. If the slack ran out, the pin lifter jammed in the knuckle and wouldn't budge. If you got going a little too fast, you'd hear, "That'll do! Now give me the pin!" So you'd shove for a little slack and then have to adjust the hump control all over again. At least while you were humping cars you didn't have to hang out the window looking for signals, the radio was used until you got close enough to the tower to see hand signs.

Soon I was bumped out of Balmer yard and was firing on an afternoon "goat" (switcher) at Stacy yard, just south of the King Dome. Even though the Northern Pacific merger with the Grea Northern was long past, it still felt like a different railroad there. I started firing for Ray Terlicker on job 235, the afternoon lead job. He was one of a group of NP railroaders who grew up in the infamous little town of Lester on Stampede Pass. They had lived and breathed the railroad life as it came through their town. From some of the stories I'd heard, it could get pretty rough! Ray was a man of very few words, so when he spoke it had true force of meaning. One night after I had shoved and spotted ten or fifteen cars into Ash Grove Cement, I had to pull a ten car cut of heavy loads back to the yard. It was uphill and always slippery, so you had to have the sanders on and the throttle in the eighth notch to keep from stalling. I had watched Ray do it before. You had to avoid car traffic on E. Marginal Way and train traffic at a UP interlocking, so it was a bit dicey at times. As we chugged out of the hole he looked over at me and said, "Someday you're going to be the best engineer out here." I never forgot that unexpected compliment, and it kept me literally on track, trying to do my best work.

There were some real characters at Stacy, like Timmy, who thought bathing and cleaning his work clothes meant slapping another coat of Old Spice powder under his arms. He was badly used by a couple of young women who claimed to be "friends", and always showed up in the parking lot on payday. And there was "Dirty Ernie", who lived in a flop house in Georgetown and spent his vacations at questionable nudist camps, always wanting to show everyone his X-rated photos when he returned. (I gladly declined.) Later he lived in his battered old camper in the parking lot at Stacy and West Seattle yard. He was known to be extremely generous, always giving his extra cash to those less fortunate in his neighborhood. And there was "The Crocodile", Dan, an ornery switch foreman who routinely barked at his engineers, "Don't think, just watch the Golden Arm!" One day when an extra board switchman showed up to work on our crew, he ignored him completely until it was time to go out the door to work. Suddenly he snapped, "WELL, are you gonna get on the goddam TIME SLIP or AREN'T you?!" Back then there was an odd method of both ignoring and hazing new-hires. The thinking was it would get them on their toes and prepared to watch, learn, and do what they were told without question. Or maybe it was just the "cycle of abuse", and that was how they were treated when they first hired out. Over the years Dan and I became good friends, and I still have a pair of antique ski poles he gave me. He had been an avid skier as a kid, but like many others, working as a switchman meant giving up sports that might cause injury and affect his ability to bring a paycheck home to his family.

I didn't see it coming, but I began to like working in the yard with shorter hours, five days a week, with two scheduled days off. When business picked up and I was able to work as an engineer again, I only worked the extra board until I was able to mark to a night tramp (yard and industry switcher) at Stacy. Suddenly I was working with people my own age. I made some great friends, many who I still enjoy knowing thirty years later. Ted and I had split up, but I didn't date guys I knew from work. I always thought it would be too awkward when we split up.

Working at night was usually interesting, as there were a lot of characters living under the viaduct and near the tracks along the waterfront. Many nights we took a train up the waterfront to Balmer, and then brought another train back to

Stacy. There were several people living in a crates and boxes draped with tarps where the tracks crossed S. King Street and S. Jackson. It was somewhat protected from rain, as the viaduct was directly overhead. One of the crates was so close to the tracks it barely cleared passing engines and cars. There were people wandering the streets that you would not see during daylight hours. Big wharf rats skittered around as the trains came through. One night I was going by the crate closest to the tracks with a small train headed for Balmer, engine bell ringing deafeningly, when a man suddenly stood up out of the crate and was clipped on the shoulder by my engine. He spun around and fell, luckily away from the train. I put the train in emergency and stopped pretty quickly, as we were only moving at about eight or nine miles per hour. I hurried back to find him sitting on the ground with his head hanging down. "Are you OK"?!!" I asked, to which he said, "I'm fine, I'm fine," and I said, "Do you realize you just got HIT BY A TRAIN?!" which he did not quite seem to comprehend. "Are you SURE you are alright?" I asked again, and he said, "Yeah, yeah, I'm OK." I called the yardmaster on the radio to tell him what had happened, and we continued on our way to Balmer. The roving yardmaster drove up from Stacy to check on the man who had been hit. He was nowhere to be found, so he asked another fellow, "Where is the man who was just hit by a train?" to which he replied, "Oh, he went uptown to get a bottle!" I am so grateful that during my entire career, I never was involved in a fatal or serious crossing injury, which is somewhat rare for an engineer.

The waterfront yard transfers were almost always made at night, as there was so much auto traffic on the crossings during daylight hours. One summer night we were headed south to Stacy light engine (engine only) after taking a train to Balmer. It was about 2:30 in the morning. I noticed a truck rushing down Alaskan Way, trying to catch up with us. As they paralleled us, they slowed down, and four girls riding in the truck bed simultaneously pulled up their shirts and flashed me!

When they saw that I was a woman they all started laughing, and so did I. I told the guys on my crew sitting on the left side of the cab, "You would love to have seen what I just saw!" Most crews never really liked making that waterfront trip though, because you never knew how long it would take you to get back. The freight tracks were removed in 1982 and until ten years ago, a tourist trolley ran up and down the waterfront.

During those night shifts at Stacy I sometimes worked with women as well. At that time there were a few female engineers and several female switchman, most of them working nights or on the extra board. They were fairly new and low in seniority like me, and it was fun and refreshing to have other women around to talk to.

As time marched on I marked to afternoon shifts when I could, and I preferred working at Balmer because it was so close to home. I ended up working quite a bit at South Seattle yard as well, which was a "piggy back" switching yard for conventional flatcar truck trailer rigs, and a few locals like crew 9 and 10. Later it was a container/stack train yard, as it had long storage tracks, especially on the east side of the mainline. Occasionally we had to spot cars at the nearby Boeing facility or at Manufacturer's Minerals. One afternoon we were on Main 2 at the hand throw crossover at Black River, ready to cross over to Main 1 to get back to the south end of the yard. We had the dispatcher's permission to line the switches for our movement. Luckily my switchmen lined the switches and stood near them, and as per the five minute rule we waited. Just thirty seconds later a southbound train came around the curve on Main 1 at about forty-five miles per hour, and there was just enough time for BJ to say on his portable radio, "Jerry, line the switch." And he did, thank God, so we all survived to be here today. That train was lined right toward me and my engine until that moment. The train continued straight past us on main one. When the engineer saw us he put the train into emergency and came to a stop, but the engines were along way past us before they did. We called the dispatcher and found out he had forgotten the southbound train was still north of Tukwila, so he should NOT have given us permission to line the crossovers. The train had already passed the last signal when we lined the switches, so their crew had no warning that the switches had been lined in front of them. I became a true believer in the five minute rule. That portion of track has since been upgraded to CTC with timed automatic switches and dispatcher controlled crossovers.

There was a time in 1992 when all I could hold with my seniority was the extra board. I made some road trips to Portland and Wenatchee with the new (to me) ETDs. The loss of cabooses was a major change, and we relied on info relayed to "Mary", a receiver on the engine, by radio signals transmitted from the "end of train device" or "Fred". That was the beginning of the end for four-man train crews.

The railroad can undeniably be a risky place to work, evidenced by the injuries and even deaths of people I came to know. I had a few close scrapes myself, once during the simple act of walking across some tracks at Stacy to get to my engine. I was preoccupied with my thoughts and didn't see a cut of flat cars drifting silently toward me as I crossed. I stepped back out of the way just inches in the clear, so close I felt the air movement as the car passed.

One particular fatality changed my outlook on life in a personal, self-centered way. I was working the afternoon hump job at Balmer when Bob was killed. He was working the west lead trim job in the deep field, and his engine had pulled a long cut of auto-racks out onto the lead. Some loaded hoppers rolled down from another track and slammed into the auto-racks. I was on my engine near the top of the hump, and had a good view of the empty auto-racks tipping over onto their sides just a few tracks east of us. My foreman burst into the engine cab saying,

"Bob's dead!" and my first thought was that the cars had tipped over on him. But when I got off the engine I could see him lying on the ground where he had been run over by the hopper cars, which I believe he had been trying to stop by setting handbrakes. It was a horrible sight, but what struck me the most was the top of his head, his long gray hair and ponytail. He always wore a hat and I had never really seen his hair. It somehow made him seem so vulnerable and mortal. An hour earlier he had been sitting with us in the lunchroom, distant in his thoughts which were probably about something that didn't matter. I was thirty-seven years old, and still not sure what my life was for.

It was a sad and terrible afternoon; we all came inside to the lunchroom to try to put together what had happened. There was a lot of disbelief and shock, head shaking and crying. Soon there were media helicopters circling over the yard. To this day I hate the sound of helicopters. Work was put on hold for the day and they sent us all home.

Against all of my own rules, I had been dating Jim Delacour, switchman and UTU #845 president for several months. He had pulled a fast one on me and suddenly gone to Europe with an old girlfriend from California. I had been getting letters from him regularly, which I had no interest in reading. For some reason he called me from Europe the night of Bob's death. I told him what had happened and he scheduled a flight back right away. His position in the union would mean he would be an active party in the investigations that would ensue from the incident. Eventually the investigation I was called to attend was cancelled, and as far as I know, no individuals were ever singled out for blame.

While I was deciding what to do about my so-called life, I went on a solo backpacking trip in the Cascades to Foss Lakes. It was raining hard and the sky was churning as I set up my tent at Malachite Lake. That night I dreamed my mom came to my house and said, "You have to get rid of all this old stuff so you can bring in something new." I dreamed the sky was divided in half, one side dark with heavy clouds, the other brilliant blue. The clouds were receding. When I woke, the morning sun was beating down on my tent and the sky was clear.

It took a while, but eventually Jim and I got back together. About a year later, we got married in a small family ceremony at Hiram Chittenden Locks. Jim had a house on Vashon Island, which was a somewhat difficult commute by ferry, so we lived at the house in Ballard. Our daughter Rachel was born at Ballard Swedish hospital on October 3rd, 1993. Of course everything changed after that. Luckily we were able to work opposing shifts, and didn't have to have a babysitter care for her until she

**Jim Delacour**

was about a year old. An old friend's mom, Carrie Schwalier, came to our house and took care of Rachel whenever our shifts overlapped.

We bought a vacation property lot at Copalis Beach, and our new neighbor's architect, Charlie Davis, designed us a house. I drew pictures of my dream house and he came up with a perfect plan. We acted as our own contractor and sub-contracted the initial structural work. Jim put together the plumbing, and I did all the electrical work after the wires had been pulled. We were busy every weekend and had to struggle to keep our days off together. Jim worked as a hostler, as the "crew consist agreement" had eliminated so many switchmen and trainmen. The yard crews were just two switchmen and an engineer. Many road crews were engineer and conductor only. Jobs got pretty tight.

In early summer of '94 I took a short medical leave, and Rachel and I stayed out at the coast in our old 1968 Silver Streak trailer. Jim came out on his days off. It was wonderful to see the framework of the house taking shape. I remember one night, after tucking Rachel into bed, I carried a chaise lounge chair up a ladder to our still wall-less main floor. In my room without walls I watched horseback riders canter by in the distance and the sun go down into the sea. I felt like the luckiest person on earth, and maybe I was.

When the tri-county commuter system was voted into existence in 1996, Jim was very busy working to acquire these new job opportunities for our division. Trains were planned to run in and out of Seattle between Everett and Tacoma, and Sound Transit had to be convinced that the BNSF crews were the best option for running those trains. It was odd how many of our union members resisted the idea or just had a lack of interest. They weren't seeing the big picture of future job elimination, and any jobs we could get would naturally be to our advantage. There was also a tradition of mistrust for anything new that was presented to us, as the unions had lost so many members, as well as the power to even hold their ground on so many contract issues. Thankfully the jobs eventually were awarded to the BNSF crews, and after many track system upgrades throughout the Seattle corridor, Sound Transit commuter service began in 2000. Jim was one of the first BNSF conductors to work the train between Tacoma and Seattle. Monday through Friday he got up before the rest of the city and drove to Tacoma. He had a midday layover in Seattle, which he was able to spend at home. Then he worked the afternoon Sounder to Tacoma and drove home or took the bus back to Seattle. He usually was home by 7:30 or 8:00 p.m. With the I-5 traffic we have today, this would just be impossible. I was unable to hold a job with weekends off, but I did manage to work days for a while, taking Rachel to morning daycare before school and picking her up from after-school daycare when I got off work. By the time Jim got home, Rachel and I had already had dinner and were working on homework or winding down from the day. His dinner was waiting and ready to reheat in the microwave. Little did we know that things were about to change quickly for the worse on the work front.

We had heard talk of the remote control engines (RCLs) being used in yard service, but were surprised when they came so quickly and extensively to our division. The Union Pacific had recently begun to use them in their yards, and it seemed the BNSF now had to keep up with the Joneses. What it meant for engineers was that nearly all the jobs with regular hours and days off would now be for trainmen and switchmen only. The ground crews moved the engines with radio control boxes strapped to a vest. There were only two crew members left to watch what was happening on either end of the movement. Most of the switchmen were sympathetic to the engineers' plight, and didn't like the cumbersome radio transmitters. But there was a lot of resentment and legitimate concern among engineers regarding the inadequate RCL operator training. Most of the training revolved around the technical operation of the equipment, with minimal experience working in the field with actual engines and cars. Like many engineers I felt I had been kicked out and pronounced unnecessary baggage. After twenty-five years of service I had no seniority and I worried myself sick about how I was going to take care of Rachel while I was working the extra board.

I wasn't getting enough sleep and began losing weight. I found out I had Graves disease, an overactive thyroid condition, and I needed to de-stress in order to get better. In 2003 I was able to get a leave of absence, mainly because of the surplus of engineers and lack of jobs. I did not think I was going back to the BNSF. We had been looking for a new place to live, preferably south so we would be closer to Tacoma where Jim was working, as well as closer to the coast house. Initially we looked in Olympia, but one day, after failing to find what we were looking for, we stopped in Tacoma to eat and look around. We happened upon a fairly nice house on the north end selling for below our price range, and decided we had better start looking at Tacoma.

In the meantime, Jim wanted me to try working for Sound Transit as an operator on the new light rail system being built in Tacoma. It wasn't exactly my dream job, but I thought I might at least give it a try. I applied and was accepted for a "light rail operator" position, and commuted from Ballard to Tacoma for training. I was one of six trainees, two voted to join the union (myself included), four against. I saw this as a bad sign. One of the training supervisors was so berating that four of us walked out on the class one day. We went down the street and discussed our options. We were already at least a month into our training, and he begged us to come back. They wanted their targeted opening day to happen on schedule. We relented, and all we got in return was a little more restraint on his part, and no more yelling, "I can make your lives a LIVING HELL!"

We learned the track, road crossings and signals by walking up and down the line as the finishing touches were being made on the system. We operated the trains in and out of the Operations & Maintenance building to practice using the controls. The brakes were touchy and difficult to apply gently, and the wheels had a tendency to slide when the rails were wet. We learned how to open and close the doors manually in an emergency, how to set up the wheelchair ramp, how to attempt to deal with angry and crazy people. (Don't touch them, or it's assault.) This was new territory for me. There was going to be just one of us on each train, and sometimes a police officer at night. But the real problem was that Sound Transit had promised the city of Tacoma to make the 1.6 mile trip from the Tacoma Dome to South 9th Street in just 10minutes. If everything went perfectly, and there were no interruptions of your speed, (such as the opposing train being late for the meet at Union Station, or a car or pedestrian in a crossing, or a passenger that needed help) you might make it in 8 minutes. Then you had exactly two minutes at the end of the line to change ends and make sure all was good to go. At least it was a free service and we didn't have to take passenger's money.

Opening day, August 22, 2003, was a big event. About a thousand people showed up at Freighthouse Square for the celebration; politicians, train buffs, curious onlookers, and reporters. The atmosphere was festive, with live music that included a mariachi band and Highland bagpipers. The Puyallup tribe gave an opening blessing. The first train was loaded with Washington Democratic politicians, including Senator Patty Murray, and all the top Sound Transit officials. They shot confetti and fireworks over the train as we left the station, the first electric train to run in the Puget Sound area for sixty-five years. I was the operator of the first train, and in a photo that appeared on the front page of the Tacoma News Tribune you could recognize me behind the windshield if you knew my face. I heard later that some local officials at the BNSF saw the photo and wondered what I was doing running trains for Sound Transit. Not long afterward I received a certified letter from Assistant Terminal Superintendent, Tom, saying my leave of absence was never approved and I was to report to work in five days.

Luckily Gary Larsen, local chairman for the BLE 518, (Brotherhood of Locomotive Engineers) was working on my case. He assured me that my leave had been approved, and he took care of the issue for me. Since the remote engines had replaced us, and there were now very few jobs with regular hours and days off, they must have known I might not return to work at the BNSF. They had nothing to lose by waiting for the remainder of my leave for me to decide. Thanks to Gary, and an old Northern Pacific agreement allowing for engineers' leave, I had until March of the next year to make up my mind.

I didn't really take to running the Tacoma Link trains. It mainly consisted of rushing back and forth over that 1.6 mile track in a constant frenzy for lack of adequate time. I was not able to talk with passengers beyond a short sentence or two as I was changing ends. I was probably considered unfriendly and rude. I am a social person, and I really wanted to have the time to at least give information if it was needed. My role was to make the trip at a mind numbing pace, not at a particularly high speed, but without any deviation from the program. One day as I approached 21st Street crossing headed north, a fire truck came flying down the hill toward the bridge. I put the brake in emergency and my windshield was so close to the truck window I could see the whites of the fireman's eyes as he looked at me, very surprised! I had a proceed signal, and could not hear the siren because of their speed, the noise of the train and the buildings blocking the sound. Afterward a woman passenger came up to me, gave me her card and said, "If you ever hear anything about this, give me a call and I will back you up. This is an incredible amount of responsibility, and I wouldn't want to be in your shoes for anything." For close to a year I stuck it out, but quit when my leave was over. I decided to go back to running trains for the BNSF. I believe they have since added two minutes each way to that written-in-stone timetable on the Link.

I started working on an afternoon switch engine at Tacoma. We had bought a house on the north end and the commute was ten minutes. The crews were very welcoming to me, and I discovered I knew a lot of people I had worked with in Seattle. It was a low-key, tight knit group. I loved it, and felt like I was back where I belonged. The remote engines had not really succeeded in Tacoma, and many of the yard jobs had gone back to engineers. There was a need for trains to go on short runs across the Puyallup River and back to the city owned Municipal Belt Line, or Tacoma Rail. (TMBL) They didn't use remotes, and remotes weren't generally used by the BNSF for transfer moves. They could also use engineers on switch engines to operate other trains in the yard, or for trains on the main line between Tacoma and Auburn.

Gradually things tightened up again as management cut costs by eliminating jobs. Soon all my seniority could get me was night shifts. I was worried about not being able to work in Tacoma at all, and possibly having to commute to Seattle. I decided to bid on the Sounder commuter train job in the fall of 2006. I visited my folks back in Michigan that summer and told them of my plan. My dad asked, "What will that mean, how will your job be different?" I answered, "It means if I screw up you'll be seeing me on CNN!"

I worked on the Sounders for a year and really enjoyed it. I am so grateful to have had the opportunity to work with some great people, (including my husband Jim, who was my conductor for most of that time). Rachel was on her own every night after school until about 7:00, and a year of that was long enough. She was the perfect age, twelve years old, and handled it really well. It wasn't until I got back to an eight hour switch job that I realized how long a stretch of time she had been taking care of herself every night, Monday through Friday. But we had enjoyed having weekends off together as well, a luxury for rails.

My stories seem to center around my training days, as they were usually the most stressful and memorable. I was fifty-two years old and trying something very new and different. There was a lot to learn on the Sounders; new high speed passenger equipment with blended braking, the territory north of Auburn which I hadn't been over since before the CTC track improvements (which were subsidized by Sound Transit), and how to go from forty miles per hour to a stop in two-hundred feet or less. For some reason, they put me in training with the engineer I was going to bump (replace). Not good, as he had no reason to hope I would succeed. The longer my training took, the longer he could stay on his job. We weren't given uniforms or uniform boots until we qualified, just in case we didn't make the cut. This engineer was not really angry or anything, but our immediate supervisor was a friend of his, and did not really want to see him bumped out of the service. After a week or two, I asked to be moved to work with other engineers. I worked with several, which was great, as you can really benefit from numerous perspectives. One of the guys I trained with was very helpful with the details of running the train efficiently. He maintained that the braking could hang you up at lower speeds, so the best method was to pass the end of the station platform at forty miles per hour, then you would have a much better chance of spotting the coach door at the wheelchair ramp. The ramp was only a few feet wide, so you had to be accurate or you would have to inch forward after stopping, or heaven forbid, back up a bit. He hand wrote four or five pages of detailed instructions for approaching stations and speed restrictions from both directions. I saved some of them, as they are one of my favorite mementos from that time:

"Tuk" (wila) "At 65 MPH when you get over Black River bridge, shut off when you get to the bungalow. Make your first set, that should get you to 55MPH for curve. Wait till you go under 405 bridge to make another little set, release if needed and whistle. 40MPH at platform. 25MPH just before you get to the 4 spot."

After about two months, I felt I was more than ready to run on my own, and our supervisor needed to qualify me. I believed he wanted to drag it out as long as he could to keep his friend on board. I asked him if he was going to be busy, and he said not tomorrow, so I said, "I want to make my qualifying run as soon as possible."

The morning run to Seattle went well and I spotted the train perfectly at every station stop. The afternoon train back to Tacoma was the same. When I pulled up to the Freight house he said, "Well, I guess I'm going to have to qualify you." I was expecting something more congratulatory, but I had done it. The next day I would be my own engineer.

It was an interesting day. Jim and I had marked up to the same train, we were now unofficially the "Delacour Express" or "slacker train" as we called it. It was the last train to leave Tacoma for Seattle, and the last one to return in the evening. We still had to be up around 4:00 a.m. to get there on time. I was wearing some dockers and a blue oxford shirt from my Tacoma Link days.

Just before we left the station, my supervisor came in to tell me the head of BNSF system-wide commuter operations was going to be riding with me in the cab to Seattle. He said to make sure I hid my improperly shod feet (street shoes without steel toes) under the control stand so they wouldn't be seen during the trip. Three men soon joined me in the cab and it was very cozy. When northbound, the cab coach consisted of a small control booth on the end of a passenger car that remotely operated the engine on the rear of the train. They chatted amongst themselves and asked me questions occasionally. As we approached S. Spokane Street, our big boss said, "Why are we going so slow?!" I told him the speed limit over all Seattle crossings was twenty miles per hour. It had been a city ordinance for as long as I had worked on the railroad. "Well, that will have to change!" he said. Not long after that, the speed limit was raised to forty miles per hour.

Passenger service could be stressful, but a lot of fun as well. I loved going seventy-nine miles per hour and having all those clear (green) signals. It was always a challenge to make an accurate spot at the stations. But you often had officials riding with you in the engine or cab coach, and your every move was constantly under scrutiny. I remember once while changing ends and walking up the platform at the Freight house, a Sound Transit employee started chewing me out for not having the wheelchair ramp in place yet. "I don't know how to put out the ramp, I'm the engineer and I have to get to the cab," I told her. Well, that made her mad. Then I had to worry all day that she was going to turn us in or write a negative email or something. I could hold a decent yard job in Tacoma again, so I left the Sounders after a year. I did eventually get a uniform, navy slacks with a vest, and some pretty cool shiny black fireman's boots that zipped on and off. The engineer I bumped a year earlier was eventually able to come back, and the happy family unit was again intact.

My dad died that fall, and I brought my mom back to Tacoma. My siblings were busy with their lives and I knew I was staying in one place for a while, at least until Rachel graduated from high school. Plus I thought it would be great for Rachel to help out and get to know her grandma better. She lived with us for a few months, but she really wanted a place of her own and didn't much appreciate Rachel's hip-hop music. Mom lived at Narrows Glen in Titlow for the next three years, eventually going from independent to assisted living as her dementia got worse. During those years it felt like I was always struggling for time.

The railroad was tightening it's belt again by having fewer jobs work longer hours, and I was compelled to work twelve-hour shifts. I made more money, but I really just wanted to work eight hours and keep an eye on my teenage girl and mom. Nine times out of ten, it's a woman who takes responsibility for the care of elders, kids, getting homework done, and after school activities. If you don't have a regular schedule it is pretty tough. So old Stuart, from my first railroad interview, was right after all; I would eventually decide to get married and have a kid. But so did most of the men I worked with. Not complaining, just stating a fact I had to deal with.

I guess in some ways working for the railroad is a little like being on a yo-yo. First they need you 24/7, then next thing you know you're getting laid off. They replace you with technology or eliminate your position entirely, like they don't need you at all, then they find they are caught short and you better be ready to mark up or be on call. Somehow I managed to survive, but not without getting numerous registered letters claiming I was not in compliance with the BNSF attendance policy! Luckily, I was never required to attend an investigation during my entire career, which is an experience I am glad to have missed. I finished up my railroad days in Tacoma and Auburn, working industry jobs and yard tramps.

The best memories are of the people I had the pleasure of working with. I know that sounds cliche', but it was true for me. Sometimes you relied on your crew and connected with them in a way that made the work go smoothly and efficiently, like a well-oiled machine. The best people were conscientious about their work and wanted to make good things happen. Like Jim holding the train at the stations for late folks running from the parking lot. Some engineers got mad when he did that, but I thought it was a nice gesture that helped make the service a success. Of course, along the way there were some bad eggs too, and sneers from guys who had their petty issues with women working a "man's job", but if you wanted to, you could let all that slide because you knew they were just so wrong!

My last day on the railroad was December 21, 2013. I showed up for my shift and there was an extra man called to take my place. A free day with pay, a nice parting gesture. Jim had retired five years earlier. My mom died of Lewy Body dementia in 2010. We had bought a condo in 2009 in Nevada near Tahoe, so we headed there for the winter. We now divide our time between Nevada and our place at Copalis Beach. Rachel studies accounting at the University of Washington, but otherwise she is usually skiing, climbing or skydiving. I now have time for my artwork, and my addiction to hiking and skiing. Somehow I've managed to live long enough to not have to explain myself or prove anything! And I've been so fortunate and lucky along the way.

# LANCE GOODWIN

Birthplace: Vancouver, WA 1957
Date of Service: November 1991
Position Held: Engineer

*It must have been February or March about 6:30 in the morning the sun was just starting to come up. There was just a light dusting of snow. The snow was just in the tree line up there. The sunrise was this orange and purple coming up. I thought, this is my office. This is the view I get when I get off work and all day long. How many people get to have a view of this?*

I hired out with the BNRR in November of 1991. It was the second go round trying to get hired here. I had a friend who hired out in 1988. I met him in 1990 and I was pretty interested in the job that he had. At the time I was a supervisor in a warehouse in charge of shipping and receiving. This friend of mine told me about the potential of working with the railroad, the money you could make and retirement and this and that. Things I didn't have at the job that I had. He told me where to go, through the employment office up there in North Seattle. I went to the employment office, filled out the job interest card, turned it in at the information desk and took off. Never heard anything at all. Ken asked me if I'd heard anything and I said no.

Thirteen months go by and Ken calls me up from Portland. He said, "Hey I understand they're hiring on the railroad again." I said, "I already turned in one of those job interest cards." He says, "Well damn it, go talk to a lady named Kathy Webb. Go up there tomorrow. They're hiring." So I go up there the next day and I get another job interest card and I ask the gal at the information desk, "Is there a Kathy Webb working here?" She showed me what cubicle she was in. I went over and introduced myself and she said, yes we're hiring but we're pretty much taken up. We've got all our applicants right now and they're all set up for interviews, so we'll keep your name on file. Well, I've already turned one of these cards in. She said, "We only keep them on file for six months, we get twelve-thousand applicants a year, who put in for the railroad. If you don't do any kind of follow up, they just go in the garbage can. If I see your face, I can place the face. Just call back periodically."

I told my friend and he said, "I'm telling you, they are hiring for the next six months, she cannot have all of these positions filled." I decided I'd talk to my boss at the job I was currently working. I said, "This is what I want to do: I need to know if I can take two days off a week at lunch, take an extra-long lunch and go and make a physical appearance at the employment office to show them that I am interested in this job". He said, not a problem. I was calling Kathy Webb at the employment office on Mondays, Wednesdays and Fridays. And I was driving up there on Tuesdays and Wednesdays.

When I found out they were doing their interviews I got there at 7:30 in the morning and I told her, hey I'm just checking in. She said, "You don't have an interview today do you?" I said, no. Well everybody had checked in for the day. I said, I thought I'd just show up anyway in case somebody had a flat tire or something, you know. I'm Johnny on the spot. She said, "No everybody's checked in, if you want you can go ahead and take off". I just grabbed a magazine and sat over there in the lounge area. She walked by about three or four times. She said, "Well I told you that you could leave." I said, I don't want to fight traffic, I figure

I'd just hang out here. She kind of chuckled and took off. Then I left. I knew they were interviewing the next day too. So I drove up there again. Kathy said, "well everybody has checked in, I appreciate your enthusiasm. I'll move your name to the top of list, but everybody's checked in for today and everybody has checked in for tomorrow too. She had confirmations for the next day too. I stuck around for another couple of hours, then I took off. I fought traffic all the way home. Didn't have cell phones back then. I had an answering machine. I got home at a quarter after five in the afternoon and I had a message on my answering machine. I go over and play it and Kathy says, "Hey Lance, its Kathy Webb from the employment office, I've got a late cancellation for an interview tomorrow. You can come in his time slot, but you got to call me back before five o'clock this afternoon". It's now a quarter after five. So I try calling anyway and it just goes to answering machine. I'm a day late and a dollar short. So I call her the next day and she says, "I wish I could have given it to you, but I needed to know by five, or I had to get somebody else. She said, they just told me two days ago that they are giving interviews for a November class in two weeks and I will put your name at the very top of the list. This was in September. I guess I was the first one in that class she called, because I was hired about five weeks later.

I've never really had a problem getting jobs before, but I guess persistence paid off. So I got hired out on November 8, 1991. We made minimum wage for the first two weeks, whatever the going rate was, maybe five-fifty or four-fifty an hour. It wasn't squat for pay but it was something that was going to work towards bigger money.

I trained in the yard, did the classroom stuff, and a couple of road jobs. It was actually December 7, which was my birthday, came in to take the final exam. Then we were going to do the Stacy extra board exam that night. Well there were ten of us in the class. We showed up at the conference room at Balmer Yard. We get in there and we're all kind of excited you know. Met all these guys four weeks ago, all our instructors. Then the terminal assistant superintendent comes in. They all looked like they had just come back from a funeral. They came around and passed these letters out to each one of us. It was pretty quiet and somber in that room after we saw the look on their faces. One of our instructors started talking. I think that it was Larry Brooks. They were our in-field instructors. They said, "Well, you know the railroad's been going in this direction, this short crew agreement, where they want to reduce the crew sizes and they have decided to discontinue this class because they are anticipating the agreement will be signed by December 31st. They said, you can go ahead and open your letters. Mine showed my name on the top with all of the other nine guys in the class. The Burlington Northern has re evaluated their personnel needs at this time and has decided to discontinue the class that started on November 8, 1991. So we're kind of all looking. What does this mean? Are we fired? Well no, you're just furloughed or dismissed. Well, do we take the test? You can take it if you want, but you aren't going to get any credit for it. So none of us took the test.

They took us all out to lunch as a good faith handshake type of thing. We're all still devastated. I hired out when I was thirty-four years old. We are all about the same age. We had all left decent jobs and here we are, out of work. So we went to lunch and after lunch was over they said that if things change in the future the Burlington Northern will look at you guys again since you did have a month of experience out here. I thought, "Oh yea." In the positions I've had over the years I'd let people go. It was a nice way of saying, we'll lay you off but never call you back. This Fortune 500 Company, the biggest company I ever worked for, I thought it was just lip service.

The last thing they said to us as we left lunch was, you guys have switch keys and lanterns, we'd appreciate it, if you'd drop that stuff off, bring it up here to

Balmer Yard. I was living south of Tacoma about thirty miles away. I thought, I just got paid squat for wages for the last four weeks and you want me to bring back a three dollar lantern and two dollars' worth of switch keys? You can drive down to my house. So I left and by the time I got home, I called my sister because she worked at the place that I was working at, we were real close. "Did you pass your test?" I said no, and told her what happened. She said, "Are you serious?" By the time I got home, about four-thirty, my old boss called me and wanted me to come back. This all happened on Friday. I got my old job back on Monday, about three weeks before Christmas. Got back there and didn't even skip a beat. I got a Christmas bonus just like everybody else did. My bosses called me in, in fact there were three of them there. They said, "Well what happened?" I told them and they said, "If they called you back tomorrow would you go back?" I said, "Well I don't know, but today I work for Northwest Technical Plastic. One hundred and ten percent as long as I'm here. We'll cross that bridge when we come to it."

Two and one half months later the Burlington Northern called. The short crew agreement of 1991 never got signed off! So here we are the first of the year. Normally when things pick up the end of February or the first of March, they are all out of people. We were the only class they let go. I was at my old job and got these messages from the receptionist to call George Smith at the Burlington Northern. My first thought, "The guy is chasing me down for those switch keys or the lantern. Are they that hard up for switch keys and lanterns? I'm not calling him back. You know it's been two and one half months". He called about two times in a couple of days and I never returned his call. All of a sudden I heard the page over the PA system for Lance Goodwin, line two. "This is George Smith Burlington Northern, you're the last one I'm able to get in touch with we're trying to get all of you guys back, we want you to come back".

I asked George, how long does it look like this time, two months instead of a month? He said, "Oh no, it looks good for six months at least." So I told him, "I'm thirty four years old, got kids, got financial obligations. I was able to come back to my old job and I cannot afford to leave here again and come to the Burlington Northern and then get let go again. He says, "I can't guarantee you anything, but it looks good for at least six or nine months." Well if you can't make a decision I need you to go in for the physical, (that was a urine test, which wasn't a problem).

So I immediately went and talked to my supervisor, and he wanted to know what I told them. I told them I am going to go in for the physical and I will make a decision on Friday. He said, "Whatever you decide, I'll back you one hundred percent. But if you go, Lance, I can't bring you back. I told him that I totally understand. So I went in and did their physical and was unsure all week. I'm just in this dilemma: do I go to a whole new adventure, or do I stay where I know everything, where I'm complacent, where I know how the system works? It wasn't until I was driving to work Friday morning that I finally made the decision that I was going to go back to the railroad. I probably made that decision because of the security. I loved the job where I worked, I loved the people, but I was in a dead end job. There was no retirement there, I made good money, it was in the aerospace industry. But at that time it was hit or miss and the railroads were going good. The bottom line was money. Money is security. So I came in Friday morning and sat down with my boss and told him that I was going to leave and that next Wednesday was going to be my last day. He said, "Okay, I support you."

So I went back to the railroad, we all went together, and we all had a week's crash course. We met at Balmer Yard in the big conference room again. They asked does everyone still have their switch keys or did you turn them back in? Everybody had them. We had about three days of classroom time. Did a little fundamental stuff, light switching out in Balmer Yard. Then we were put to the Stacy switchyards. I wasn't much of a switchman. I switched for about three days in a row, didn't know what I was doing and at that time the Stacy switchman's extra board was a supplemental road board for brakemen, extra board for the road jobs. So instead of switching I was getting called mostly to go to Wenatchee as a brakeman. Sitting up there, I didn't know where I was going or where I was at. You had two brakemen a conductor and an engineer. The new guy always sat up at the head end of the train.

After I did that for about two and a half months I got forced into a hostling program where we moved the locomotives in the roundhouses at Interbay. Did that for about three and a half months, you had to stay in there until you were able to train someone younger than you to take your spot. I kind of liked that. I was scared out of my wits by the locomotives at first. I know the first night that I got there and I had to hostle I was working the service pad. One guy named Mike Hamilton comes out and says you can work with me. He probably had a year longer than I did. He wore bib overalls and he had about four reversers in his pockets. That's a set of car keys he used to move all these locomotives. I thought that was cool and I wanted to be like him. He had all these reversers and we were going to go work the service pad that night. He says, "Okay we need to move these engines off the service pad." There's four of them, its five miles an hour there and I wasn't familiar with the controls or anything like that. I had all the lights turned on because I was working nights, a midnight job. I'd take a notch, go back to idle and put on the brakes. I was scared; this is a big piece of equipment. Within a week I was doing track speed, almost speeding sometimes. I got familiarized and I really liked that. I liked the roundhouse and the locomotives. Things like that, I didn't have any ambitions to stay in the roundhouse, but running the locomotives, the light power around in the terminal, around the roundhouse facility was quite interesting and I enjoyed it.

So I couldn't hold anything except the switchman's board when I went into hostling. But when I got out I was able to hold the brakeman's extra board. I was living down in Tacoma out by Steilacoom. Your phone was ringing every six hours to go to work. I was only making seventy five percent of the one hundred percent going rate for a trip rate. So I worked quite a bit. I got this buddy of mine who originally helped me get the job there, named Ken. He was running in the engineer's program in '91. That's the same time I got hired out. He was telling me about this and he got called to work a switch engine in Tacoma. He said, "Why don't you come on down and I'll give you a ride on one of these switch engines?" So I went down there and got sat up in the fireman's side while we were switching cars down in Tacoma. I thought I could like this. So I started putting in for the Locomotive Engineer's Class. I didn't want the conductor's side. I thought that's too much paper work and stuff like that. I wanted to kind of be in charge here and running the show. So I started putting in for the engineer's class. The first one I put in for was probably November 1992. It was based on seniority and I didn't make it. There were one hundred and eighty-some people in front of me. I thought I'm going to have to be here for ten years before this takes place. So another class comes up four months later. I put in for it, now there are only eighty people holding it away from me. I finally got into the engineer's program. I started in May of 1994. Once I got in the engineer's program my wages automatically went to one hundred percent. I was only at eighty five percent before that period of time. But the engineers had an agreement that as soon as you became an engineer you went right up to the top. So I got a fifteen percent raise as soon as I went in the program.

You had to send off your application by registered mail and return receipt. I lived about a quarter of a mile from a post office. I filled this application out, took it up to the post office, mailed it, then I just sat in the parking lot and thought, what in the hell did I just do? I wasn't the smartest kid in school and this is two shots and you're done, fail twice and you're out of a job. You don't get to go back hostling; you don't get to go back working as a brakeman or switchman. You're dismissed, you're terminated. I never had real good study habits, I wasn't a dumb kid in school, and I was average. I excelled in the industrial arts, PE and Woodshop. But in the academic classes I got C's. I was concerned about study habits. Hadn't been in school for fifteen years or something like that. I was kind of concerned about studying for this stuff. So one of my buddies got in, the guy that I hired in with, we were one number apart. He and I both got into the engineer's program. I told him, Randy you know I'm a little concerned. This guy is a whiz, photographic memory, knows how to apply himself. He says, don't worry about it cause I'll help you as much as I can. Have some confidence in yourself. I bet you'll do better than you think, you'll be in the top ten per cent of the class. So we started this program. We got to run these trains for thirty days before we had to go to Kansas City for the classroom portion. We had an engineer instructor and for the thirty days I ran between Seattle and Wenatchee. Didn't do Portland, didn't do anything else. Everything I did was between Seattle and Wenatchee. There was one particular guy, Jim Headrington, was the instructor I worked with. He said, "Well this is your last trip, you going to sign up for this?" You going to show up tomorrow for your air fare?" I said, 'absolutely." I flew off to Kansas. Three weeks later I came back and marked back up with him. Worked with him for about three weeks, then I did my runs on the south end between Seattle and Vancouver. And then I did my north end stuff between Everett and Vancouver BC. Did all of my runs. Went back and got out of class and my service date as a locomotive engineer is October nineteenth, nineteen-ninety four.

I always liked the road, I never liked the switch jobs. You get beat up in the yard. I still have neck and shoulder issues that you get from hanging out of those window boxes on a switch engine and running backward looking for hand signs and then getting hit into a cut of cars. I mean it just tears you up. It takes its toll and the money wasn't as good in the yard, but the flip side to that is you were home every night. I worked Board Thirty at Interbay, the engineer's extra board for ten years. Occasionally I would go and work on a temporary vacancy. Somebody's vacation vacancy for four days or something like that. I'd work a switch job, just get a little reprieve and be home a little bit. The extra board you got to work every eight to ten hours. Your phone was ringing every eight or ten hours. I didn't have enough seniority to hold the Wenatchee pool. I tried to a few times I was on the pool the next day but I was getting bumped, that went on and on.

That's when I finally decided to go work the engineer's extra board for ten years. Once I got the seniority, I told my wife I can't do this anymore. They got so many new people and I got to be qualified on seven hundred and fifty miles of track. That's what you had to be qualified on as an engineer. Seattle Board 30 at Interbay covered everything. After ten years on the extra board my seniority changed and I sat in a comfortable spot. I sat down and told the wife, we got so many new people coming on and its scary when you're at this end of the train and you got a brand new conductor a mile back in the train and you got to back this thing up and he's brand new. I just told her it's a lot easier to babysit them for a hundred and fifty miles, Seattle over to Wenatchee than seven hundred and fifty miles on territory I only see maybe once a year. When that phone rings I need to know I'm going to Wenatchee. I'm tired of going to Portland, Vancouver BC tomorrow, a switch engine the next day. Just the variety.

I got the "Traveling Hoghead" job because over the years they had these mountain mentors up here, especially winter mentors. Basically it's a winter program because these trains operate a lot differently when it's snowing up here, than when its sixty five degrees and sunshiny. They've had this mentor program to help the younger guys for probably that I know of, for the last ten years and it would usually go from November until March or until the snow disappeared. I went through the engineer's program. Started in May and got out in October. I never trained up here in the winter time. But the guy that I worked with, Jim, always said, do this but if it's snowing, do that. He was very, very thorough. I knew what summertime running up here was and what wintertime was. But until you actually run a train up here in the wintertime you don't have a clue. Even if you have all this knowledge of what your instructor had told you, until you get up there and set the brakes to have this train slow down and it keeps on picking up speed, it's kind of a hair-raising experience. We're not talking your bicycle with wet brakes. We're talking tonnage heavy trains up here. I'd seen these older senior guys get the opportunity to work up here as a mentor. I thought that would be kind of neat, but you know, it wasn't a really big desire of mine. Then here they asked me about five or six years ago if I wanted to do it. I was having some marital issues at home and I knew what kind of time that I would have to put into this job and I said it's just not a good time for me.

Well ultimately my marriage ended about five years ago. We're good friends today but we just grew apart. You know, this life is tough, especially working the road. When I first took the job, my wife knew all about it. I said this is the way it's going to be because in order for us to maintain some kind of a lifestyle with me working the road, this is what I got to do. Going to work every eight to ten hours, no set days off. Okay, but after about nine months she says, you're never home and I'm not doing well with it. I said, "Well if you want, I'll take a switch engine job, we'll sell the house, we'll go to dinner once every two weeks, we won't go here we won't do that. Well, no, but about a year goes by and it rears its head again. She says, "It gets lonely, every time I go someplace, I'm always going by myself. We didn't live high on the hog, but we lived comfortably and we were still able to do stuff.

You develop a lifestyle, I had my family here at the railroad, she had her family and her friends at home and then we had one together. So I'd be gone for two days and I'd come home and all of a sudden I'd want the kids to be whipped into shape and stuff done and twelve hours later I'm walking out the door. They learned after a period of time to do exactly what I wanted them to do for the ten or twelve hours I was home and then I'd take off and be gone for two or three days. I was grumpy and tired and they knew when to stay away from me. So anyways the marriage ended back in 2009. And this opportunity came up in 2012.

Some of these extra board engineers or younger engineers who worked this east end pool over here had started asking me in September if they were going to put a winter mentor up here. I told them that I had no idea. So I talked to the superintendent of operating practices, Mike Rogers. I said, "Hey I'm getting a lot of people inquiring, if you're going to put a winter mentor up here?" He said, "Matter of fact we were just talking about that. Would you be interested?" Over the last three or four years there was an issue over pay, when there was a company vehicle involved, mileage reimbursement. I just told him I'd be interested in discussing it. This was the end of September. He got back with me about three weeks later in October 2012. He said, "We got the okay from the general manager to put a mentor program up there for the winter, let's get together next week and we'll talk." I had my list of questions that he answered and he told me what I wanted to hear, all the numbers were right. There was a vehicle involved, a gas card involved, the pay was good. I'd just put my dog down after thirteen and a half years. All the stars were lining up. The marriage wasn't there anymore, the dog was gone, there was no commitment for me to go home every day like there was when my puppy was alive. The first day that I started as a mentor was December 8, 2012. I thought the job was going to last until March or so because it was the winter program. March comes around and I asked the SOP again when this thing was going to end? He hadn't heard, nobody had heard, so he said just keep going. They were having engineer classes about every two and a half or three months. About ten students per class. Not only did I work with the younger engineers who were out here by themselves. I started having contact and an active role in working with the student engineers. Being in touch with them at the very beginning of their classroom portion before they went to Overland Park, I stayed in touch with them on their student runs over here on the Scenic sub division. I would ride with them when they started in their program. Ride with them when they were about two weeks into it when they were brand new over here. Then usually when they were about halfway through their training program. And then towards the end to see how they had developed. It didn't always work out that well because there is only one of me and sixty of these guys that I got to keep tabs on. All you can do is try.

You know it wasn't as critical with the student engineers as it was with the younger engineers. The student engineers are working with a seasoned engineer already. I just kind of got up there and quizzed them to see where they were at. So I've been doing that and I've gone through about three different road foremen out of Wenatchee. That kind of change and every time we've gone through a different manager I've thought the job was going to end. I've had a lot of support from management because I'm still a scheduled union employee but I just do this on the side. I've had a lot of support which I'm very grateful for from some of the local management. In December 2015 it will be three years that I've been doing this. There is good and there is bad, there are certain days that I'm just tired. You know I just don't like to ride trains every single day. I don't like to go through that Cascade Tunnel everyday but you know there are certain days out here like last night I showed up to go ride trains. We had an eight-thousand ton train that stalled on the other side over there. It needed water in the rear locomotive. We went over there and got them going, thought we had the problem solved and I talked to the chief dispatcher and said after we get this thing watered up and stuff, I'm pretty much done over here and can head back over to Skykomish. I ended up getting back over here about 10:30 p.m. I got over there about 5:30 in the afternoon. So I decided to leave here about 10:45 p.m. or so to go home because I have about an hour and a half drive from my house up to Skykomish on a good day. Eighty one miles. I'm just about down past Zekes in Gold Bar and my phone rings and it's the chief again, I've got another one of those engines over there but it's on the head end they need to get water. What's the best way to do it? Do we cut the power out? I said,"Take the whole train up there." "Do you want me up there?" He said, "If it was my personnel opinion, well yea, I'd want you there but I know you're probably an hour away." So I went back over to Merritt and they'd just filled it up with water and they made it back up and over the hill at sixteen miles an hour and they came down the hill and once they got to Skykomish I left.

I left Sky at 12:30 last night and got back home at 3:00 in the morning. I just get tired, it doesn't matter how you look at it it's a minimum of an hour and a half drive up here. I live down at Federal Way. This is a whole different lifestyle. You can't tell somebody what the lifestyle is until you live it. I don't need a lot of sleep, I can get up and answer the phone at two in the morning or six at night, it's just not an issue.

I'm glad that I took the job. I love this town of Skykomish. People recognize me here that I don't even know. They know me because I'm here all the time. I remember the first winter I started up here December of 2012. It must have been February or March about 6:30 in the morning the sun was just starting to come up. There was just a light dusting of snow. The snow was just in the tree line up there. The sunrise was this orange and purple coming up. I thought, this is my office. This is the view I get when I get off work and all day long. How many people get to have a view of this?

# MARTIN BURWASH

### Photographer / Train Buff / Farmer

*Once the train left Skykomish it would set off a bell at Tonga, then that guy
there would know that there was a train coming up, he would get the staff
ready so you could go from Tonga to Alpine and so forth. They had orders too
and telegraph, but what controlled the signals at the station was that staff.
That's how they funneled trains through the old tunnel, with that staff.*

By trade I am a farmer and I work in a
feed mill. For many, many years my hobby
has been railroad photography. I did it with
my dad in the early sixties which brought
me to Skykomish and Stevens Pass to begin
with. Dad and I came up in 1968 in the fall
and from that point until I went to college in
the early 1970's we would do that every fall.

Since then I have always been interested
in railroading and particularly how the history and the railroad run together. Stevens
Pass is a great place because there is so much
history that you can still see. For that reason

Railroad historian and author
Martin Burwash

I have been up here at least once or twice a year since the early sixties taking photographs of the trains and what is left of the old railroad grade.

The history of Stevens Pass has kind of evolved. When I first started coming up here it was just all about getting pictures of the various trains and of course when you are young its all about what engine is on the front and what engine is next. Of course there is always the chase, because it is so easy to chase trains from Skykomish clear to Merritt if you want to, or beyond. Why do people chase trains? My point of view was more not how many pictures I could get of the same train. But getting it in a scenic backdrop or getting it in the light just right and that might entail following the train from point A to point B to point C. The other thing that I always tried to do with my photographs was to tell some kind of a story. Whether it was a mini story or a grand story. In doing that you had to sometimes follow a train from point A to point B to point C, to round out a story. Many times you would come upon a train that was stalled up at Scenic or something like that. So to try to photograph that entire story, these poor guys trying to get this train going, of course you had to realize they were not having a good day. You had to stay out of their way but at the same time other people are very interested in this kind of stuff so that might involve chasing the train once it gets going to see it finally get to the top of the pass and go onto Wenatchee.

The older that I got the less I was interested in that and the more I was drawn to the history especially the history of the old grade. I mean, I was aware of it from early on, but it kind of occurred to me that the modern day railroad that I was seeing was very much built on what had happened years previous. When I started blending that together, the historical perspective started taking more of a front street and the modern trains started taking more of a back seat. I realized for instance that with the Eight Mile Tunnel you could probably make a pretty strong case that if it were not for the Wellington Avalanche that tunnel might not even exist and if that tunnel did not exist what would be the route over Stevens Pass now? Would there even be a railroad there? With the BN merger would they have opted for the old Milwaukee Line over Snoqualmie? Or the Northern Pacific over the Stampede Line? I don't know, you start asking yourself these questions on the profile of this pass. Is it one of the better crossings over the Cascades because of the history that came before it?

I was always on the outside of the railroad looking in so I don't remember many of the men but there were a couple that stick out in my mind. The trouble is that I'm not sure of names.

The first year dad and I came up here it was still the Great Northern and the helper crews were still stationed here in Skykomish and living there at the Cascadia. We were talking to a crew that was getting ready to ride over to couple in at Cashmere. A guy by the name of Chase, (he was a little short guy had kind of a limp) but anyway we were talking to him at breakfast and he said, "Yah, they were taking the helper over." So dad and I went up to Foss River to get a picture of them coming across the trestle. We were standing there and we heard them coming up and then on the far side of the trestle, where you couldn't quite see the end of the trestle,we heard the units throttle down and stop. "That's weird," but pretty soon they started up again and were coming across the trestle real slow and we got our pictures. They come up alongside of us and stopped. I don't know who the conductor pilot was but Engineer Chase hung out the window and said, "Hey do you want a ride?" Well yea I did! Poor dad he had to go over to Merritt to pick me up. They gave me a ride from the Foss Rive over to Merritt. The stories they had to tell! When Chase hired out the new tunnel wasn't quite completed, Chase said that the first year he was hired out he went up over the old grade.

In 1970 we were up here, that's when they were rebuilding the Foss River Bridge. We got a couple rides with Elmer Dahl. Elmer was pretty entertaining.

He had just gotten off of the Woodinville job, the merger had just started. Elmer had such low seniority that he ended up here on the helper. He wasn't too happy about that because he loved that Woodinville job. If Elmer was on a train you had to kind of hustle up the highway to meet him at Scenic. I liked Elmer.

Someone asked me a while ago what I thought is the biggest change up here? I think that it is just the lack of people. You don't see railroaders anymore. Even when you go by an engine they have those dark tinted windows. You can't tell whether there's a guy in there or not. I think just the lack of personalities is the biggest thing I've seen. It's not their fault, its almost against the law to stop and talk to anyone anymore. That's the biggest change I've seen. It makes it hard. Who's going to tell the stories now? These great stories that you're recording, they're gone. That's kind of too bad. When I first started coming up here you could go in the station and talk to the operator, ask "What's going on today"? That's gone.

About my books, I've actually done three books. The first one is photos and stories called, "Cascade Division." I did that about 1990. It was a collection of photographs I'd taken up to that point. It was actually an overview of all three passes. There was a section on the Milwaukee, Snoqualmie Pass, and then by that time the BN running on Stampede Pass, prior to it being quote, unquote "mothballed". Then of course a section on Stevens Pass. What happened when I did that book, I tried to do it in equal thirds but because my main focus and interest was always Stevens Pass, it ended up being a little more about Stevens Pass. And quite frankly back then if a guy wanted to take train pictures you came up here because this is where the trains were. There weren't that many on the Milwaukee, same on Stampede. That was not the main route for the BN so they had a couple of junk freights there and Amtrak went over Stampede for a while but that was it.

After that book came out I still had a ton of material just on Stevens. By then I'd really started getting interested in more of the historical aspect of it. So a couple of years later I put together the second book called, "The Great Adventure". It is strictly my photographs of Stevens Pass along with blending in the historical with the photographs I was taking. Then kind of in conjunction with doing that book, I met Bob Kelly. He had just kind of started getting interested in Wellington and I had done some writing in both books. Once we met up he and I would talk for hours about Wellington. I used to come up to the Lions Railroad Swap Meet here in Skykomish. I met Bob Norton there.

By then I was really enthralled with Wellington. I was aware of it! The first time I read about it was in the November 1961 issue of *Trains* magazine. They had a two-part series in November and December on Stevens Pass. There were about three paragraphs in that article that talked about Wellington, I don't know why but I thought oh that's interesting. You know I was just a kid., It would sort of come and go. You'd get interested for a while then maybe five years would go by and you didn't even think about it, then something, a little tidbit would come and you'd think "oh yea". Bob Kelly and I finally linked up and he turned me onto the book, "Northwest Disaster". So I read that book and all the time I was reading the material about Wellington it always occurred to me that there's something kind of missing. I couldn't put my finger on it for a long time, finally it dawned on me, most of everything that's written even in more modern times is from the perspective of the passengers. You never saw it through the eyes of the rank and file. Those were the guys who really knew what was going on.

So I thought it would be fun to try and write a book from that perspective, let's get it down on the level of the guys who were actually shoveling the snow and see how that whole thing developed from their point of view. So I started doing some research from that aspect. You always figure it actually happened, it is historical fact. You need to write it as a non-fiction story. I just could never pull it off. I tried a couple of times and either I was just kind of rehashing what was already done or it was just garbage. Then I'd give up for a while. Bob would come by, he was a great mole, he's all about the search and finding everything. I kept telling him "You should write this". He said, "I don't want to write, I just want to look." I'm trying to write this story and he just kept getting more and more information. Bob is extremely generous, he is just an awesome guy. My wife is a librarian so she checked out a DVD about the Battle of Gettysburg. Now I'm not a Civil War buff but I watched the movie and actually it's really good. So my wife Janice, the librarian said, "If you name your wife she becomes a part of the story." She really helped me get started with the suggestion that the movie was based on a book. Based on a book? Now how would I know that? She said, "Would you want to read the book?" Well, I'm not a big reader, but she brought the book home. The book was titled "The Killer Angels". So I'm reading this book, it's historical fiction. I started reading this thing and its very, very good. There are times I'm not the sharpest tack in the drawer, but I'm about three quarters of the way through this book when it finally dawns on me, oh this is how I can tell the story of Wellington through the eyes of the railroad men. The reason I couldn't do it with non-fiction is that there is nothing there to report. There are all of these documents through the railroad. All of these depositions taken from the men who lived through it. You read the depositions and they are all virtually the same, with the name signed at the bottom, "here sign this." When they go to trial, there again, just because they were fighting over the physical evidence, the railroaders had very little to say.

So the only way that you can go about telling that story is, number one, you need to be really familiar with how they operated the railroad back then. Number two, find what men you can with enough information that you can kind of get into who they were, what they were and from there you just draw on what you know about the working rank and file and tell the story. That's how I pulled it off. This is one time I had to actually go into fiction to be able to tell the story. I always thought that I did okay, because I had the relatives of some of the people say, "Oh yea, that sounds just like so and so." or, "My mom knew so and so." I felt good about that.

One thing that I felt was that I had to be very strict and very accurate in the time line. I wasn't going to go clear off here and make up a bunch of stuff. I stuck with the actual timeline of the events that happened up there. The real savior is a document that Bob found. I've had it for years. I'm sure it was for the 1912 court case, a long deposition and it has this horrendous title: "The Positions of Trains and Rotaries on the Hill between February 22 up to the Slide." It's about a four-page document. It is fantastic because not only does it list where all the trains and all the snowplows were at this point in time, it also lists the crews. It listed who was there, so you could follow these guys. That was the breakthrough. I started seeing the patterns.

I had a couple of rough maps and I'd say at this time this plow was here, this train was there. I'd try to put the whole thing in motion. Once I got that, then I started to see, here's what was going on, here's why this happened. I tell people you have to throw your cell phone or telephone away to get into that mindset to understand how things happened up there. When a train went around a corner from the station the crew literally did not know what was going on till it came around the corner at the next station. That's why they had so many little stations along the way. They had kind of a crude phone system but it was on again off again at best. So it was strictly by telegraph, by sight, by staff and if you didn't have the staff, you didn't go into that block period! The staff was literally like a baton in a relay system. Each station along the way had a machine, the big signals outside for them to let the train go by. They would have to pull a staff out and you would hand it up to the crew. The crew would hand you the staff down from the previous station. You'd put that in your machine and that would release it from the previous station. If an engineer started out here in Skykomish he'd get a staff and your next station, I think was Tonga on the Foss River. Once the rain left Skykomish it would set off a bell at Tonga, then that guy there would know that there was a train coming up, he would get the staff ready so you could go from Tonga to Alpine and so forth. They had orders too and telegraph, but what controlled the signals at the station was that staff. That's how they funneled trains through the old tunnel, with that staff.

One of the big questions was why didn't they take those passenger trains and back them up off of that siding into the tunnel? Well one thing they didn't have the staff to do it. That was just so ingrained and against the rules. The other thing was you put a train in that tunnel, you have blocked off any possibility of any relief coming from the east. They knew at that point that was probably where the soonest relief was going to come. It wasn't coming from the west side it was coming from the east. You tell me, you've got a steam engine on the point which is a natural wedge. You've got six or seven cars but back end of rear car is blunt. Now you're going to back that up through three or four feet of snow, plus switches, bucking against snow, around a corner and into a tunnel bucking snow the whole time? You're going to do that? How far across those switches are you going to get before you start jackknifing those cars? But you see, people don't think in those terms. You have to think how the railroaders were thinking. They had numerous times they had gone through with the rotary plow. A rotary plow with that much snow you literally dig yourself a canyon. Then the snow fills in and you can have an army of shovelers but you're not just shoveling it off the track you have to shovel it twelve feet up and over to clear the track. From the sidings you are a good quarter of a mile away at least, maybe closer to half a mile before you get to that tunnel. Now you've got people in that tunnel and your source of food is maybe a half a mile away. You have to realize that to the railroad men all of that would seem like nonsense because there would be no reason to do it. These guys had spent ten winters on the pass and because of that experience they absolutely believed that hill wasn't going to slide, no reason to slide. Who are they to question??

That's the kind of thing that I tried to do, show it from the perspective of the actual railroad men, they were the ones who were literally on the front line knew what was going on and why they were making the decisions that they were making.

The men told the story. Thirty-five passengers perished and sixty-five railroad men and postal employees perished.

On the Iron Goat Trail the site of the old railroad grade over Stevens Pass, if you stand at Windy Point and look down on the modern tunnel, you realize just how much elevation was lopped off by building the other tunnel. I always said that the Cascade Tunnel was an eight mile snow shed. They knew where to drill that tunnel. They knew just where that heavy, heavy snow line was.

My dad was a career firefighter. I don't know why he was into trains. My dad started out as a logger right out of high school. Then he was in the army during World War II. He came back home and went back to logging. Started dating my mother. My mother would not marry him unless he got a steady job, (not logging), something safer. So he became a firefighter in Tacoma and immediately his life insurance went up.

Dad grew up along the Milwaukee in Tacoma. He always liked trains. Dad took train pictures so I would always go along with dad. That is how I got into taking train pictures. It was dad's idea to come up here to Skykomish in 1968. My dad is still living, he is ninety-three going on ninety-four. We moved him off of the farm about a year ago. He is doing very well.

# "THE HILL"

*People interviewed for this book often talked about "the hill".*
*When asked to be more specific they would mention the area between*
*Merritt in the east and Skykomish to the west.*

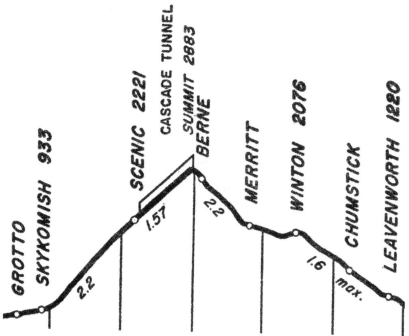

Inspecting the track profile on a Great Northern employee time table, illustrates "the hill" as that portion of the Cascade crossing with the 2.2 percent grade and the 8 mile long Cascade Tunnel.

Merritt station on the east side of "the hill" where the track begins to climb at 2.2 percent or over 100 feet in elevation for each mile traveled. Skykomish Historical Society Collection

**Skykomish on the west side of "the hill". The first name assigned to his location by the Great Northern Railway in the 1890's was "Flat spot at the west end of the 2.2% grade." Walter Ainsworth Collection, PNRArchive.org**

## My Railroad Town

"I want to go back to my Railroad Town.
Back to my engines so big and brown,
Back where a whistle could put me to sleep,
Sooner than all of the lulls of the deep.
Back where one tells time by a train,
Always there, in sunshine and rain.
Where one sees engines the whole day through,
And lots and lots of boxcars, too.
So now when I hear a train from afar,
I wish I were on the very last car,
And a grand old engine, big and brown,
Was taking me back to my Railroad Town.

*Gayle Tiller*
*Whitefish Pilot, April 16, 1929*
*Used with permission*

# The Language of the Rails

*A selected glossary of some of the railroad terms used in this book*

BAD ORDER—A tag or note applied to a defective piece of equipment. Generally, equipment tagged as bad order is not to be used until repairs are performed and the equipment is inspected and approved for use

CABOOSE HOP—Taking an engine and a caboose only, with no cars, to the destination

CLEAR BLOCK—Authority to proceed (green light) between two consecutive signals governing movements in the same direction.

COVERED WAGONS—Older locomotives with enclosed walkway or running board. Non covered wagons have open walkways alongside the engine on both sides. When walking back through covered wagon types for inspection or other reasons, the diesel engine noise was so great that you could almost feel the wax jumping in your ears. Newer locomotives have running boards that are not covered, with side doors to access the diesel engine.

CRUMMY—Another term for caboose

DEADHEAD—Crew needed at a distant station, hauled by auto, train, bus or other conveyance to the station where their work on a train will begin, is called a deadhead or deadheading crew.

DIED ON THE ROAD—No he wasn't hauled off in a pine box, it simply meant the crew had run out of working time. (There is a legal limit to the amount of hours a crew can work. When that limit expires, the crews are "dead".

DOG CATCH—When a crew dies (runs out of working time) on the road, another crew is sent out to bring the train in.

DYNAMITE THE BRAKES—To apply the brakes very suddenly

EXTRA BOARD—A list of engineers, brakemen, firemen, switchmen that fill personnel vacancies when someone on a regular job lays off. The extra board person covers the job for the person laying off or on vacation. It could be a yard switch engine, a local, an east end, south end, north end pool job, a passenger job or ten days in some point such as Burlington, Portland or Vancouver BC. When you come in you mark your name at the bottom of the list and as other people whose names are above you get used and your name gets to the top of the list, you must take the job that comes up when its your turn to go out. Sometimes you deadhead to the place that you will be working.

FIRING—A worker whose primary job is to shovel coal into the firebox and ensure that the boiler maintains sufficient steam pressure.

FLAGGING—marking the track with flags to warn approaching trains

FROGS—The area of the track through a switching point that allows for the wheel flange to pass through it

FUSEE—A pyrotechnic device similar to an automotive flare that is used in signaling.

GANG—a group of laborers often with special tasks such as working on the track or repairing bridges.

GEEP—Any of the GP ("general-purpose") series of Electro-Motive four-axle diesel locomotives

GOAT—A switch engine.

GOING TO BEANS—Going to eat

GOING IN THE HOLE—Putting the train in a siding or yard track, usually to meet another train.

GOING IN THE POOL—The Pool, (chain gang on some railroads) is like an extra board, only it is assigned to specific territory, such as Seattle to Portland, Seattle to Wenatchee or north to Canada. If you are assigned to the Wenatchee pool, all of your trips will be to Wenatchee, likewise the Portland pool goes only to Portland and so forth. It is like an extra board with respect to your not knowing the exact time that you will be called to go to work or to return home from the distant point. The pool covers most jobs in freight service and (before Amtrak) often in passenger service also. Some jobs were assigned and went to the same place and back at approximately the same time every day and were not considered "pool" positions.

GRIP—The valise, suitcase or bag that's used on a trip to carry your belongings

HI BALL—Means "Everybody is on the train, take off or proceed." (multiple uses)

HOGHEAD—The engineer of the train

He BIG HOLED IT—Go into emergency with the air brakes

HOSTLING—A job held by a fireman that moved all of the engines around a designated area, usually the round house or the engine house. When an engineer and fireman came in from a trip it was the job of the hostler to move the engine, to fuel them, sand them, wash them and to move them into the roundhouse.

HOT BOX—An axle bearing that has become excessively hot due to friction

KICK—To shove a car a short distance and uncouple it in motion, allowing it to roll free under gravity and/or its own inertia onto a track.

LEAD TRACK—A non-main track from which several others branch within a short distance, such as within a rail yard or engine terminal (pronounced "leed").

LIVINGSTON tool—a tool with very long handles used to cut rivets. Often used by a bridge gang.

MALLET—A type of articulated locomotive designed by the Swiss mechanical engineer Anatole Mallet (pronounced "mallay")

MILE POST—a sign marking locations along the track in miles

RAIL GRINDER—A machine used to remove irregularities in the surface of the rails that may be self-powered

RIP TRACK—Where railroad cars are repaired

SPUD LOCAL—a local train that picks up lots of potato shipments

STEEL GANG—A group of employees engaged in the maintenance of the railroad. Steel gangs repair and replace the track.

TIE GANG—A group of employees engaged in the maintenance of the railroad. A tie gang, maintains the ties that support the track.

TIE UP—When the tour of duty is finished, clock time crews go off duty, their "tie up".

WASHOUT—Putting brakes into emergency, or a hand signal to make an emergency stop

WHISTLING POST—An advance warning sign for the engineer of an upcoming grade crossing

WYE—A triangular arrangement of tracks forming the letter "Y", typically used for turning railroad cars and locomotives

YARD SERVICE—Switching railroad cars to make up trains and for deliveries of box cars and tank cars to different businesses that are within yard limits. "Yard limits" is a designated area that yard crews and switch engine crew can work in.